Library and Information Studies in the Digital Age
(Professor K.A. Isaac Commemoration Volume)

Library and Information Studies in the Digital Age
(Professor K.A. Isaac Commemoration Volume)

Edited by
Prof. G. Devarajan Ph.D.
Head, Deptt.of Library & Information Science
University of Kerala
Thiruvananthapuram

Ess Ess Publications

4837/24, Ansari Road, Darya Ganj,
New Delhi-110002
✆ : 23260807, 51563444
Fax : 011-51563334
E-mail: info@essessreference.com
url:http://www.essessreference.com

ISBN: 81-7000-459-4

Rs.650/-

Published by:

Ess Ess Publications

4837/24, Ansari Road, Darya Ganj, New Delhi-110 002

Tel: 011-23260807, 51563444 Fax: 011-51563334

E-mail: info@essessreference.com

url: www.essessreference.com

Printed in India at:

Printline, New Delhi

Dedicated to

Prof. K. A. ISAAC

"A true disciple of Dr.S.R. Ranganathan and a friend, philosopher and guide to thousands of Library professionals in India"

CONTENTS

Preface

Technological change is a major contributor to economic development. The rapid development of information and information technology has tremendously increased the capacity to process information and accelerate growth in the information intensive sector. The impact of information technology arises from its attributes such as enabling technology which can be applied in a wide range of different circumstances, the capacity of the technology increases at an exponential rate. These attributes of information technology will trigger a new wave of economic growth stimulating the development of information society. It is indeed the avenues of information technology that should be utilized to the possible extent in libraries and information centers to make use of the information speedily, effectively, efficiently and with precision. This book is a compendium of selected studies that highlight the application of information technology in the scientific management of collection, organization and dissemination of information in the various types of libraries. These studies have got contemporary significance in the present digital world.

This book contains fifteen learned articles contributed by authorities in the field. Topics selected by the authors are current and significant in the present day information world.

The editor considers it a matter of great privilege, honour and respect to dedicate this publication to Prof.K.A,Isaac on the occasion of his 80th birth anniversary. He is a friend, philosopher and guide to thousands of library and information professionals in India and who spent his lifetime for the cause of library development and library and information science education in India in general and Kerala in particular. I sincerely thank Prof.K.A.Isaac, my teacher who obliged my request for dedicating the publication to him.

The editor records his profound thanks to the authors for contributing articles in this book. The editor also records his great appreciation and profound thanks to

Mr. Sumit Sethi, M/S ESS ESS publications, New Delhi in bringing out this book in an excellent format within record time.

Trivandrum.
01-09-2005

Prof. Dr. G. Devarajan

PROF. K.A. ISAAC: DOYEN OF LIBRARY SCIENCE

Prof.K.A.Isaac was born on 10th July 1925 in a Jacobite Syrian Christian family named Kaadaapuram at Kanjiramattom, Ernakulam District, Kerala as the youngest son of Mr & Mrs. K. V. Itten. Father was the founder manager and head master of St.Ignatius High School, Kanjiramattom. He was also the local Panchayat President for about fifteen years and passed away in 1962 at the age of sixty four. Mother, Mrs.Mary Itten was a house wife and died in 1969 at the age of sixty eight.

Prof. Isaac had his primary education at Kanjiramattom and high school education at Mulanthurthy. He studied Intermediate and B.Sc with Physics as the main subject in the Union Christian College, Alwaye. Both in the high school and college he took part in dramas and other items of entertainment and became known for his histrionic talents.

While in the college he was also active in student politics and was President of the Students Congress unit of the college for a year. In that capacity he led an agitation against Sri.C.P.Ramaswami Iyer's independent Travancore movement and invited an arrest warrant which however, was not executed.

After a stint of work as demonstrator in Physics in the Union Christian College for two years and a science teacher in the St.Ignatius High School, Kanjiramattom, he joined M.Sc (Physics) in the Wilson College, Mumbai. But due to certain unforeseen developments he was not able to continue in the course after the first year. Later, he joined the Library Science course in the University of Delhi. He chose the Delhi University because of the presence there of Dr.S.R.Ranganathan, world renowned library scientist and also because the Master's course in Library Science was offered only by that University at the time. He took the Diploma in Library Science in 1952 and the Master's degree in 1953 with a I class and first rank in the University.

He worked as Librarian of Nirmala College, Delhi, a college started by American Jesuits, during the year 1952-53. As the college was closed down in 1953 he applied for and was selected for a newly created post of librarian in the Forest Research Institute and Colleges, Dehra Dun. He was there from 1953-59.

It was when he was working in Dehra Dun that he got married to Chechamma, daughter of Advocate Mr.P.K.Kurien of Kottayam in 1955. His elder son Abraham Isaac was born in Dehra Dun in 1956. He is now a lawyer practising in Trivandrum. His second son Kurien Isaac, born in 1958, is now a Professor in the Mechanical Engineering Department of the IIT, Powai, Mumbai.

In 1959 he joined the Kerala University as the University Librarian. Since 1961 he was heading both the University Library and the Department of Library and Information Science until he relinquished the post of University Librarian in 1980. But he continued to be the Professor and Head of the Department till his retirement in 1985. After this also, Prof.Isaac held almost continuous assignments. During 1986 he served in the University of Calicut as a U.G.C. Visiting Professor; He worked on a U.G.C. Book Writing Project during 1987 and 1988; and later he served in the Mahatma Gandhi University as Special Officer (Library) on a contract basis for two years.

Prof.Isaac has worked in a number of bodies, both academic and professional, at the local, State and national level, in responsible capacities. In the University of Kerala, he was the Dean of the Faculty of Arts for two terms, Chairman, Board of Studies in Library and Information Science from 1961 to 1986, and member of Senate, Academic Council, Faculty of Arts, and Finance Committee for different terms. He was also a member of the Board of Studies of several other universities. At the national level, he served as a member of the Review

Committee on Library Science, Standing Advisory Committee on University and College Libraries, and Convenor of the Library and Information Science Panel of the University Grants Commission. He was also U.G.C National Lecturer in Library and Information Science for a term in 1984. He also served on several other committees of academic and research institutions like the Executive Committee of the Indian National Scientific Documentation Centre, Delhi, National Social Science Documentation Centre, Delhi, National Guide Committee of the National Archives of India, Delhi, Manpower Development Committee of the Department of Science & Technology (Government of India), Delhi, the Committee appinted by the Department of Culture, Government of India for drafting National Library and Information Science Policy, Raja Rammohan Roy Library Foundation, Kolkatta, and several others. Prof.Isaac has been very closely associated with the activities of the national and state level professional associations. He was the founder President of the Kerala Library Association, and member, Indian Library Association and Council of the IASLIC, Calcutta. Now he is the Patron of KLA. He also served as a member of the Bhrana Samithi of Kerala Granthasala sangham from 1959 until its take over by the government in 1977 and in that capacity made significant contributions to the cause of public library movement in Kerala.

Prof.Isaac has widely travelled all over India and has maintained a high degree of intimacy with library professionals working in almost all important libraries in the country. During 1960-61 he visited U.S.A. and U.K. to study the organization and operation of university libraries and Library Schools.

Over 200 papers on various aspects of Library and Information Science are there to the credit of Prof.Isaac, many of them being papers presented in various national conference/ seminars/symposia,etc. He has also authored five books, viz Librares and Librarianship, Literature Search,Libraries in Distance Education (ed.); Glimpses of Library and Information Science and Library Legislation in India. He has a large wealth of disciples as he has been a teacher all along. Four research scholars have taken the Ph.D degree under his guidance and there are other research scholars still being guided by him.

He re-organized the Kerala University Library on modern lines and introduced several new forms of library service which enabled the library to acquire reputation as one of the best University libraries in India. In 1980 when he left charge of this library, it was a large system comprising themain university library, the campus central library, 28 departmental libraries, and a number of outstation study centres. This called for the development of sound library policies, careful planning and execution of work and a high degree of team spirit in the staff. This bears testimony to the professional competence and leadership qualities of Prof.Isaac. Further, the development of the Kerala University Library under Prof.Isaac could create in the minds of the enlightened public and the academic community in Kerala a sense of respect for qualified librarianship. Prof.Isaac was, therefore, invited by many new and old institutions to help in the re-organisation of their libraries. Thus, he prepared a number of project reports for the development/ reorganization of libraries in the State, like the State Legislature Library, the Kerala Agricultural University Library, the High Court Library, Quilon Public Library ,Calicut University Library, Library of the Institute of Management in Government, Trivandrum etc. Almost every important library in the State is indebted to him for the timely guidance and counsel it received from him in the course of its development.

The establishment of the Department of Library Science in the Kerala University and the starting of the B.Lib.Sc. degree course in 1961 marked not only the beginning of university level Library Science education in Kerala but also the continuous growth of the community of professional librarians, Prof.Isaac thereby took upon himself the task of producing a new generation of librarians with the required technical knowledge and professional motivation and attitude. Over the years he could bring out about 700 new librarians most of whom could find positions in the State itself while others have gone to other States and even to other countries to hold responsible positions.

Prof.Isaac's students have been, accepted everywhere as persons of both calibre and character. Such was the care and interest he took all along in shaping the librarians of the future. It is well known that as a teacher Prof.Isaac has excelled in the field emulating the example of his own great Guru, Dr.Ranganathan, and adding his own personal qualities of utmost sincerity, concern and openness to all his academic endeavours.

The leadership that Prof.Isaac gave to organized professional activities in the library field in India in general and in Kerala in particular have been most significant.

Therefore it was most befitting that, in recognition of his contributions, he was selected for the award of the Fellowship of the Raja Rammohan Roy Library Foundation (RRRLF) Kolkatta for the year 2003. This was the fourth award of the Fellowship since its inception in 2000 and the first to be given to any one from the southern part of the country. The Fellowship was formally conferred on Prof. Issac by His Excellency the Governor of Kerala on the 6th January 2005 at a well attended function in the V.J.T Hall organized by RRRLF. The citation read out on the occasion and presented to Prof.Issac succinctly describes his contributions and underlines his exalted professional status in the library sector in India. The citation is reproduced below in full:-

"RAJA RAM MOHAN ROY LIBRARY FOUNDATION (Established by the Department of Culture, Govt. of India) Block DD-34, Sector -1, Sell Lake City, Kalkatta-700066.

CITATION

Prof. K.A.Issac, the doyen of Library science, has distinguished himself by selfless service, remarkable academic scholarship and admirable administrative acumen for the past four decades. His contributions towards the development of library education and professionalism in library services at the state level and the national level are gratefully remembered and widely acknowledged.

He served as the Librarian of the Kerala University Library and retired as Professor and Head of the Department of Library and Information science in 1985. During his stewardship, the Kerala University Library could scale new heights and acquire its status as a library of eminence. It was Prof. Issac who pioneered Library and information Science Education in Kerala.

Right from 1953, Prof. Issac was engaged in research projects on the theoretical and practical aspects of librarianship. In these activities he was closely associated with the late Dr.s.R.Ranganathan. Prof. Issac has authored a number of books including "Library legislation in India: A critical and comparative study of State Library Acts."

Prof. Issac has gained unparalleled experience in the library sector, spanning from the grass roots to the national level. He has served on the Board of the Raja Rammohan Roy Library Foundation from 1984-89; he was also a member of the committee on National Policy on Library and Information Systems. Besides, Prof. Issac has been actively associated with Kerala Granthasala Sangham, Quilon public Library and Trivandrum Public Library.

A teacher of eminence, a professional with commitment, Prof. Issac stands out as a role model, with his gentle disposition, quiet confidence and inspiring vision In recognition of his rich contribution towards professionalisation of library services and library education in the country and enrichment of the library sector through his research and studies, Rammohan Roy Library Foundation confers its Fellowship on him".

Trivandrum
6-01-2005

Prof.Dr.G.Devarajan

1

Economics of Information and Knowledge

Prof. C. A. Augustine

0. INTRODUCTION

"Economics is a science which studies human behaviour as a relationship between ends and scarce means which have alternative uses" (Lionel Robbins). In other words, the basic problem with which economics is concerned is that of economizing on the scarce resources. Since all activities directed towards creation, collection, processing, organization, dissemination and use of information involve spending of scarce resources, like men, materials, and money, information is a fit subject for economic analysis. That explains the reason behind the origin and growth of the specialty called "economics of information / knowledge' or more recently the "information economics".

D.M. Lamberton (1971) has explained:

"The economics of information and knowledge, an emerging topic of interest for both economics and managerial science, analyses the processes by which information and knowledge is produced, diffused, stored, and used. It is not only because these processes absorb such a large share of resources that economists should accept responsibility for their analysis. There are additional reasons (Machlup, 1962, pp.9-10): government finances a large part of these activities; they give rise to important externalities; inelasticity of supply of labour exist in the information and knowledge industry; the lack of markets for the industry's products creates difficult problems of valuation for social accounting; one product, technology, results in continuing changes; the employment structure may be responding to demand shift from physical to 'brain' labour that is possibly related to the rate of economic growth; and some of the component activities and their associated institutions may be operating inefficiently."

1. TWO SIDES OF THE STUDY

The subject is studied from two different angles. One looks at the role of information and knowledge in the overall economy of a nation or the society as a whole. This angle is special to economists and management scientists. The second is concerned with the economic aspects of production, distribution and consumption (use) of information products and services. This is from the side of the library and information professionals. The purpose of this paper is to introduce some of the basic concepts and contributions in economics of information and knowledge (EoI & K) from both areas that are relevant to the understanding of this subject by library and information professionals.

2. INFORMATION AND KNOWLEDGE

A discussion on economics of information and knowledge presupposes some clear understanding about both the terms 'information' and 'knowledge'. There are many writers who employ these terms interchangeably, while others make clear distinction between these terms. Basically, "information is that which is communicated, it may be a message, a signal or a stimulus" (Jesse H. Shera, 1972). But, human communication can be either verbal or non-verbal, between individuals, or between human beings and machines, or between machines and machines (as humans programme them). All that are transferred in the process of communication (a message, a signal or a stimulus) from one point (the source) to the other (the destination) are information. In human communication what is so transferred most often takes the form of a record. For example is a graphic representation, a handwritten document, a printed book or journal article, a photograph, an instrument tracing like that of an ECG output, a computer print out, an e-mail message, or an e-book/journal. This is not to say that there is no possibility of any unrecorded information but there is the possibility that even unrecorded information will become eventually recorded. The concern of the library and information profession is almost entirely about all forms of recorded, and eventually recordable information.

In the above sense information is not knowledge. To quote W.L. Saunders (1980), "...information is not in itself knowledge, any more than knowledge is wisdom, But at least information provides raw material, which in due course can lead to new knowledge, if only via the restructuring of existing knowledge". It is only the precursor of knowledge, meaning thereby that it is information that leads to the building up of knowledge, either in the individual or in the society.

3. THE ECONOMISTS' VIEW OF INFORMATION

This phrase "Economics of information" appeared in the literature of economics only in the 1960s. Nevertheless, economists were aware of the place of information in economic activities much earlier. Adam Smith (1776), who is considered to be the father of modern economics, had realized that the learning process (involving input of required information) was the key to economic development because increase in the productive power of labour, which is the major factor of production, involved a knowledge process in the form of development of skill and dexterity. Adam Smith was also conscious of the role that information plays in market performance as he illustrated through the case of a street vendor who successfully markets his goods by 'crying' out the price to the potential buyers and thereby giving information to the buyers. Since then, many economists have studied the role of information / knowledge in areas like marketing of goods and services, controlling monopoly and competition, decision making, reduction of uncertainty and risk, policy making, resource allocation and development planning, etc. As early as in 1921 Frank H Knight of the London School of Economics and Political Science is reported to have made a pioneering contribution to EoI through his work "Risk, Uncertainty and Profit" (Lamberton, 1984).

The earlier economists were working on EoI&K in two different fronts. The first was the incidence of information / knowledge as a necessary input in different economic activities. Here information is recognized as an important resource. The second was the treatment given to information /knowledge as a commodity almost similar to economic goods.

4. TWO GREAT PIONEERS

Lamberton who reviewed the subject EoI for *ARIST 1984* paid a tribute to the two pioneers in the subject and wrote: "Both Jacob Marschak (1898-1977) and Fritz Machlup (1903-1983) were economists whose interests and contributions ranged widely but included major developments in information economics, and both appear to have taken up information economics in an attempt to analyze more completely problems already defined in economics" (Lamberton, 1984).

Marschak's interested areas were expected-utility theory, statistical decision theory, and subjective probability theory. In these areas of economic behaviour he investigated the importance of anticipating information. His basic idea was that the value of information is governed by the benefits generated by its optimal use and there he recognized the importance of communication and the factors limiting the transmission of information. From early 1950s he brought out a series of papers like "Towards an Economics Theory of Organization and Information" (1954), "Remarks on Economics of Information (1959), and "Economics of 1984). Inquiring, Communicating, Deciding" (1968) (Lamberton, 1984).

Fritz Machlup studied the role of information in a different perspective. His crucial publication *The production and Distribution of Knowledge in the United States* came out in 1962. In this he defined the 'knowledge industry' and produced statistical data to prove that this industry accounted for approximately 29% of the U.S. gross national product (GNP) in 1958. This pioneering work stimulated several other studies of the knowledge industry or information sector of other industrialized nations for the purpose of comparative economic analysis. Machlup planned to bring out a second edition to his book in 8 volumes. But only the first two were published, in 1980 and 1982 respectively, while two others were in the press when he died. In the words of another reputed economist "the very concept of knowledge industry contains enough dynamite to blast traditional economics into orbit" (Boulding, 1963).

Marschak and Machlup together had done much to shape the pattern of development of information economics. Marashak's studies were theoretical and aimed at establishing the concept that 'organization is an information handling decision system', while Machlup was providing detailed statistical account of information activities (Lamberton, 1984).

After Machlup the first all encompassing study of information activity in the US economy was done by Marc Uri Porat in 1977. Freeman and Katz (1978) described his work in these words: "For Porat, information is a collection of many heterogeneous goods and services that together comprise an activity in the economy. The information activity includes all the resources consumed in producing, processing, and distributing information goods and services. He also gives examples of information capital and information labor and goes on to define two major types of information activity – "one in the primary information sector where information is exchanged as a commodity, and one in the secondary sector where information is embedded in some other good or service and not explicitly exchanged."

5. INFORMATION AS A RESOURCE

As stated earlier the interest of economists in information was first manifested as the different analyses of its role in various economic activities where decision-making was involved. G.J. Stigler who published his first paper on EoI in 1961 made the following opening remark:

"One should have to tell academicians that information is a valuable resource: knowledge is power. And yet it occupies a slum dwelling in the town of economics. Mostly it is ignored: the best technology is assumed to be known; the relationship of commodities to consumer preferences is a datum. As one of the information-producing industries, advertising, is treated with a hostility that economists normally reserve for tariffs or monopolists."

"There are a great many problems in economics for which this neglect of ignorance is no doubt permissible or even desirable. But there are some for which this is not true, and I hope to show that some important aspects of economic organization take on a new meaning when they are considered from the viewpoint of the search for information."

Stigler was analyzing in this paper one important problem of information, viz. 'the ascertainment of market price'. He was exhorting against the general neglect of ignorance that then prevailed and advocating for the search for information. According to him, prices change in all non-centralized markets and the buyers and sellers want to know the prevailing prices in order to ascertain the most favourable price for selling or buying. This is done by 'canvassing' various sellers or buyers, as the case may be. This phenomenon he was calling 'search for information'. He wrote: "Price dispersion is a manifestation – and indeed, it is the measure – of ignorance in the market." The more the buyer search for prices the more savings he will have from reduction in price. But all search incur costs in terms of time and money. The cost of search for consumers is approximately proportional to the number of sellers approached and hence the cost need not be equal for all consumers. Sellers also incur costs in the search for prices. In their case, the marginal cost of search equals the expected increase in receipts as in the case with buyers. Advertising is obviously the method of identifying buyers and sellers. This reduces drastically the cost of search. There are also alternatives to advertisement, like trade fairs or dealer markets where both buyers and sellers can meet and know the prices. According to

Stigler, "The identification of sellers and the discovery of their prices is only one sample of the vast of role of the search for information in economic life. Similar problems exist in the detection of profitable fields for investment and in the worker's choice of industry, location, and job". He concludes: "Ignorance is like subzero weather: by a sufficient expenditure its effects upon people can be kept within tolerable or even comfortable bounds, but it would be wholly uneconomic entirely to eliminate all its effects. And, just as an analysis of man's shelter and apparel would be somewhat incomplete if cold weather is ignored, so also our understanding of economic life will be incomplete if we do not systematically take account of the cold winds of ignorance". Hence, recent research in the economics of information focuses largely upon the information structure of markets (Spence, 1974).

6. MARKETS WITH ASYMMETRIC INFORMATION

Many markets are characterized by asymmetrical information: actors on one side of the market have much better information than those on the other. Buyers for example often know less about the product than sellers. This can be called an "information asymmetry". There have been considerable amount of research work relating to the effects of informational asymmetries on market performance and on how well buyers and sellers can be matched up in respect of information. Most outstanding among them are by the three eminent economists of our time, A. Michael Spence, Joseph E. Stiglitz and George A. Akerlof, who were awarded jointly the Nobel Prize in Economics 2001 for their crucial contributions in the area of the markets with asymmetric information. These Nobel laureates had in the 1970s laid the groundwork for a general theory of markets with the so- called asymmetric information. According to the Royal Swedish Academy of Sciences the contribution of these three "form the core of modern information economics" and their works have led to real-world applications in areas ranging from agricultural markets to modern financial markets. For example, borrowers know more than lenders about the repayment prospects, managers and boards of directors know more than shareholders about the firm's profitability, prospective clients know more than insurance companies about their accident risks (Augustine, 2001). This information asymmetry is indeed an imbalance caused by the absence or availability of correct information. Whoever has better information is in an advantageous position who can even exploit the interests of the other party.

7. INFORMATION AS A COMMODITY

That information / knowledge is a commodity is a big idea in economics. But it was too slow to get general acceptance. K.E. Boulding's paper "The economics of knowledge and knowledge of economics" in 1966 contained a survey of the ideas connected with information as a commodity. He pointed out that the commodity aspects of knowledge have been neglected in the theory of the market, the theory of development, and the theory of decision making. He was concerned with "the role of knowledge in social systems, both as a product of the past and as a determinant of the future". It is relevant to note the commodity concept as explained by Boulding: "As it is exchange or potentiality of exchange or relevance to exchange that make things commodities, one would think that economist would be interested in knowledge as a commodity. It is certainly something which is bought and sold". But economists were reluctant to think of knowledge / information as a commodity, because, unlike other commodities, information is not amenable to measurement and therefore to pricing, it cannot be fully appropriated like any other property, it can be duplicated or reproduced, its possession is not generally exclusive, and it can generate further knowledge once in possession of an individual.

Michael D. Cooper in *ARIST 1973* discussed the commodity concept of information in the context of the market mechanism. According to him there are a number of problems in applying the market mechanism in allocating information. "First, if it is assumed that equal access to information is a right, just as is freedom of speech, freedom of religion, and privacy, then a decision must be made whether the market mechanism is adequate for allocating information to individuals ... Alternative institutional arrangements other than the price system may have to be made to insure the equality of the distribution. Second, if the market mechanism is used to aid the allocation of information, then there is the implication that a certain quantity of information is available at a stated price....A third problem with use of the market mechanism to allocate information has to do with the characteristics of information. A decision cannot be made as to the price to pay for the information until the information has been examined and evaluated...Thus information *about* the information is required before a value can be assigned. Still another problem relates to the fact that, in the process of transferring information from one individual to another, the resource is not depleted...When information is disseminated, both parties have the information ...Thus there may be no economic incentive to engage in the transfer process" (Cooper, 1973).

8. RESOURCE ALLOCATION

If alternative institutional arrangements other than the price system have to be made to insure the equality of the distribution of information and knowledge it becomes a subject matter for consideration in welfare economics. "Welfare economics is concerned with the extent to which the objectives of society as a whole are satisfied, rather than the individual objectives of its members"(Cooper, 1973).

In welfare economics decisions are based on evaluation of the social welfare function and cost–benefit analysis can be employed in aiding the allocation decisions. In this context it is relevant to know the important contributions of Kenneth J. Arrow who was awarded Nobel Prize in economics in 1972. During the 1960s and 1970s Arrow's research was mainly on uncertainty and information and that was recognized in his Nobel Prize. One of his significant papers was on "Economic welfare and the allocation of resources for invention" which came out in 1962. By invention he meant the production of knowledge. He wrote; "From the viewpoint of welfare economics, the determination of optimal resource allocation for invention will depend on the technological characteristics of the invention process and the nature of the market for knowledge". In examining how far the perfect competition will lead to an optimal allocation of resources he identified three reasons for the possible failure of perfect competition in achieving optimality in resource allocation and they are 'indivisibilities, inappropriability and uncertainty'. According to him a given piece of information is by definition an indivisible commodity. The economic characteristics of information as a commodity and, in particular, of invention as a process for the production of information, lead to uncertainty in resource allocation. "The central economic fact about the processes of invention and research is that they are devoted to the production of information. By the very definition of information, invention must be a risky process, in that the output (information obtained) can never be predicted perfectly from the inputs" . In a free enterprise economy there can be only under-investment in invention and research because it is risky and because the product can be appropriated only to a limited extent. For optimal allocation to invention, therefore, it would be necessary for the government or some other agency not governed by profit-and-loss criteria to finance research and invention." Research and development activities undertaken in the private sector usually will not be adequately funded. "If the government and other nonprofit institutions are to compensate for the under-allocation of resources to invention private enterprise, two problems arise: how shall the amount of resources devoted to invention be determined, and how shall efficiency in their use be encouraged?" (Arrow, 1962). These questions might have engaged the attention of subsequent researches.

In economics when choices have to be made in the allocation of funds to competing projects different tools such as welfare economics, cost-benefit analysis, demand analysis, cost-effective analysis and operations research techniques are used. These tools can be employed also to information service institutions such as libraries, information retrieval systems and even to the entire spectrum of the information industry. According to Cooper (1973), "Resource allocation tools have two major functions: they serve as external allocation aids and as internal allocation devices. External allocation refers to decisions made with respect to allocation of resources among competing institutions, while internal allocation tools aid in allocation within an industry or an organization".

9. INFORMATION INDUSTRY STUDIES

There have been numerous studies on the information and the information industry and they range widely in scope and emphasis. "There is need to look beyond individual case studies of either an information supplier or a user to broader analysis of the economy-wide input-output interdependence of economic activities." (Lamberton, 1984.). A study of that dimension was the OECD project on the international comparison of information sectors that came out in 1981. The typology used in this study is reproduced below in Table 1.

Table 1. Typology of Information Occupations (OECD Project on the International Comparison of Information Sectors)

Information Producers:	Scientific and technical workers (Components) Market search and coordination Specialists Information gatherers Consultative services
Information Processors:	Administrative and managerial Process control and supervisory Clerical and related (Components)
Information Distributors:	Educators Communication workers
Information Infrastructure Occupations:	Information machine Workers Postal and telecommunications

Source: OECD, 1981 Vol.1; p.24.

10. MACRO-ECONOMICS OF INFORMATION

Macro-economics is concerned with the analysis of economies. Macro-economics of information deals with the aggregate inputs to and outputs from the information sector. Machlup's study described earlier was the most comprehensive survey of the resources devoted by the US economy to the acquisition and transmission information. Edwin B. Parker (1973) 'added 'some intriguing extension and projections of the Machlup's work' (Spence, 1974). Together they gave the impression that the information/ knowledge sector is both large and growing. Based on their statistics Cooper (1983) presented estimates of the continuous growth information economy. But the difficulty is in estimating the effects of information on economic growth as there is difficulty in measuring information. Researches have to be directed towards developing more direct measures of the productivity of information (Cronin & Gudim, 1986) . There are ample studies on measuring the investment in human capital, like education, training, and work experience, as knowledge embodied in people. Such studies are there also in respect of the human capital in the information sector.

11. MICRO-ECONOMICS OF INFORMATION

Micro-economics is generally devoted to the study of households and firms. Micro-economics studies the information processing behaviour of individuals. It analyzes the information an individual needs in the rational decision-making process. Marschak (1971) has mathematically formulated this problem in terms of the costs and delays involved in obtaining the necessary information. The whole process is a chain of events consisting of 'inquiring, communicating and deciding' and in this process the cost and benefit of the information are calculated and the value of the information is determined. The process is almost the same whether it is in a single-person decision making or in decision-making by a group of individuals (teams) or in decision-making by networks of teams or organizations (Marschak & Radner,1972).

12. DR. RANGANATHAN AND ECONOMICS OF INFORMATION

Librarian community has a reason for special pride in the subject of EoI. The very basis of EoI is the premise that information is a commodity. This idea was first mooted in the library field by Dr. S.R. Ranganathan (1944). He brought out the Economico-Bibliographic Chain (EBC) to illustrate the classes and kinds of bibliographies of books. He treated books as commodities and bibliographies as catalogues of these commodities prepared from the special point of view of the various parties involved in their production, distribution and consumption. According to Dr. Ranganathan books are 'double entities'. People are interested in them either (1) as mere material commodity, or (2) as thought made tangible and communicable. Table 2 below gives the diagrammatic representation of the EBC showing the parties who are concerned with this commodity and their different interests, and the classes and names of bibliographies they may compile.

Table 2. Economico-Bibliographic Chain of Dr. S.R. Ranganathan

Phases/classes	*Agents*	*Types of bibliographies*
1. Consumers (Thought)	1.1 Readers	1.1 Reading lists
	*1.2 Authors	1.2 Authors' biographies
2. Distributors (Thought)	*2.1 Reference Librarians	2.1 Subject bibliographies
	2.2 Library Cataloguers	2.2 Library catalogues.
	2.3 Book Selection Agents	2.3 Book Selection lists.
3. Distributors (Material)	3.1 Bibliophiles	3.1 Bibliophilic bibliographies.
	3.2 Book Sellers	3.2 Book seller's catalogues.
	3.3 Publishers	3.3 Publisher's catalogues.
4. Producers (Material)	*4.1 Governments	4.1 Copyright lists.
	4.2 Binders	4.2 Binders' bibliographies
	4.3 Printers	4.3 Printers' bibliographies.
5. Producers (Thought)	5. Authors	5. Author bibliographies.

The 5 phases in the EBC correspond to the 5 classes of bibliographies. Each of these 5 phases has its own links and each link corresponds to a type of bibliography. Some of the links are appearing at junctions of phases (marked by asterisk) and they represent overlapping of both material and thought interests. Although Ranganathan's commodity concept in EBC was related to books, the fundamental idea that information / knowledge is a commodity involving economic activities was first introduced by him. This commodity idea, however, did not attract librarians for a long time until economists began to research and publish profusely on this subject.

13. ECONOMICS OF INFORMATION IN LIS

Although the phrase "economics of information" began to appear in the terminology of economists in the 1960's, in the field of library and information science this made its entry probably in the 1980's. This was primarily in connection with the information system evaluation studies. At first, it was mainly centered on the costs and effectiveness of information services, followed by studies on the value of information for the user, and on the productivity of information work. Later phases showed increasing interest in pricing of information products and services, particularly in the context of a profit oriented market and fee-based library and information services. There were three central areas of concern for library and information managers in economics of information (Casper, 1983; Van House, 1984). They were:

(a) Information supply- economics of information production, and pricing of information products;

(b) Information demand - acquisition and use of information; and

(c) Special problems of information as a product or resource - e.g. pricing of use; public funding of information production, etc.

14. INFORMATION PRICING AND PRICE STUDIES

Information pricing and price studies is an area closely

identified with the economics of information production. Although it is difficult to assess the potential value of information to its users, producers and vendors go on fixing the prices of information products and services. In the modern context pricing studies form part of the subject marketing of information products and services. The marketing aspect will be discussed later.

Pricing and price studies are a fond area of research of librarians. Hence there are innumerable studies in this area. They may be either directed towards the rate and range of price escalation, especially in S & T journals, trying to analyze the factors contributing price rises or the alternatives to paying increased subscriptions, etc. Repo (1987) who surveyed this subject for *ARIST,* remarked: "The price of information hardly arise from information itself and its value-in-use but from transfer or equipment costs and sometimes also from commercial profit". He added that although information is partially a public good its dissemination is largely commercial. A later work by Frans Spigai (1991) surveyed the price studies mainly under three heads: 'the serials crisis', 'the book crisis' and 'electronic publishing'. According to him the studies relating to serial prices fall into two categories: (1) those examining the causes for the extra-ordinary price increases; and (2) those examining the possible measures to stem these prices. Some possible causes as identified are: exchange rates, rising cost of doing business (especially due to journal page growth), inflation, and rampant profiteering. So too are the suggested solutions: boycott certain publishers, educate faculty (authors and readers), justify larger budgets, stimulate competition and alternative technologies, and share resources. (Dougherty & Barr, 1988). A report of the Economic Consulting Service based on the study of four large publishers (Elsevier, Pergamon, Plenum and Springer-Verlag) estimated the publisher costs and resultant profits form 1973 to 1987. It showed that during the period studied publishers' profits rose from 40% to 137%, the average funding support to ARL libraries rose to 243%, average per cent of library expenditure for materials rose from 29% to 33%, total budget for serials rose form 40% to 152%, and average serials holdings of the estimated universe of serials dropped from 32% to 26% (quoted by Spigai, 1991). Similar studies were done in different places and in different contexts. Recently a study was done in the Kerala University Dept. of Lib & Inf Science about costs escalation in botany periodicals (Deepthy & Varghese, 2004) during the period from 1976 to 2003.They found significant association between the costs escalation and country of origin. For example journals from the Netherlands showed the highest price rise with an average annual increase of 117.09% (=745.23% in Indian rupees).

The question that is usually asked in this context is 'how can the publishers continue to increase prices and expect libraries to continue to subscribe?'. Bebensee, et al (1989) have posited that "publishers understand well that libraries simply must subscribe in order to provide current /essential information to faculty and to maintain collection continuity. This demand inelasticity is common when products have few substitutes; buyers believe that the product is needed regardless of cost. Even if there are a few cancellations resulting from an increase in price, publisher costs decrease, profits increase, and total revenues often increase as well. The authors conclude that econometric studies are needed to estimate demand curves and elasticities of various scholarly and professional journals.

The serials crisis has contributed substantially to a book crisis also, that is in the prices and pricing of books and monographs. Some studies have pointed out that book prices are increasing faster than inflation to cover smaller unit sales; this phenomenon seems particularly pronounced for science, technology and medical (STM) titles. Perhaps the recent aspect in the price and pricing studies is what pertains to electronic literature. There are many issues that influence price structures, pricing strategy, price discrimination and differentiation. licensing, leasing and buying, and even price tolerance by buyers and users. As already stated, pricing has a crucial place in marketing. Questions like: what are the costs involved? what should be the criteria for pricing? what is the ethics involved in pricing and charging library & information services?, etc. are discussed in professional literature. Most of these topics are occurring in the studies related to marketing and they are taken to the next section.

15. INFORMATION MARKETING

Jennifer Rowley (2001) has defined information marketing as 'the marketing of information-based products and services'. According to her, "Typical information based products include books, CDs, videos, journals, journal articles, databases, electronic journals, newspapers and databanks. Typical information-based services include public libraries, academic libraries, workplace information centres, access to databases, electronic current-awareness services, business consultancy services, subject gateways, and Web-based information services. Libraries, bookshops, database producers, online search services, business intelligence services and portals act as the interface between the consumer and the producer in respect of these products. Within the marketplace there are also a host of other organizations that often interact with the consumer through one of these 'retailers'."

The above passage sets the scenario of the present information market place very clearly. The definition given by the Chartered Institute of Marketing (UK) reads: "Marketing is the management process which identifies, anticipates, and supplies customer requirements efficiently and profitably". The key aspects in this definition are: (1) marketing is a business process, and (2) marketing is for meeting customer requirements. Therefore, organizations that stand for meeting customer needs should have a marketing orientation in their overall functioning. According to Webber (1998) "marketing is an all-pervading philosophy that should be practiced by everyone in the organization. The point of difference between the traditional and the modern outlooks towards library and information services has been explained by the oft-quoted statement that "you sell what you have and you market what the buyer needs".

Present day librarians and information professionals have much to learn from modern marketing. Marketing includes three stages: planning, implementation and evaluation. There are 6 steps in the planning stage: market segmentation, product development, promotion, distribution, pricing and evaluation. Among them market segmentation is the most crucial step which in turn involves market research and analysis. In the context of library information marketing, market research includes user need studies, identification of users and target groups.

16. DEMAND ANALYSIS

In the context of information marketing a special area that has proved attractive to pursue for information economists and found potentially important for the information professionals is 'demand analysis'. Objective assessment of the usage of information services are necessary for identifying the services to be operated and for their investment needs. The purpose of demand analysis is to find out the relationship between price and quantity. It is possible to develop a function that describes the quantity of information to be supplied at a given prices. There are some researchers who have developed models to predict demand for information services. Among several others in this category Sanford V. Berg (1970) could do a prediction of the demand for scientific journals. In his models, two subscription-demand curves were distinguished: one generated by institutions such as libraries, and the other generated by individual subscribers. He mathematically formulated demand as a function of the price of the journal, number of pages published, number of researchers in the field, and number of institutions employing the researchers. Empirical estimates of these parameters were made, the elasticity of curve was examined, and pricing and page policies were evaluated in light of the functions. (Cooper, 1973). Demand analysis involves marketing research as it has to rely on information about consumer needs in making predictions about preferences and behaviour. For data gathering various marketing research techniques are to be employed.

Sheila Anne Elizabeth Webber did the survey of "Pricing and Marketing On line Information Services" for *ARIST 1998* has brought out many salient information on marketing generally as well as the prices and pricing of electronic information in particular. She surveyed the ideas that have emerged out of the studies in the area of on line marketing from 1991 to 1997. For this purpose, she defined online services "as remotely held electronic information services accessed via networks". Stephen E. Arnold (1990) introduced a new concept called 'relationship marketing' which became a buzz phrase of the mid-1990s. This is meaningful in the context of the Internet, which is seen as 'an enabling mechanism for creating one-to-one relationships'. The traditional producer-oriented marketing theory based on a marketing mix defined as 'the 4 Ps: Product, Price, Promotion and Place' has met with opposition and a paradigm shift centered on customer-oriented relationship building came to be advocated. A replacement for the 4 P's was suggested by Bob Lauterborn (1990) viz. 'the Cs: Customer needs and wants; Cost to the customer of satisfying those needs and wants; Communication; and Convenience'. Virtually, it is the replacement of 'price' by 'cost' to the customer. In online services the customer incurs cost of telecommunication, hardware and software, as well investing of time and training required which is the bigger part of total cost than the database price. For Rowley (1995) electronic information is a mixture of product and service, and online information exhibit the characteristics of a service more strongly than some other forms of electronic information. Some key problems are there in marketing information services arising from their intangibility, variability, perishability, inseparability, etc. (Kotler, 1997). Because of these and other characteristics of information as a product or service, special strategies are needed for pricing them according to the value obtained by users. Barry & Yadav (1996) have proposed three strategies: 'satisfaction pricing', 'relationship pricing', and 'efficiency pricing'. Coming to the question of marketing high-technology products there are some obvious common characteristics in them, such as the high cost of initial production and low cost of reproduction and the fact that customers may need to experience the product before being able to estimate its value to them. Cahill (1996) suggested that pricing in the electronics information industry may follow the pattern of the software industry, with decreasing prices or increasing functionality for the same price. In the case of international online services the problems are more special. The value of the same information to customers in different countries may not be equal depending upon the language, the foreign currency involvement, the inadequate coverage of local information, etc. Further, they have to bear more telecommunication charges. There is an extensive amount of writings on the value of information. Saracevic & Kantor (1997) had identified three research approaches to the value of information: normative value, realistic value, and perceived value. One important question is the connect-time charging as a policy. There are arguments for and against this policy. Collier (1993) has identified four pricing methods: (1) connect time, (2) an amalgamation of connect time and other elements, (3) subscription, and (4) payment according to quantity of data retrieved. There are advantages and disadvantages for each of these options. Collier stresses that pricing should reflect value to the customer and notes that pricing must be a marketing decision. There are some important issues that have influenced pricing strategy from the start of the online industry. These are mainly borne out of intermediaries in the information chain. The relationship between information producers and hosts on the one side and information professionals and intermediaries on the other side need to be studied in detail. Arnold (1989) expressed the view that "information providers who rely on third parties to distribute their information in electronic form have little influence on prices". Normally the vendor knows more about the product and its value than the customer does, and therefore the vendor has more control of the pricing market. (Webber, 1998). Recently, a major influence on pricing of online services is the Internet. Internet has lowered costs, which normally influence pricing decisions. Webber had concluded her survey with the following optimistic note: "The effect of Internet as a low-cost distribution channel and the entry of more players into the online market seem bound to prolong this area of change. There will certainly also be more changes in the pricing of electronic journal and magazine articles. The one consolation is that, in this continuingly complex environment, there seems to be more need than ever for alert, informed information professionals who can steer end-users to the best pricing deals".

17. EVALUATION OF LIBRARIES AND INFORMATION SERVICES

EoI has a special place in the evaluation of libraries and information services. A library as a whole and every one of its services specifically has a defined goal. Once this goal is correctly described it is possible to measure how well a particular library or any of its activities helps to realize the goal. This type of evaluation can be done by using the methods of economic analysis. Cost-benefit analysis is one of the aids used in these methods.

18. COST-BENEFIT ANALYSIS

It was in 1972 that *ARIST* dealt with EoI for the first time. This chapter was authored by John H. Wilson and was titled as "Costs, Budgeting, and Economics of Information Processing". It shows that the very first area of concern for information professionals in EoI was cost studies of information processing or other aspects closely connected to the evaluation information services and libraries. Interests in such studies surfaced at a point of time when people began to depart from the accepted faith that information services were to be supplied free, particularly in R&D establishments. Gradually, economics began to be considered as the key factor in all information activities.

Information services began to incur increasing costs to the managements and they became more and more eager to assess the benefits accrued from services to both the users and their organizations. But, costs and benefits of information services, (for that matter of any other social activity) cannot be measured in terms of money. Welfare economics, that branch of economics in which economists categorize non-profit information activities, warns that the total welfare of the community must be considered in the matter of the benefits derived from information. This emphasizes the question of social benefits accruing from libraries and information services. Similarly, there are also the social costs involved because welfare economics is concerned with the conditions that determine the total economic welfare of a community. The benefits to one individual can be increased without diminishing the benefits of anybody else. According to Beaumol (1965) the basic difficulty is in stating all input and output data in terms of money. In the words of Wilson (1972) "The cost to society of producing some item may contain elements which can never be expected to show up in the books of the producing firm...Similarly, the production of the item may provide social benefits such as improved technology...and other advantages which are not collected in the revenues of the firm". Therefore, cost studies should take into account not only the marginal costs as in the classical economics. The cost that information managers are to be concerned with are the working costs including total costs, unit costs, average costs, and costs of particular operations. Further, the cost of setting up in business (the establishment costs) and the social costs have to be considered. Wilson concentrated attention on matters like defining costs and delineating the ingredients of costs in the information processing and services environment, cost-effectiveness analyses of storage and retrieval systems, and cost-benefit analysis. He surveyed extensively the literature on costs until then and had to agree with Mick (1979) who observed that "although the methodologies for measuring costs were available, application of them was hampered by the lack of standards". Flowerdew & Whitehead (1974) had worked on cost-benefit analysis and cost-effectiveness in information science. This paper, as Mick had commented, "provided a benchmark on the measurement of costs, effectiveness and benefits in scientific and technical information". In 1978 Kleijnen developed a critical survey of the theories and tools for quantifying financial benefits of information. Wilkinson (1980) worked on the criteria for counting the costs and benefits. These authors have emphasized the advantages of cost-benefit analysis in economics of information. Repo (1987) who surveyed the literature has summarized the advantages of cost-benefit analysis as follows:

"Cost-benefit analysis aids decision making when we seek answers to the following questions:

(1) How much should the organization invest in information products and services (e.g., compared with competitors)?

(2) How much of the organization's running costs should be invested in information services and how much in other activities?

(3) Is the size of the present information budget adequate, or should it be changed?

(4) How the resources are allocated among different information services?

(5) Are the investments in particular information services Successful, or should they be changed?

(6) How useful are the individual information service projects?

(7) How is the information services priced?

(8) How should information production and dissemination be supported or taxed?

(9) Is pricing suitable for management and investment plans?

(10) What kind of measures is needed to monitor the performance of the information services?"

Since then such studies have become numerous in LIS literature. But they were mostly using the measures of money, which is a characteristic approach of economists. But in LIS this approach is not found generally agreeable because benefits derived from library and information services by the individual or the society, or the value of information and knowledge cannot always be measured in monetary terms. Nevertheless, many empirical studies were undertaken and these studies mainly focused on analyzing the three basic concepts involved, viz. costs, effectiveness and benefits, and identifying their ingredients. By combining those basic concepts researchers could separate five levels for examining the economics of information.(Lancaster 1977). These levels are: (a) costs, (b) effectiveness, (c) efficiency, (d) benefits, and (e) value (or cost-benefit analysis).

19. CONCLUSION

The merits of an economics of information and knowledge have been its potential contribution on furthering economic analysis in particular areas like consumer theory, welfare economics and economic developments. There can be other merits of wider significance also. For example it can contribute to a dis-equilibrium economics. It can bridge the gap between micro-economics and macro-economics. "This claim may raise a query: in what ways does an economics of information and knowledge differ from the spate of new sub-disciplines (e.g. ...economics of education, defence economics, health economics...) that have emerged in recent years? These new subjects have been plagued by the same old problems of reconciling the parts or sub-models with the aggregate or macro-economic schema. The answer is that these subjects represent the application of the tools of economic analysis to an area of interest, whereas information and knowledge problems are embedded with in the corpus of economic analysis itself". (Lamberton, 1971). This statement explains the real difference between economics of information as studied by economists and by library and information professionals. For the latter, perhaps, it is more convenient and meaningful to accept the terminology used by Cooper (1973), namely "economics of information science".

In conclusion I should say that what have been described

in this chapter does not constitute the whole of economics of information. I have only tried to present before the readers a general overview of a very large subject as it has developed over the years. I don't claim that it is a comprehensive survey nor that I have made any original contribution here. I have been reading on this subject for quite a long time and of late also teaching some aspects of this subject. These are my only qualifications in writing this. For this I have used mainly the annual surveys brought out by the ARIST in this subject and the book of Penguin Readings on the subject edited by D.M. Lamberton. It is my wish that library and information professionals with economics background should come forward to engage in more serious research on specific aspects of the economics of information and for them this work can help in the choice of research problems.

REFERENCES:

1. Arnold, Stephen E. (1990), "Marketing electronic information: theory, practice and challenge, 1980-1990" in Williams, Martha Ed. Annual Review of Information Science and Technology (ARIST) 1990 (Vol. 25) pp.87-144; American Society for Information Science.
2. Arrow, Kenneth J. (1962) "Économic welfare and the allocation of resources for invention" in The rate and direction of invention activity: economic and social factors; Princeton, National Bureau of Economic Research; Pp 609-626.
3. Arrow, Kenneth J. and Scitovsky, T. eds. (1969) Readings in welfare economics; selected by a committee of the American Economic Association, Illinois.
4. Augustine, C.A. (2001) "Editorial" KELPRO Bulletin 5(1) June 2001; Pp. i-ii.
5. Augustine, C.A. (2001). "Some aspects in the economics of information" (K. Kunhamed Memorial Endowment Lecture given in the University of Calicut on 25th May 2001) published as part of Library co-operation in a networked world ed. by M. Bavakutty, et al.

6. Beaumol, William J. (1965). Economic theory and operation analysis. ; N.J. Prentice-Hall.

7. Beaumol, William J. (1967). *On the economic theory of library operation*; Princeton, Mathematica.

8. Beaumol, William J. et al. *Manual of pricing and cost determination for organizations engaged in dissemination of knowledge*; N.Y. New York University.

9. Bebenesee, Mark, et al (1989). "Elasticity of *journal* pricing" *The Acquisition Librarian* 2(2):219-227.

10. Berg, Sanford V. (1970). Structure, *behavior and performance in the scientific journal market*; Washington DC, National Bureau of Economic Research.

11. Berry, Leonard L. and Yadav, Manjit S. (1996). "Capture and communicate value in the pricing of services" *Sloan Management Review* Summer 1996; 37(4)' 41-51.

12. Boulding, K.E. (1966). "The economics of knowledge and knowledge of economics" *American Economic Review* 56 (2)1`-13.

13. Cahill, Denis J. (1996). "Further issues in pricing strategies for electronic information" *Pricing Strategy and Practice* 4(1):34-38.

14. Casper, Cheryl A. (1983). "Economics and information science" in *Information science in action; system design* ed by A. Debons. London, Mauritius Nijhoff Publishers; Pp. 565-572.

15. Collier, Harry (1993). *Strategies in the electronic information industry: a guide for the 1990s*. Ed.2; Celine, Infonortics Ltd.

16. Cooper, Michael D. (1973). "The economics of information" in *ARIST 1973* (Vol 8) ed. By Carlos A. Caudra.

17. Cooper, Michael D. (1983). "The structure and future of the information economy" *Information Processing and Management* 19(1):9-26.

18. Cronin, Blaise and Gudin, M. (1986). "Information and productivity; a review of research" *International Journal of Information Management* 6(2):85-101.

19. De Saez, Eileeen Elliott (1993). *Marketing concepts for libraries and information services*. Ed. 2; London, Facet Publishing.

20. Deepthy, K. and Varghese, M *(2004)*.. "Cost escalation of scholarly periodicals in Botany: a comparative study of British,American, Dutch and Indian Publications". *KELPRO Bulletin 8(1&2),48-57.*

21. Dougherty, Richard M. and Barr, Nancy E. (1988). *Paying the piper; ARL libraries respond to skyrocketing journal subscription prices.*

22. Flowerdew, A.D.J. and Whitehead, C.M.E. (1974). *Cost-effectiveness and cost benefit analysis in Information science.* London School of Economics and Political Science.

23. Freeman, James E. and Katz, *Ruth* M. (1978). "Information marketing" in *ARIST 1978* (Vol. 13).

24. Griffiths, Jose Maria (1982). "The value of information and related systems, products, and services" in *ARIST 1982* (Vol. 17) Pp.269-284.

25. Hindle, A. and Raper, D. (1976). "The economics of information" in *ARIST 1976* (*Vol.*11) 27-54.

26. Kleijnen, Jack P.C. (1978). *Quantifying financial benefits of information; a critical survey of theories and tools*; Tilburg, Katholeke Hogeschool Dept of Business Economics.

27. Knight, Frank H. (1921). *Risk, uncertainty and profit.* Boston, M.A. Houghton.

28. Kotler, Philip (1997). *Marketing management: analysis, planning, implementation and control.* Ed. 9; Upper Saddle River, Prentice-Hall.

29. Lamberton, D.M. (1971) "Introduction" in *Economics of*

information and knowledge: selected readings, ed. By D.M. *Lamberton*; Penguin; Pp7-17.

30. Lamberton, D.M., Ed. (1971). Economics of information and knowledge: selected readings. Penguin Modern Economic Readings ed. by B. J. McMormic. Penguin.
31. Lamberton, D.M. (1984). "The economics of information and organization" in *ARIST 1984* (Vol. 19); Pp. 4-30.
32. Lancaster, F.W. (1977). *The measurement and evaluation of library services*; Arlington, Information Resources Press.
33. Lauterborn, Bob (1990). "New marketing litany:four P's Passe: C-words take over" *Advertising Age*, October 1990. 2(9):22-26.
34. Machlup, Fritz (1962). *The production and distribution of knowledge in the United States*: Princeton University Press.
35. Machlup, Fritz (1980). *Knowledge: its creation distribution and economic significance. Vol I: Knowledge and knowledge production*; Princeton University Press.
36. Marschak, Jacob. (1968). "Economics of inquiring, communicating, deciding" *American Economic Review* 58(2):1-18.
37. Marschak, Jacob (1974). *Economic information, decision and prediction: selected essays. Vol .II;* Boston, MAD Reider.
38. Marschak, Jacob and Radner, Roy (1972). *Economic theory of teams: Cowler Foundation Monograph*, No.22. Yale University Press.
39. Mick, Colin K. (1979). "Cost analysis of information systems and services" in *ARIST 1979* (Vol. 14), Pp. 37-64.
40. OECD (1981). *Information activities, electronics and telecommunication technologies; impact on employment, growth and trade*. Paris, Organization for Economic Co-operation and Development.

41. Parker, Edwin B. (1973) "Information and society" in *ARIST 1973* (vol.8) Pp. 345-373.

42. Porat, Marc Uri and Rubin, Michael R. (1977). *The information economy; definition and measurement.* Washington DC. US Govt. Printing Office.

43. Ranganathan, S.R. (1944). *Document bibliography and reference service*; Madras Library Association.

44. Repo, Aatto J. (1987). "Economics of information" in *ARIST 1987* (Vol. 22) ed by William Martha E. Pp. 3-35.

45. Rowley, Jennifer(1995). "Issues in pricing strategies for electronic information". *Pricing Strategy and Practice* 3(2):4-13.

46. Rowley, Jennifer (2001). *Information* marketing; Aldershot, Ashgate.

47. Saunders, W.L. (1980). "Information, the 'unscarce' resource"; opening address in the Joint Conference of the ASLIB, the Institute of Information Scientists, and Library Association, held in September 1980.

48. Saracevic, Tefko and Kantor, Paul B. (1997). "Studying the value of library and information services. Part I: Establishing a theoretical frame work" *Journal of American Society for Information Science* June 1997 48(6):527-541.

49. Schackle, G.L.S. (1972). *Epistemics and economics: a critique of economic doctrines.* Cambridge University Press.

50. Shera, Jesse H. (1972). *The foundation of education for librarianship.* Becker & Hayes.

51. Spence, A. Michael (1974). "An economist's view of information" in *ARIST 1974* (Vol.99) ed by Carlos A. Cuadra. Washington DC. American Society for Information Science.

52. Smith, Adams (1776). *The wealth of nations.*

53. Spigai, Fran (1991). "Information pricing" in *ARIST 1991* (Vol. 26) ed by Martha E. Williams. Pp. 39-69.

54. Stigler, George J. (1961). "The economics of information" *Journal of Political Economy* 69:3 ; June 1961; 213-225.

55. Stigler, George J. (1983). "Nobel Lecture: the process and progress of economics" *Journal of Political Economy* 91(4):529-545.

56. Stiglitz, J.E. (1977). "Symposium on economics of information: introduction" *Review of Economic Studies* 44:389-391.

57. Van House, Nancy A. (1984). "Research on the economics of libraries". *Library Trends* 32(4): 407-423.

58. Webber, Sheila Anne Elizabeth (1998). "Pricing and marketing online information services" in *ARIST 1998* (Vol.33) ed. By Martah E. Williams. Pp. 39-83.

59. Wilkinson, J.B. (1980). "Economics of information: criteria for counting the cost and benefit" ASLIB Proceedings 32(1):1-9.

60. Wilson, John H. Jr. (1972). "Costs, budgeting, and economics of information processing" in *ARIST 1973* (Vol. 7) ed by Carlos A. Caudra. Pp. 39-67.

2
Continuing Professional Development of LIS Teachers: A Strategy

Vijayakumar, K.P.

0. INTRODUCTION

This is an era where changes are taking place so rapidly in all spheres of life that constant updating of knowledge and sharpening of skills have become inevitable. The best method of achieving this target is by continuing professional development (CPD). Here, the concept CPD is used in the place of continuing education (CE), the common term used to denote the programmes aimed at updating the knowledge of individuals, because of the specificity in the meaning of the former concept. CPD, the term popularized by the Library Association (UK), can be defined as "the planned and systematic updating of professional knowledge and improvement of professional competence throughout the individual's working life."[1]

CPD is aimed at:

i. Developing the existing skills;

ii. Acquiring new skills;

iii. Remaining in touch with relevant issues in the job and in the profession;

iv. Increasing the knowledge, understanding and the skills required for the job; and

v. Developing personally with in the job.

1. IMPACT OF INFORMATION TECHNOLOGY ON LIBRARY SERVICES

The advent on information technology has brought in unprecedented changes in the philosophy and practice of Librarianship that information professionals are compelled to change themselves in the quest for existence. IT has a major impact on the following areas of Library services:

i. Raw materials

While traditional library systems are geared to the identification and retrieval of the artifacts like books, journal articles, videotapes etc., IT converts all these types of information carrying artifacts into digital data for the purpose of storage, processing and transmission. Naturally, the focus on the format and location of these artifacts has changed to the content and access of information.

ii. Operational Processes

Because of the repetitive nature of many of the library routines like issue and return of books, reservation, recording of the receipt of the books and journal issues etc., computers can be effectively used for automating these procedures.

iii. Management processes

The main management processes like planning, directing, co-ordinating, control, reporting, budgeting etc. can be considerably enhanced by IT. Management Information Systems and Decision Support Systems make the management task easy.

iv. Customer Interaction

IT can influence the nature of customer interaction in three ways:

* By speeding up routine processes at the library counter.
* By widening the choice of available information sources and services.
* By making library services more accessible.

2. CHANGING ROLE OF THE INFORMATION PROFESSIONAL

The knowledge and skills required by the faculty members of LIS schools can be assessed only examining the changing role their products are expected to play in their organization. It is a fact that IT has brought in unforeseen changes in the LIS profession. But it is not enough for the library and information professional to be a master of IT alone. In addition to the technical and professional skills, they have to possess managerial skills too. This is all the more necessary in the context of libraries becoming large enterprises in terms of men, money, materials and machines.

Library professionals have the onerous responsibility of constantly justifying themselves to their parent organizations that they contribute more than they cost. Also they have to stand as a model for the profession demonstrating that "putting knowledge to work" is a dynamic and creative process that requires highly developed skills in planning and co-ordination. As Evelyn Daniel puts it"the model will be that of the information counselor and the independent broker, which contributes knowledge of subject areas with that of contemporary information technology. The information field will require individuals who understand the business of information, how it works, how it is marketed and how it realizes profit. The challenges for all librarians will be fiscal, technological and managerial. "The technique of information resource management seems to be the best available tools for new librarians to assume a leadership role in the larger world of information, be it inside or outside a traditional library."[3]

As information managers, librarians have become part of the corporate management team, at least in the special library atmosphere. In addition to providing information services to all the users in the organization, librarians have to assist top management with strategic decision making. The growing complexity of organizations coupled with advances in information systems and technology have begun to test the validity of many classical forms of organizational structures and managerial techniques.[4] These aspects have been succinctly stated by Prof. Tom Wilson, Head of the Dept. of Information Studies, Sheffield University as follows:

"To all intents and purposes, a great deal of the professional technical skills have been overtaken by events and the skills that are now required in this sector have more to do with information technology and the management of the relationship between the technology and information users, than they have to do with established library practice."[5]

3. SKILLS NEEDED BY THE NEW INFORMATION PROFESSIONAL

There is a need for today's information professional to develop new skills to meet the increasing demand for information. The much needed skills are discussed below:

3.1 Use of available technologies to create services.

It is not essential for a professional to be a programmer or software expert, but he/she should have an understanding of the technologies available to offer new services or redesign the existing services. It is necessary for him/her to sell the potential with in those to be able to repackage service aided by the technologies and to meet the customer's present and future requirements.

3.2 Use of Internet tools and services.

Though this skill can be discussed under the heading in section 4.1, it is treated as a separate section due to its overriding importance. If even the software giant Microsoft has been obliged to bend on to the INTERNET, it is better not to speak of other small organizations. As a provider of services at the global level, INTERNET offers exciting potentials and avenues to the information professionals.

3.3 Business and finance

Today's information manager who controls millions of rupees must surely know accurately the unit cost of each services, staff costs, overhead expenditure, capital expenditure and so on so that wisely planned spending is made possible.

3.4 Public relations and marketing

There is no meaning in developing new services unless these are publicized and marketed. Before any service is launched, a business plan is necessary which will include research into the potential market, identification of target groups (market segmentation), staff skills needed to develop and sustain the services,costs involved in the development and continuation of the services and products, and the promotional methods to be used for publicizing them.

3.5 Communication skills

It is absolutely necessary that all information staff develop good communication skills- both oral and written- to be able to talk to groups of people or individuals with confidence in order to present their ideas efficiently and effectively.

3.6 Training skills

It is perhaps in this role of a trainer that the information worker will be able to succeed and exert most influence. He/she should be able to offer to all levels in the organizations, the opportunity to enhance their own information skills and knowledge base.

3.7 Moving and Shaking Skills

Prima-facie, these terms appear to be ludicrous, but they are important. This stands for the ability to recognize opportunities, point them to the organization, making the users feel that without a regular flow of up-to-date information neither the individual nor the organization can succeed. It is a matter of common knowledge that there are some people in all organizations who believe that they do not need any information because they know it all. This is a challenge which no worthy information professional can ignore.

3.8 Pro-active role

Information professionals have to shed the passive role hitherto assumed by librarians and try to develop a modern image which includes professional skills coupled with business acumen. This calls for an understanding of other sections and departments deadlines and ways and means of meeting these deadlines realistically and cost-effectively.

Nick Moore predicted the emergence of four complementary groups of information professionals-creators, collectors, communicators and consolidators[6].

Creators are those who can develop and produce information services and products. Their skill sets should consist of navigation and ability to develop maps and other tools needed to find one's way round the system.

Collectors constitute people who build up collections of information by employing all the traditional skill of the profession. Ability to understand the needs of users and organizations as a whole is the key skill required by them. *Communicators* should be skilled in analysis of requirements, information selection and evaluation. *Consolidators* are people who make sense of the world for managers. *Consolidators* need a high level of skill in analysis and synthesis of information and the ability to present results effectively.

4. TOPICS TO BE COVERED IN THE CPD OF LIS TEACHERS

The skills needed by the information professionals serve as a pointer to the skills to be possessed by the LIS teachers to function effectively in the capacity of trainers. As stated by Ewen Sutherland of University of Wales, " it is no longer enough to talk about continuing professional development on to staff masters courses in the hope that one day students will be able to recall the material, years hence when they need it."[7] Therefore, he advocates regular updating courses for the practitioners. He terms this as 'life–long strategic learning partnership'.

This practice can be adopted in the CPD of teachers also. Just-in-time learning i.e. imbibing the skills as and when needed, rather than imparting them as part of long term course, is advisable. Taking into consideration the profile of modern information professional, the essential skills to be imparted to LIS teachers are summarized below:

4.1 Skill to serve as a facilitator

The widespread use of IT calls for crucial changes in pedagogy and in the roles available to the academic staff. They have to serve as facilitators, i.e. those who can add to the experience of students using technological means and enhance discussion and interaction. This involves the extensive use of INTERNET tools and services.

4.2 Proficiency in content development

Information professionals have to become content developers also if they want to encourage uploading of worthwhile information. For this, teachers have to be familiar with:

* HTML
* Still pictures (GIF, JPEG, TIFF etc) formats
* Image maps
* Moving pictures(MPEG,AVI)
* Programs like

  Common Gateway Interface (CGI)

  C and C++

  PERL

  Hot Java and JavaScript

  Virtual Reality Modeling Languages (VRMLs)

4.3 Facets of Management

A critical analysis of the syllabi of the BLISc and MLISc courses offered by Indian Universities would clearly show that the management content is very low. Whatever is discussed under the guise of management is nothing but the organization of libraries rather than planning and other aspects. At the same time, as stated earlier, libraries are becoming monolithic enterprises, the governance of which calls for extensive use of management skills. Therefore, it is necessary that at least the top and middle level professionals have to be given training in modern management practices.

This should include topics in:

* Financial management
* Staff management
* Marketing management
* Strategic management
* Stress management
* Crisis management
* Systems analysis
* Space management
* Quality management

4.4 Information Consolidation

This involves adeptness in collecting information from a variety of sources, combining it and interpreting it. It requires a high level of skills in analysis and synthesis of information and the ability to present results effectively.

4.5 Presentation and Communication Skills

Education in our country is still class room centered. Advancement in Information and Communication Technology (ICT) has little impact on the methods of presentation. At the same time Computer-Aided Instruction (CAI) and Computer-Aided Learning (CAL) are become popular. Graphic packages and presentation packages like Power-Point have enabled effective presentation of topics. Hence teachers have to be introduced to the use of these devices too.

5. MODUS OPERANDI OF OFFERING CPD

Having examined areas to be included in the CPD, the next question is how to offer the programmes. For convenience, the topics listed earlier (in section 4) can be categorized into three modulus. They are:

Module 1

Use of computers in libraries

Internet-tools and services

(With extensive hands on)

Content development

Web design

Module 2

Facets of management

Module 3

Information consolidation

Technical Writing skills

Presentation and Communication

Each module can be offered as a package or programme and the duration of each programme should be not less than 3 weeks, as in the cases of Refresher Courses prescribed by UGC. Attendance in at least two such programmes should be made mandatory for L & IS teachers. The second question to be answered is who should offer such programmes? The faculty should consist of experts in the field of Information Technology, Management, Communication and Library and Information Science. It logically follows that only Universities having strong Departments or schools of computer science or IT, Management and LIS can offer these programmes.. The DLIS has to take the lead in enlisting the co-operation of other departments for organizing such programmes. In order to ensure quality, only one or at the most two Universities in each zone-north, south, east, and west- of the country should be given full financial assistance by the UGC for organizing these programmes. All the three courses (modules) should be offered in a year successively so that teachers get an opportunity to pick and choose the topic of their interest.

Naturally, a question as to the desirability of offering these programmes as refresher courses offered by various Academic Staff Colleges arises. The fact is that at present the refresher courses are meant for librarians of academic libraries and library science teachers where the former outnumber the latter. In such programmes it is a matter of common experience that the course contents are diluted to make them palatable to library professionals who hail from various backgrounds. The intensity and seriousness of the programmes envisaged in this paper cannot be achieved in such a heterogeneous group. That is the rationale of suggesting exclusive programmes for teachers. Professional forums like IATLIS can take the lead in convincing the UGC of the need for organizing such programmes, exclusively for LIS teachers.

6. THE E-LEARNING METHOD OF IMPARTING THE PROGRAMME

Once, considerable experience is gained in organizing such full-time programmes lasting for at least three weeks, this can be offered through e-learning. One of the biggest advantages of e-learning is that it makes knowledge easy of access by a large number of people. Moreover it can make the varying place of the individual learner such that the knowledge worker learns only as much of a chosen subject as he/she perceives as relevant.

E-learning allows for different kinds of learning experience through:

i. On-line participant groups — which allows participants to interact with each other.

ii. On-line tutoring — where faculty and participants connect one-to-one through e-mail and scheduled chats.

iii. On-line counselling — which helps in decision making

iv. On-line libraries and resource centers — where collections of all types of related literature are available

v. Contact with experts in the field — which bring participants to well known authorities in the field.

vi. Bulletin boards — which offer participants a common place for posting topics, queries and comments.

E-learning is often self-paced, thus training needs to be broken down into small nuggets of information that can be tailored to meet individual skills, gaps and delivered as and when needed. These chunks of information are called learning objects, examples of which include pre-test, games, assessments and e-mail links to subject experts. Content providers and designers must be able to produce learning objects that can be searched and indexed easily.

Nearly, half the approximately 4000 institutions for higher education is the US provide some variety of distance education through e-learning, according to a study made by US Dept. of Education. A few years back in India, the T.A. Pan Management Institute (TAPMI) and Aptech joined hands in offering an MBA course through the INTERNET, which received a good response and many more institutions followed suit. Spurred by the success of on-line courses available at the international level, many more institutions are coming up with new programmes. If such full fledged academic programmes can be offered through e-learning, there is no reason why such short courses cannot be offered in the same way.

REFERENCES

1. Ives,Liora. CPD and you-four years on. The Library Association Record 98(10) Oct 1996:526
2. Daniel,Evelyn H. Educating the academic librarians for a new role as information resource manager. The Journal of Academic Librarianship 1(6) Jan 1986: 363
3. Cortez, Edwin M. Developments in special library education: implications for the present and the future. Special libraries, Fall 1986.
4. Cortez, Edwin M, Kazlanskcs,Edward J. Managing information systems and technology. New York: Neal-Shuman,1986
5. Wilson,Tom. Professional education-the ever changing face. The Library Association Record 95(4) April 1993: 224.

6. Abell,Angela. New roles? New skills? New people? Library Association Record 99(10) Oct 1997:539

7. Sutherland, Ewan. Global virtual graduate schools: learning in cyber space.Aslib proceedings 48(10) Oct 1996: 229

8. Varadan,M.S.S. HRD- the e-learning way. The Hindu (Thiruvananthapuram) 25 Jan 2001:BS-3

3

Role of Harijan Welfare Libraries Among Rural Women

Dr. S. S. Jagnayak

0. INTRODUCTION

Education, today, is beyond the primitive stage of instruction and training but has basically individual and social meanings-individual in that education is concerned with the whole development of the person; social in that it is essentially a process by which the material, mental, moral and cultural inheritance of society is transmitted to each generation. By transmitting knowledge from one generation to the next can help civilization maintain itself and make advances upon the knowledge of the past. In this context, reading is an efficient means of absorbing, comparing and contrasting knowledge, which produces an individual reaction conducive to imaginative and mental development. The intellectual metabolism of reading skill is an essential to the educational process in a society so heavily dependent upon letters. By organizing knowledge as contained in books and related materials the library plays an important role in individual and social meanings of education. By transcending the isolation of subjects the library caters for an interdisciplinary approach in keeping with modern educational practice[1].

One of the most important mention about the purpose of a public library is given by UNESCO Public Library Manifesto (as revised in 1972) as follows " .... the Public library must offer to adults and children the opportunity to keep in touch with their times, to educate themselves continuously and keep abreast of progress in the sciences and arts. Its contents should be a living demonstration of the evolution of knowledge and culture, constantly reviewed, kept up-to-date and attractively presented. In this way it will help people form their own opinions and developed their creative and critical capacities and powers of appreciation. The public library is concerned with the form in which these may be expressed"[2].The remaining section of the Manifesto say the basic principles of public library services as it exist to serve the needs of individuals and through them the community at large.

The Library

Library, defined by R.S.P.Singh as "a collection of books and other literary material kept for reading, study and consultation or a place, building, room or rooms set apart for keeping and use of a collection of books"[3].

According to Dr.SS.Jagnayak, library means, "a social institution which collects, preserves, organizes, interprets and makes available the printed as well as audio-visual materials and helps the implementation the extension activities for socio -cultural, educational, economic and political development of the people"[4].

Libraries can be classified into three categories via; academic libraries, public libraries and special libraries. Academic libraries are mainly established to cater to the academic needs of the people. Special libraries are established to obtain and exploit specialized information for the private advantage of the organization, which provides its financial support[5]. Public libraries are meant for the public irrespective of age, sex, education, occupation, caste, class, creed, politics etc and all round development of people.

The Internationally accepted definition of a public library that it is a library which[6] :

1. is financed out of public fund;
2. charges no fees from readers and yet is open for full use by the public without distinction of caste, creed or sex;

3. is intended as an auxiliary educational institution providing a means of self- education which is endless
4. houses learning materials giving reliable information freely and without partiality or prejudice on as a variety of subjects as will satisfy the interests of readers.

Functions of Public Library

Public libraries have a prominent role in supplementing formal education and providing for a life long and continuing education according to the needs and convenience of individuals. In a country where illiteracy is rampant the public libraries can help in spreading literacy and preventing people from falling into illiteracy.

In a participatory democracy, abdication of illiteracy and spread of education are of most important for its success. And public libraries can contribute a lot to eradicate illiteracy and help in spread of education. A library makes a substantial contribution to socio-economic change in a social milieu. It can serve as pillars of national system of education. Even though librarians deal with books and teachers with persons, both are complementary to each other since books provide guidance and enlightenment to people. It is undeniable that the key to understanding is the key to a library.

Public libraries are essential support to socio-economic development of a nation. There is a remarkable unanimity of opinions among political leaders that facilities for reading books and newspapers must be brought within the reach of people at large, especially those in rural areas.[7] . Reading will free a citizen of his narrow attitude and outlook and well lift him to a higher plane. Education is an effective media to transmit the social ethos on desired lives and improve the economic lot of the people. Science and technology grows faster and if people are not keep pace with such advancement, they will be left behind in the technological and economic fields. Reading will help people to open one's windows to outside of the nation and also to whole world of knowledge. Literacy is the gateway of knowledge and libraries can promote this. The greater the literacy in a country, the larger will be the reading public. Public libraries can bridge the gap between the increasing number of literates and readers and the increasing number of books and other library materials. The establishment of a network of public libraries with a view to providing free and equal facilities to all, whether they live in rural or urban areas will go a long way and opportunity to think and rethink and integrate the best thought of the greatest minds into their lives. In the socio-cultural field, libraries have an important contribution to make flow the wisdom of the ages found in books. Libraries are, no doubt, active agents for building a nation's socio-cultural, economic, educational and political development. Apart from the socio-cultural goal that libraries are capable of achieving, it has also a plain to enrich personal lives of individuals. Individuals can become useful citizens and improve their vocations and professions through libraries particularly through reference books in the libraries. In India, Public libraries have got importance as a vital means to the progress of civilization. It is an important function of the public library that to kindle interest in the illiterate through the audio-visual materials and thus promote adult education. Further, it is the main duty of the library to supply necessary reading materials to neo literates. A modern library is not confined in stocking of books and other reading materials but in stocking films, filmstrips and audio-visual cassettes. These media will help them to make interest in reading books and other materials, which ultimately result in becoming regular users of the library. Besides, this will help library to become a powerful medium for eradicating illiteracy. A public library is a public utility concern and should be viewed in the same commercial point of view i.e.; library must be a pay and use form which was the opinion of the philosopher, Herbert Spencer also.

The UNESCO's declaration of Human Rights states that it is the birth right of every individual to have free access to the results of human ingenuity exercised in the arts and sciences. Free access to accumulated and recorded thought helps individuals and communities. If free fundamental education is an essential pre-requisite, then the free use of public libraries are, no doubt, essential for the same. Now, it is clear about the functions of a public library i.e. collecting printed and audio-visual materials needed for individual and group advancement. The main features of a modern public library are to collect, organize, distribute, interpret and guide the individuals. The function of a public library is to serve all people irrespective of age, sex, education, occupation, class, caste, creed and politics.

The libraries have to foster the habit of reading needed to broaden one's vision and to sharpen one's power of understanding. The main duty of a library is not to interfere in the interests of the readers but to initiate their development. It would be a proper function of the libraries to provide reading materials to children of all ages and tastes and also to women of various categories. A Public library is not simply a center of book distribution but a center where having various extension activities like seminars, debates, exhibitions, symposia, conferences, competitions, social service activities etc. All now accepts it that the establishment of free public libraries can be an important measure of social reform. Public libraries can be considered to be an important index to the cultural level of a country as well as significant integral part of the socio-cultural complex of a socialist, democratic, secular republic. The public libraries help in bringing into being a community of thinking people whose opinions are independently arrived at which would render a democracy meaningful and purposeful.

It is well known that India had an excellent tradition of economy, knowledge and important libraries of conserving knowledge and important libraries existed in the country in various centers of learning, temples, theological centers and palaces during the ancient and medieval times. Although these libraries conserved knowledge and passed on knowledge from generation to generation these libraries attributed little emphasis on library services in the modern sense, as was the case with several other countries in the east[8]. The pivotal role, libraries could play in the educational, scientific, industrial, social and economic development of the country came to be recognized only in the middle of the present century. After independence, as part of the industrialization and literacy rate, libraries too received encouraged from the government for its growth and development.[9]

There has been uniform development among various libraries and also among the same category of libraries[10].

The religious and spiritual leaders, writers and thinkers, poets and priests, artists and philosophers, scientists and technocrats, all regard libraries as great store-houses of knowledge. Even the informed public, though they scarcely know what a public library is and certainly not what it could be, consider it important to the education of common man. Libraries encourage readers to keep in touch with the best minds of the world, give them time and opportunity to think and rethink and integrate the best thought of the greatest minds into their lives. In the socio-cultural field, libraries have an important contribution to make flow the wisdom of the ages found in books. Libraries are, no doubt, active agents for building a nation's socio-cultural, economic, educational and political development. Apart from the socio-cultural goal that libraries are capable of achieving, it has also a plain to enrich personal lives of individuals. Individuals can become useful citizens and improve their vocations and professions through libraries particularly through reference books in the libraries. In India, Public libraries have got importance as a vital means to the progress of civilization. It is an important function of the public library that to kindle interest in the illiterate through the audio-visual materials and thus promote adult education. Further, it is the main duty of the library to supply necessary reading materials to neo literates. A modern library is not confined in stocking of books and other reading materials but in stocking films, filmstrips and audio-visual cassettes. These media will help them to make interest in reading books and other materials, which ultimately result in becoming regular users of the library. Besides, this will help library to become a powerful medium for eradicating illiteracy. A public library is a public utility concern and should be viewed in the same commercial point of view i.e.; library must be a pay and use form, which was the opinion of the philosopher, Herbert Spencer also.

The UNESCO's declaration of Human Rights states that it is the birth right of every individual to have free access to the results of human ingenuity exercised in the arts and sciences. Free access to accumulated and recorded thought helps individuals and communities. If free fundamental education is an essential pre-requisite, then the free use of public libraries is, no doubt, essential for the same. Now, it is clear about the functions of a public library i.e. collecting printed and audio-visual materials needed for individual and group advancement. The main features of a modern public library are to collect, organize, distribute, interpret and guide the individuals. The function of a public library is to serve all people irrespective of age, sex, education, occupation, class, caste, creed and politics.

The libraries have to foster the habit of reading needed to broaden one's vision and to sharpen one's power of understanding. The main duty of a library is not to interfere in the interests of the readers but to initiate their development. It would be a proper function of the libraries to provide reading materials to children of all ages and tastes and also to women of various categories. A Public library is not simply a center of book distribution but a center where having various extension activities like seminars, debates, exhibitions, symposia, conferences, competitions, social service activities etc. All now accepts it that the establishment of free public libraries can be an important measure of social reform. Public libraries can be considered to be an important index to the cultural level of a country as well as significant integral part of the socio-cultural complex of a socialist, democratic, secular republic. The public libraries help in bringing into being a community of thinking people whose opinions are independently arrived at which would render a democracy meaningful and purposeful.

Public Libraries: Extension Activities

The Librarian's Glossary defines the term 'Extension

Work' as activities which are undertaken with object of reaching groups of people who might otherwise be unaware of the library such as lecture societies, reading circles, discussion groups and the provision of books for hospitals, clubs etc. and it is also defined as the provision of lectures, film shows, talks, book displays in order to draw attentions to library services and book stocks[11]. Extension activities of the library can better be called as extra-library activities or co-library service activities. Since library is a socio-cultural institution, its activities should reflect the socio-cultural trends of the locality where it exists. These activities suited to the local culture will attract the people to the library. But, the purpose of such activities is much wider than that of attracting the people. Acquisition of knowledge and information is continuing and unending process and it is that function which a good library must continuously and competently promote through the library services as well as extra-library service activities. These co-library services are not a new phenomenon but were also present in the early days of public library. But, such activities of that time were of limited and gradually gathered momentum and now have great variety of activities.

Extra library activities have certain aims. First, it brings the library into contact with individuals, groups and people in all walks of life. Second, it can meet the needs of various categories of individuals and groups. Third, to remind the users as well as non-users of the existence of libraries and their services. Forth, to inform the readers of all the facilities which the library provides for them. Fifth, to organize fund raising programmes for some specific purposes. Sixth, to remove illiteracy and socio-economic backwardness. Seventh, those who are able to organize various activities can utilize their resources to do the same with the co-operation of the library. All extension activities spell out some positive benefits.

The Public Library and Development

The modern library is a living force in the society where it functions, with the potentialities to determine its shape and quality. At the same time, it is also a product of that society. So the library may be described as a social institution as well as a vital societal force. It may be observed that at different stages of history, social forces such as religion, industrial revolution, the accumulation of surplus wealth, universal education etc have made their impact on the origin and development of libraries. "A study of society and culture or man's continued existence culturally through the ages, has revealed that the library existed in all ages as part of the social fabric. As the culture has advanced, the libraries have also developed"[12]. In other words, "the development of a nation, historically, is reflected in its cultural advancement and the development of libraries, a cultural signpost of any nation, is conditioned by a popular urge for social, economic and intellectual improvement: and to a large extent by the size and organization of the social order in which the libraries have to function. Thus, the library is a part of general cultural scene"[13]

As a social product library is meant to fulfill social needs of the community and is a multi-purpose social institution, which cannot remain as an isolated rigid institution resisting the various social changes, which affect the daily life of the people. Ogburn remarks, "the public library is a part of our social fabric and cannot remain independent and immutable amid social change, but as one of the social institution, it must adapt itself to the social order as it changes"[14]. Being a social product the library has in its functioning certain social objectives such as the acquisition of documents, giving reliable information, promoting research potential, helping the productive drive, giving intellectual recreation, developing social homogeneity, socializing the individual, cultivation of friendship, giving people the opportunity to mix with others belonging to different classes, castes, religions etc, helping people to learn social behaviour and helping to promote socio-cultural, educational and economic activities suitable to each community for its development.

It has been remarked that the public library has "a social mandate"[15] to serve the whole community. The library has an integrative role, as a cultural unit constituting an organic part of the society, to resolve conflicts in terms of the interests of the whole society. Thus, it contributes towards the unification of society. That is why J.H. Shera gives importance of the library in the society as "it is one element in the total communication system by which society is held together and a culture is created and maintained"[16]. A public library is a community center around which the cultural life of the community revolves[17]. Thus, library acts as a center for all round development of the community where it functions. The public libraries play a vital role in building up a healthy and progressive community. " A well organized library system can deeply influence the future development of the society"[18]. Society needs libraries in order to make the records of the human adventure available over long periods by giving them protection. The more sophisticated the society, and the more complex its social organization, the more it needs the libraries[19]. The public library as a social institution, works for greater enlightenment of the people and gradually and culture life of community.

Public libraries function as an effective instrument in the socio-cultural, educational, economic and political development of both individual and society. According to Rogers and shoemaker, development "is a type of social change in which new ideas are introduced into a social system in order to produce higher per capita incomes and levels of living through more modern production methods and improved social organization"[21]. Saul Ross interprets development as, "with reference to human beings developments connotes a change or changes in the functional capacity of the individual or group or the nation, brought about by education or by practice or by therapy or by social interaction"[22]. In the words of Seetharamu, development refers to the production and utilization of material resources or to the enrichment of human resources. Enrichment of human resources is referring to the non-economic factors such as political, social, educational or ethnic background of the people[23].

Development means people. Developments in the new connotation refer to as an overall process of transforming men and societies leading to a social order in which every human being can achieve moral and material well being. It can also be referred as a whole, an integrated value-loaded cultural process encompassing social relations, education, production, consumption and well-being. Thus, development is a process of giving up or modifying old habits, beliefs, attitudes and values and also cultivating some new ones, which are necessary to live in modern society.

A public library in which has an important role to play in the national programmes of social reconstruction and nation building. These centers are not for revolution but for change which could eventually bring people to a more equitable and integrated society since "the library service enriches whole aspects of living and reaches persons of all age groups and occupations helping them to become balanced, integrated and satisfied individuals and valuable citizens[24]. A research group and library association say, public library contributes to sustain the quality of life in all its aspects-educational, economic, industrial, scientific and culture-and promote the concept of a democratic society in which equal opportunity exists for all develop into true citizens with whole and balanced personalities. The contribution is effected through its multi-purpose dissemination of information, education and culture[25]. Its books and other printed matter as well as audio-visual materials are powerful and indispensable agents for bringing enlightenment, encouragement, inspiration and information to every member of the society[26].

Dr. RSP. Singh summarizes the role of libraries in development as given below[27]. A well-planned and efficient system of library and information services is an indispensable aid to all activities undertaken in the promotion of economic and social development. The more advanced the stages of economic and social development in a country the greater the benefit derived from these services. So, one of the indices of the social development of a nation is the quality, effectiveness and state of development of its information services.

Since, full development is impossible without proper education and adequate information, the absence of library system in the developing countries helps to widen the gap between the rich and poor. The concentration of nation's riches in information resources in a few countries and their unwillingness to give up this monopoly because of the profits they derive from it, force some countries to be culturally dependent on others This in turn gives rise to the brain drain of specialists from the developing countries to developed countries.

A library and information system in a society constitutes a dynamic agency to facilitate the use of all information regardless of the level of education, profession, place of abode, political belief and religious creed; to offer adequate training to users of information in the methods and the techniques and intellectual work; to support education in all levels especially life long education by developing in users the attitudes and skills; to provide recreational reading etc. According to SR.Mittal, the objectives of a rural library are [28].

1. Disseminating authentic news and information;
2. Providing motivation for learning, reading and writing and helping in maintaining, main enhancing and feeding literacy among the people;
3. Helping to keep alive and enhance the cultural heritage;
4. Increasing vocational competence in raising the technological level of a village occupation;
5. Promoting information of the various functions of the village population wherever they exist;
6. Helping the village institutions and organizations to improve their programmes;
7. Developing aesthetic sense and refined taste;
8. Helping the people to spend their leisure time profitably.

1. THE PUBLIC LIBRARY AND EDUCATIONAL DEVELOPMENT

The Oxford Advanced Learner's Dictionary of Current English defines education as knowledge and the development of ability in the formation of character and mental powers resulting from systematic training and instruction[29]. Durkheim puts "education is the influence exercised by adult generations on those that are not yet ready for social life. Its object is to arouse and to develop in the child a certain number of physical, intellectual and moral taste that are demanded of him by both the political society as a whole and special mileage for which he is specially destined[30]. Education is a "process of meaningful interaction between a person and a stimulus resulting in changed behaviour beyond the level of simple reflex [31].

Whether a country is affluent / advanced or a developing one, acquisition of knowledge is the very basis of progress and strength. The library preserves knowledge and kindles thoughts and ideas. It serves as the cause of peace as well[32]. New knowledge is for human benefaction i.e.; for a better social order, political order and economic order[33]. Education is not simply stuffing minds with information, but to change the attitude and outlook of a person. Reading is helpful for education and it provides information, status, spiritual satisfaction, emotional release and pleasure. It is also significant for the creation of intellectual, moral and aesthetic values. The library is the only institution, which is fully engaged in the creation of reading habit. Library enriches the community by providing knowledge recorded in books and other graphic materials of great importance for development programmes. Libraries provide necessary facilities to the people to attain proficiency in the fields of their specialization and to stimulate general knowledge[34] . The library is intended for improving reading habit and educational development through books and other extension activities.

The Public Library And Socio-Cultural Development

Soreson says, "by social development we mean increasing

ability to get along well oneself and others". In the words of Freeman and Showel, social development "is the process of learning to conform to group standards, mores and tradition and becoming imbued with a sense of oneness, intercommunication and cooperation"[35]. Gandhiji says, "social development is development out of or away from man's present state in any society"[36]. Nittala V.Ratnam and B.Bhaskara Rao used social development or social infra structural development in a comprehensive sense to emprise the component via, social services and social amenities or facilities" [37].

As a recreation the habit of using books and frequenting libraries frees the mind and emotions from the routine and drudgery of the immediate present and immediate surrounding. It inspires the ordinary man who is less self-confident and finds his path in the darkness, to live a noble and useful life through the potential books or ideas of yesterday and today. The information dissemination form the library should improve the competence and self confidence of the people, increase the problem solving capacity of the people and enrich personal and social life. It is essential for the progress of individual and national development. It is needed to perform his/her duties efficiently, to develop individuality and to be partner in social and cultural life and thus enrich the quality of life. Books and information stimulate interest and ideas; widen the horizons of minds for quick understanding. " Its role is that a medium of mass communication, it acts a social institution which inculcates fellow feeling. It imparts the essence of discipline, which gives a strong foundation for the social behaviour of people. The pivotal role in the process of searching for ways to improve the quality of life belongs to the library[38].

Libraries provide vocational, career, academic and recreational materials. It creates suitable environment for family living and provide necessary technical and professional literature concerned with family welfare and also provide with reliable information needed to take intelligent decisions on home management, childcare, family adjustment and other equally important topics. Some of their leisure time may be spent in activities, which are socially useful because they release tension and restore energy. Thus it helps for further participation in socio-cultural, educational, economic and political life of the community[39]. The libraries also perform various social activities such as construction of houses, thatching of huts, road repairs and constructions, market and slum cleaning etc through which these centers act as an agent of social development. Besides, libraries help to change the unfavorable attitude of the people and give a chance to mingle with various categories of the people irrespective of class, caste, creed, sex, education, occupation, politics etc which no doubt improve social capacities and calibers.

By Raymond Williams, culture is "artistic and intellectual activities"[40] . Ronald C.Benge points out "the word culture includes all forms of recreational activity including reading"[41].Robert J.Stalcup snapped culture like "as the characteristics and the products of the learned behaviours of a group of people"[42]. Thus, it is a product of human endeavors and reflects among other things, the level of education enjoyed by a group of people, culture is the patterned behaviour learned by each individual from the day birth as he or she is socialized, encultured and educated by parents and peers to become and remain as a member of the particular group into which he or she was born or joined. Cultural development invariably involves certain transformations, even distortions of traditional art forms life styles and values.

Public libraries can be considered as cultural institutions encompassed with the goal of transforming traditional art forms life styles and values And for providing artistic and intellectual activities. It helps to create progressive and scientific outlook while at the same time retaining the basic values of our ancient culture. Library is a center for many cultural programmes such as film shows, music recitals, dramas, sports, group discussions, short stories, lectures, seminars, debates, quiz programmes, elocutions, etc and indoor games like chess, caroms, cards, table tennis etc which kindles interest among clientele. This in turn induces cultural development of the people. Thus libraries can make them highly moral in character and good citizens of the country. These institutions are centers of revolution in the cultural life of the people[43].

2. THE PUBLIC LIBRARY AND ECONOMIC DEVELOPMENT

Economic development is defined by Everyman's Dictionary of Economics as "it can be used to describe the underlying determinants of economic growth such as in techniques of production, social attitudes and institutions"[44]. Okun and Richardson say "it is a sustained secular improvement in material well being which may considered to be reflected in an increasing flow of goods and services[45].

Without public library service, it is not possible for all around development of society and economic progress in modern age of democratic set up[46]. Public libraries in villages are centers of development programmes conducive to national development like agriculture, health, nutrition, social welfare, small scale industries, community development programmes etc. Books concerned with daily needs written in simple language are necessary to improve local ways of making a living by agriculture, industry, health, hygiene, maternity welfare, childcare, home management etc for rural development. It can also provide commercial, technical and scientific information in rural areas, which can eradicate economic problems. They conduct several programmes for economic development like construction and thatching houses, anganwadi, crèche, scholarship programmes and agricultural development programmes.

The Public Library Development in India-An Historical Perspective

Public libraries are considered as democratic agencies for the life-long self-education of the citizenry. Public library is vital societal force. J.H.Shera points out the importance of the library in society as "it is one element in the total communication system by which a society is held together and a culture is created and maintain"[47]. The modern Public library has penetrated deep into the societal life through socio-cultural, educational and economic activities.

In the matter of development of public libraries, India is about hundred years behind the developed democratic countries of the world. Infact, public library movement in Europe and America started with the growth of democratic institutions and Men of Wealth like Andrew Carnegi. Libraries were started in ancient and medieval India by the patronage of the emperors, by capitalists and other scholars of that period. The monumental works like Vedas , Upanishads, Mahabharatha, Ramayana, Arthashastra, Manusmrithy, Kamasustra etc. produced by great scholars and thinkers of this land have been preserved here despite the passage of time and ravage of nature. The learned Brahmins, memorized, became "living" or "ambulatory libraries" that were the real sources of knowledge for the young generation. The new religions, Jainism and Buddhism, encourage in making and copying of religious manuscripts to spread and propagate their philosophy, which gave birth to monastery libraries. Evidences are available to show that well developed libraries were existed even in the sixth century A.D. The famous universities like Nalanda, Taxila and Vikramshila had magnificent library with a massive collection of manuscripts. Besides monastery libraries, there were small libraries attached to various temples and mathas spread all over the country for the use of all people[48]. During the Sultanate period various libraries were attached to the palaces, mosques, Makatabs, Khanqah, Madrasas and other educational institutions. Efflorescence of library movement could be seen during Mughal period in the country as evidenced by Babar's Mughal Imperial Library. The other Mughal Emperors like Humayun, Akbar, Jahangir, Shajahan and Aurangazeb were showed remarkable interest in libraries

The Calcutta Library established in1784 was made opened to the public in 1820.The Madras Library Society was emerged in 1812. In 1900 Calcutta Public Library opened a reading room to the public, which became the National Library of India and hence this year is considered as a landmark in the history of public library movement. In 1914,1928,1929,1929 and 1936 the Andhra Desh Library Association, the Madras Library Association, the Punjab Library Association, the Bengal Library Association and the Bihar Pusthakalaya Sangh were established respectively.1937 is considered as another milestone in the history of library movement. In 1939-40 the Bombay Government appointed a library development committee for the establishment of regional libraries, district libraries, town libraries and village libraries.

"It is a sad commentary on 185 years of British Rule in India that on August 15,1947, when India attained independence, there was not a single Public Library in the country. Trivandrum Public Library was then 48 years old. However it took caution money and subscriptions and still take such fees. It is uncredible that when NewDelhi was designed in the second decade of this century and completed in 1930 as the capital city there was no provision for a public library. Whatever libraries existed, had been established by voluntary organizations or endowments and were without exception, subscription libraries. They were used primarily by the English speaking elite who constituted one percent of the total population"[49]. At the time of independence, only 15 percent of the population could read and write of whom only 3 percent had received schooling for eight years or more. During the British rule, the public libraries primarily acquired English books. It is no wonder that in 1947 only6,455 books were published in India in 15 Indian languages, making an average of 430 books per language, against 1627in English alone. Out of 5,63,133 towns and villages, only 2,767 or0.49 percent had public electricity supply and only very few of the towns and villages were connected by roads. These were the constraints under which the National Government planned to provide free universal public library service in the country. Under the Republican Constitution, enforced on January 26,1950, provision of public library service was made a state concern"[50].

The British Parliament passed Indian Independence Act,

1947 which provided for transfer of power to Indians. But political independence did not bring about intellectual and cultural independence. In the beginning the national government did not give much interest to the intellectual and cultural aspect of the life of the people.

After Independence, Ranganathan thought of promoting Library Movement here by establishing libraries and constructing a new-edifice of public library system for free India. He criticized the Report on the "Post-war reconstruction of the educational development in India" made by Sir John Sargent by saying that it has omitted patting up the roof. To avoid the expected huge national waste due to the very defect in the Sargent edifice, Ranganathan then himself worked out a library development plan to build the super structure of libraries, which was published in book form in 1947 under the title "Library Development plan with a draft bill for Bombay". Mr.R.S.Parkhi in his article on "Renaissance of Library Movement in India" published in March,1948 issue of "Indian Librarian"after studying the Ranganathan Plan, suggested as "So Sargent Plan for the development of free public schools and the Ranganathan plan for development of free public libraries require to be integrated for the proper development of the human resources in our country. And this can be well achieved only if the Provincial Governments hasten to enact at once Acts a Free Public Schools and Free public Libraries. The sporadic efforts that are going on at present in quarters of the country will not ultimately serve the purpose of killing the archdemon ignorance in the first instance, in order to burn out by irradiation of knowledge the other five demons sapping away the life out of the people-dependence, idleness, want, squalor and disease. The legislation of the two agencies of education will automatically solve the problems of finance, organization and co-ordination of the fields of education and libraries[51].

3. THE DELHI PUBLIC LIBRARY

The most significant development in library movement after independence is the establishment of Delhi Public Library in 1951. It was started as the first UNESCO Public Library Pilot Project under the joint efforts of UNESCO and the Government of India. The purpose of this library is "to adopt modern techniques to Indian conditions" and to serve as a model public library for Asia. This library provides complete free service to all, taking into consideration, the modern concept of Public library service. It is controlled by a library board with the President of the Delhi Municipal Committee as its Chairman on behalf of the Ministryof Education, Government of India. The library has now developed into a system and provides an efficient library service to the people of Delhi and its suburbs through its central library, branch libraries, sub-branch libraries, mobile library stations and deposit stations. It has extension programmes like lectures, story tellings, radio and television programmes etc. It serves school and college students and has a children section also.

The National Library, Calcutta

Men of great vision got together in the year 1636 and resolved upto setup a library. The Prince Dwarkanath Tagore was the first "Proprietor" of the Calcutta Public Library. The Pyari Chand Mitra, the father of the Bengali novel was its librarian during those days. The library was located in a part of the Fort William College in 1481. By 1903, the dynamic Lord Curzon, the Viceroy, vitalized it into an Imperial Library by buying of the rights of the Proprietors of the Calcutta Public Library and amalgamated with Fort William College Library and the departmental libraries.

Even in Lord Curzon's time the library possessed a hundred thousand books. In 1947, the collection of books in the library reached 7,50,000.With the advent of independence every institution in the country geared itself into national needs. The National Library was formally opened in its new home at Belvedere, Calcutta on February, 1st,1953 by MaulanaAbdul Kalam Azad, Minister of Education, Government of India. Shri.B.S.Kesavan was the first National Librarian appointed by the Ministry of Education. He compartmentalized into an independent section of each of the major languages of India and ornamentalised the Library with modern furniture and steel racks and shelves. Mr.Benoyendra Sengupta compiled for the first time classified catalogue code of periodicals, Newspapers, and Gazettes in the Library.

"Under the delivery of Books (Public Libraries) Act, 1954, every publisher in the country including government agencies, is required to send a copy of every publications to the National Library at Calcutta"[52].

The Rajaram Ram Mohan Roy Library Foundation

The Raja Rammohan Roy Library Foundation was established in 1972,ie. During the Fifth year plan, at Calcutta on the recommendation of the National committee for the Bicentenary Celebration of Raja Rammohan Roy for supporting and promoting library movement in the country by providing adequate library service, and popularizing reading habits among the people.

Objectives

The main objectives of the Foundation, as given in the Memorandum of Association are as follows:-

* To promote library movement in the country.
* To enunciate a national library policy and to work towards its adoption by the central and state Governments.
* To help build up a national library system by integrating the services of National Libraries, State Central Libraries, District Libraries and other types of libraries (Children's, Academic and Special) through inter-library lending system.
* To propagate the adoption of library legislation in the country.
* To provide financial and technical assistance to libraries.
* To establish Regional Library Service Centres.
* To act as a clearing house of ideas and information on library development in India and abroad.

* To advise the Government of India on all matters pertaining to the library development in the country.
* To take all such measures conductive to the promotion of library development and its utilization in the country.

4. THE PUBLIC LIBRARY DEVELOPMENT DURING 1970'S

Tamil Nadu, Andhra Pradesh, Karnataka, Maharashtra and West Bengal had only public library laws during the period of Seventies. But other states and Union Territories had yet no public library law for providing a well knit and organized public library service, both in urban and rural areas. Dr.D.N.Marshall, Librarian, Bombay University, at All India Library Conference at Patna in 1964 mentioned the importance of libraries in administration and education as under[53].

The Government of India launched a massive adult education programme in 1978, from October 2,1978, the Gandhi Jayanti Day, for five years period with a view to provide adult education to nearly 10 crore people. In 1979, the West Bengal was able to enact, the West Bengal Public Libraries Act, 1979.

History of Library Legislation in India

The history of public library legislation starts with the efforts of Dr.S.R.Ranganathan whose efforts in this direction became materialized by the enactment. Madras Public Libraries Act, 1948 which was put on the statute book on 29th January, 1949. Madras was the first state to provide the public library system though library legislation. The act has failed to raise enough funds to provide adequate service to the entire public[54].

The All India Library conference at Nagpur in 1949 called the attention of the Government of India to the question of libraries and library movements reaching the masses of India. The conference demanded the provincial Governments to enact public library law for establishing a network of public libraries in each province. In the working paper on "Library Service in Five Year Plans" by Ranganathan at the Tenth All India Library Conference in 1953, stressed the need for enactment of public library law in the states to implement the scheme for development of library service in Five year plans.

An Advisory committee for Libraries was appointed by Government of India in 1957 for conducting a general survey to find out the state of libraries in India. The report submitted by the committee had eight recommendations including the necessity of enacting public library act in each state of India for establishing an integrated public library system.

Hyderabad state enacted Hyderabad public Libraries Act in 1955. this became defunct due to the merger of Hyderabad with other states. Andhra Pradesh Public Libraries Act, 1960 came into force in 1960 [55]. It was amended during the year 1969.

A regional seminar on library development in south Asia organized by UNESCO in New Delhi in 1961 stressed the importance of law for establishment and development of a State Library System.

The seminar of 14th All India Library Conference in 1964 organized by the Indian Library Association on State Library Legislation suggested for necessary changes in the Model Library Bill drafted by the Advisory Committee for libraries.

Karnataka was the third state to enact library legislation and The Mysore (Karnataka) Public Libraries Act, 1965 was passed in the year 1965 was passed in the year 1965. It came into force on April,1, 1966[56]. The Government of Karnataka realized the defects in the Madras and Andhra library acts and enacted their act by which the state Government is empowered to constitute a State Library Authority and Local Authority and also a Department of Public Libraries.

The Maharashtra Public Libraries Act, 1967 was passed in 1967. In the year 1979 the West Bengal Public Libraries Act, 1967 was enacted[57].

Manipur Library Association mobilized all the libraries in the state and drafted the Manipur Public Libraries Bill, which was passed and came to force with effect from 1st October, 1988. The Act was drafted mainly on the basis of Madras and

West Bengal Public Libraries Act. The Haryana Public Libraries Act, 1989 was passed in 1989, which primarily meant to provide comprehensive library service on statutory basis in the state of Haryana. Several attempts were made for enacting library legislation for the state of Kerala since 1940. Finally, in 1989 after more than 12 hours discussion on the bill and la large number of amendments, the Kerala Public Libraries (Kerala Grandhasala Sangham) Act, 1989 had entered into the Statute Book[58].

Different states in India had passed Public Library Legislations. Firstly, the Princely State of Kolhapur had enacted Kolhapur Public Libraries Act, 1945. Followed by, other states like Madras (1948), Andhra Pradesh (1960), Karnataka(1965), Maharashtra (1967), Bengal (1979), Manipur (1988), Kerala (1989), Haryana (1989), Mizoram (1993), and Goa (1993). Efforts for library legislation is continuing in the states like orissa, Uttar Pradesh, Madhya Pradesh, Rajasthan, Delhi, Gujarat etc.

A permanent and continuous public library service can be ensured by way of legislation. Dr. S.R. Ranganathan had desire to have a National Public Library Act which helps the smooth working of a library system by providing a framework for organization, administration, and financing of libraries. Recently, in 1987, the Committee on National Policy for Library and Information System recommended to the Government of India for the need of the enactment of library legislation as a sure way to set up public library system in the states.

Public Library Development Through Five Year Plans

The important milestone in the development of library service after 1947, is the inclusion of the scheme of "improvement of Library Service" in the Five Year Plans.

First Five Year Plan (1951 to 1956)

For educational development, a programme for improving library service was included. In this scheme District Libraries were planned to establish in each state supported by a State Central Library. With support of the State Governments, a Scheme of Integrated Library Service was initiated by the

Government of India. The scheme was to select an area where five model community centers with a main library with branches to distribute books to 20 villages. In 29 areas in the country, this project was implemented.

During this plan, Delhi Public Library(1951), Central reference library, Calcutta (1955), State Central Library, Madras (1950) etc. were established. In 1954, the Delivery of Books Act was passed. At the end of March, 1954, there were 32,000 libraries were present in the country[59]. Under the first plan, 142 district libraries and nine libraries were established.

Second Five Year Plan (1956-1961)

The target for development of public library in this plan was that "by the end of plan, the whole country would have been covered with a network of Central, State and the district libraries, thus realizing the first of three major objectives, the other two being to secure foundation of a well thought legislation and an organization by which the district Libraries would, in their turn, be linked up with the library system of the whole world"[60]. In this plan, 9 states in India set up State Central Libraries and 254 District Libraries. In 1960, Andhra Pradesh passes library Act.

The Advisory Committee for Libraries was appointed in1957 with K.P. sinha as the Chairman. The main recommendations of the Sinha committee are:[61]

* Enact library legislation in all constituent states, to establish public libraries
* Build nation-wide library service with detailed suggestions for financing through the State and Central Governments.
* Extend public library service to the blocks, panchayats and villages.
* Create an independent department of Social Education and Libraries.

Third Five Year Plan(1961-1966)

In this plan there was provision for public library

development which could not be achieved in the second plan. Besides, there was a plan to set up and develop all the four National libraries at Delhi, Bombay, Calcutta and Madras.

A working Group on Libraries was appointed by the Planning Commission in 1964 . The Group's recommendations are:[62]

I) By the end of the Fifth five year Plan set up libraries at block headquarters and in every village having a population of 5,000.

II) Encourage the programme of Adult Education to use the service of the Public Libraries to eradicate illiteracy.

In Karnataka and Maharashtra Library Legislations were passed in 1965 and 1967 respectively.

Fourth five Year Plan (1969-1974)

This plan outlay on Education was fixed at Rs.1,950 crores out of which 20 crores was estimated to be available for libraries.

In 1972, the Working Group on Development of Public Libraries was constituted by the government of India Planning Commission. In this plan the Government of India established the Raja rammohan Roy Library Foundation. Fingures Provided in 1973 concerning the number of Public libraries are:[63]

* 15 out of 21 States/Union territories had State central Libraries.
* 235 out of 376 districts had District Central Libraries.
* 1500 out of 3100 Sub-Districts had sub-district Central Libraries.
* 50,000 villages out of 5,66,878 had Village Libraries .
* 1,800 out of 2,641 towns had Town Libraries.

Fifth Five Year Plan (1974-1979)

In this plan it was proposed to expand the network of libraries in every district. To get access to books by the people, a large outlay had been proposed for the establishment of libraries at State and Regional levels. And also planned to establish village libraries in the country. Adult education was also the emphasis of the plan. In order to give strength to village, block, state and central libraries, steps were taken. Raja rammohan Roy Library foundation assisted the State Governments in this regard. Ministry of Education in the Department of Culture, a library section under the charge of an Under Secretary to promote development of Public Libraries in India. It was in 1979. The only state that passed library legislation during this plan period was West Bengal which was in 1979.

Sixth five Year Plan (1980-1985)

In this plan, it has been proposed to allocate funds to such State governments and Union Territories as have not so far established Central State Libraries. It is expected that by the end of this plan the state and Union Territories that have not established Central State Libraries will be able to complete the task of the same. A working Group on Modernization of Library Services and information in the Seventh Plan was appointed by the Planning Commission in 1983.

During this Period (1982 figures) number of libraries are as follows:

* 26 States/Union Territories, out of 31 existing in 1982 had established/designated State Central Libraries.
* Out of 401 districts, 1,798 Development Blocks had Block Libraries.
* Out of 5,75,936 villages, 41,828 had Village Libraries.
* Out of 2,643 towns, 1.280 had Town Libraries.

Seventh five Year Plan (1985-1990)

In this programme, Planning commission decided to provide literature to neoliterates through network of libraries. In 1986 the National Literacy Mission was adopted which emphasized the establishment of rural libraries. A Committee on National Policy on Library and Information System was appointed by Department of Culture, Government of India in 1985. In 1989, there were 7,180 libraries in India.

The National Book policy of 1986 had an impact on

libraries which recommended for the provision of reading materials for children and 10 percent of the annual education budget of the Government should be used to purchase books for libraries.

Eighth five Year Plan (1992-1997)

The promotion of books was given importance in this plan. The organization responsible for this is National Centre for children's Literature which has to produce 3,000 titles annually

Many important books had to be translated into the various Indian Languages.

THE DEVELOPMENT OF PUBLIC LIBRARIES IN DIFFERENT STATES AND UNION TERRITORIES

The libraryn movement in the states may be reviewed by grouping the States into three broad categories.

States belonging to South India.

States belonging to North India

Union Territories.

States belonging to south India

Kerala

The Library movement in Kerala had its origin in the early part of 19th century. Libraries came to be stated as a result of the interest taken by the Government and the Public.[65] During medieval period Christian Missionaries started a few libraries because education became not the concern of Missionaries. These purposes and not for the educational and cultural development of the people.

The year 1945 is a milestone in the history of library movement in Kerala. In 1947 the All Travancore Grandhasala Sangham was registered under Section 9 of the Travancore company Act, 1939 and in 1948 the government approved the Sangham as the Central Agency of the Libraries. With the integration of Travancore and Cochin States in 1948 the

Sangham become All Travancore-Cochin grandhasala Sangham and later after the formation of Kerala State in 1956 with Malabar, it assumed its present title as "Kerala Grandhasala Sangham". The sangham was founded with the principal aim of establishing a network of libraries throughout the state so as to enlighten and encourage the rural population in its social, cultural and educational pursuits.[66]

Distribution of public libraries in Kerala.
Development of Libraries from 1945-1985.

Year	*Total Number of Libraries*
1945	47
1950	1023
1955	1747
1960	2918
1965	3297
1970	3780
1975	4280
1980	4625
1985	4928
Total No. of Libraries at present	5189

(***Source***: Dr.S.S. Jagnayak, 'Role of Libraries in Socio- Economic, Cultural and Educational Development among Rural people', Classical Publishing Company, New Delhi, 1997, p.35

Tamilnadu

Tamil Nadu has a rich traditon of Public Libraries. The government of Tamil Nadu has passed the Libraries Act in 1948 and it provided for the establishment of State Library committee, Directorate of Public Libraries and Local Library authorities in each district.

The number of libraries as on 1991-92 are as follows:-[67]

Type of Library	*Number*
State Central Library	1
District Central Library	18
Branch Library	1538
Mobile Library	7
Part-time Library	1099
Total	2663

Karnataka

It has a history of Library development for more than a century. Under the provisions of the Karnataka Library Act, Central Libraries have been set up in the State at state level, City level and District level. Besides, there are many Branch, village Centres were started in 1985.

Statement of Number of Public Libraries in Karnataka:1994-1995

Type of Library	*Number*
State Central reference Library	1
Public Technical Library	1
City Central Library	15
District Central Reference Library	10
Branch Library: City Central Library	: 125
District Central Library	: 324
	449
Mobile library service	10
Service Station	295
RRRLF	1905
Mandal Panchayat Library	1051

(***Source:*** V.K. Thomas; Public Libraries in India; Vikas Publishing House Private Limited. 1997, p. 51)

Andhra Pradesh

It is one of the leading States in the matter of Public Library development. The Andhra Pradesh Public Library Act of 1960 was later amended in the years, 1964,1969,1987 and 1989. The state has a State Central Library, Panchayat Libraries, village Libraries and Book Deposit Centres. Besides regional libraries, District Central Libraries and Branch Libraries are existing in the State.

Number and Types of Libraries in Andhra Pradesh as on 31st March, 1994.

Types of Libraries	*Number*
Government Libraries:	
a. State Central Library	1
b. Regional Libraries	6
c. Mobile Library	1
Zila Grandhalaya samstha Libraries.	
a. City Central Libraries	1
b. District Central Libraries	22
c. Branch Libraries	1426
d. Mobile Libraries	98
e. Village Libraries	344
Book Deposit Centres	546
Aided Libraries:	
a. Gram Panchayat Libraries	1197
b. Co.Operative society Libraries	34
c. Private Libraries	653
Total:	4329

(*Source*: V.K.Thomas, 1997, p.37)

STATE BELONGING TO NORTH INDIA

Maharastra

The Maharashtra Public Libraries Act of 1967 makes provisions for grant-in-aid, building and equipment, grants to nongovernmental libraries, grant-in-aid to library associations and libraries of the research and library institutions. The number of different types of libraries are as follows:-

(Year 1995-96)

	Types of Libraries	*Number*
A)	Government Library State Central Library	1
B)	Government Divisional Library (Including Sub-centre of Bombay)	5
C)	Government district Libraries	8
D)	Aided Library (Including 28 district Libraries)	
	i) Grade A-125)	5597
	ii) Grade B-469)	
	iii) Grade C-1887)	
	iv) Grade D-3116)	
	Recognised Libraries of) Research and Literary) Institutions)	32
	Total	5643

(*Source:* V.K. Thomas, 1997,P.55)

Madhya Pradesh

The first Public Library was opened in 1954 in Indore. The Madhya Pradesh Library Association was formed in 1957. This association is trying for passing the library Bill for the development of the Library System in the state. Madhya Pradesh has a State Central Library, Regional, district, Subdivisional and Village Libraries.

The number of libraries functioning in the State of Madhya Pradesh are:[68]

Type of Libraries	*Number*
Regional Library	5
Information Centre	6
District Library	42
Private Public Library	80
Gram Panchayat Library	15800
Total	15933

Uttar Pradesh

Attempts for enacting a legislation is going on since 1949 and Dr. S.R. Ranganathan has drafted two bills in 1949 and in 1958. The Government of Uttar Pradesh has established a Library Cell in the Education Department in 1980 to look after the matters of public libraries by the recommendation of the Public Libraries Enquiry Committee. A bill was drafted and submitted to the Government in 1983 by Prof. C.G.Viswanathan Committee.[69] There is a State Central Library (Allahabad) Government public Library (Allahabad) and 57 District Libraries are functioning in the State. About 250 voluntary organization libraries are also working here.

Himachal Pradesh

The library movement here was started with the establishment of State Central Library at Solan followed by 11 district libraries. Government action for starting of libraries was initiated in 1952. Here school libraries are also used as public libraries after school hours. There is one State Central Library, 11 District Libraries, 15 Community Central Public Libraries, 1 State Public Library and 101 Senior Secondary School (Public) Libraries in the State during the year 1989-90.

Arunachal Pradesh

The Government of Arunachal Pradesh started a Central Library at Itanagar, the capital of the State.7Block and 14 Circle libraries were established in different areas. Now there are total 82 libraries working in the State. A few mobile libraries are also functioning in the capital city.

Bihar

The ancient educational and Cultural Centres like Nalanda, Vikramashila, pataliputra and Taxshila had magnificent libraries. Attempts are going here to enact a library legislation. The library service at Government level is under the supervision of Commissioner of Education.

During 1985-86, there were libraries in Bihar as follows.[70]

Type of Libraries	No. of Libraries
State Central Library	1
Divisional Library	7
District Library	25
Sub- Divisional Library	25
Block Library	440
Village Library	4000
Total	4498

Gujarat

The State has not yet adopted library legislation. It has started two State Central Libraries, District Libraries in all districts and sub- Divisional Libraries in several Taluks. Gujarat has 7,589 libraries which are divided into Government Public Libraries (72) and Grant-in-aid Public Libraries (7,517) and 300 Book Service Centres.

Haryana

A State Central Library was started in 1967 by the Government of Haryana. Besides, it has started District Libraries in all 12 districts, 11 sub-Divisional Libraries and 11 Municipal Libraries. The Haryana Library Association was started in the year 1967. The Haryana Libraries Act was passed in 1989 behind of which was Haryana Library Association. The Act provides for a comprehensive rural and urban library service and network of libraries. According to this Act, Chairman is the Minister-in-charge of the Libraries and Secretary is the Director of Libraries.

West Bengal

By the efforts of the West Bengal Library Association, the State could enact a library legislation in 1979. there were total 2421 libraries in the State in 1986. This includes the State Central Library,21 District Libraries, 3 Central Libraries, 120 Sub-Divisional/Town Libraries, and 2276 Rural/Area/Primary Unit Libraries.

Orissa

At present there are 3 administrative departments which provide library service in the State. They are Department of Sports and Culture, Department of Housing and Urban Development and Department of Information and Public Relations. 1116 Libraries are functioning under Department of Culture,39 Libraries –cum-reading rooms in all 57 Sub-Division and 12 Cities and towns of Orissa. The Utkal Library Association formed in 1944 is constantly pressing the government to bring out a library legislation.

Rajasthan

In 1962, Rajasthan Library Association was formed. The Association drafted a Bill and submitted to the Government in 1965. Department of Education controls the functioning of public libraries in the State. A state level Permanent Advisory Committee for Libraries advise the Government in the matters of Libraries.42 Libraries and 18 Reading rooms are functioning in the State at present.

Assam

The first public library namely the Government public Library which merged with the State Central Library in 1956. The Public Library Services in Assam was started almost during the first Five Year Plan. The State has not yet enacted a library legislation although attempts were made several times in this direction. The Directorate of Library Services controls the entire library services throughout the State. There are 217 libraries functioning in the State.

Goa

The Government of Goa has constituted a State Library Advisory Board in 1983 for the development of Library service in the State. The Board appointed a Sub-Committee to draft the Public Libraries Bill which drafted the Bill and presented to the Government.

The public libraries in the State can be categorized into Government Libraries, Government-Aided Libraries,

Municipal Libraries and private Libraries. There are total 132 libraries work in the State.

Jammu & Kashmir

In 1975, government appointed a Committee under the chairmanship of Dr.Randhava, who examined the necessity of the Public Library Act and drafted a Bill and submitted to the Government. After 1947, a number of libraries, one Research Library and two small Children's Libraries.

Manipur

Manipur got status of a state in 1981. Imphal Public Library was started in 1983. Manipur Library Association was formed in 1987. This Association drafted the Manipur Public Libraries Bill and passed it in 1988 and came to force with effect form 1st October, 1988. The State has got one State Central Library,5 District Libraries and 101 Libraries run by Voluntary Organizations.

Meghalaya

It became a State in 1972. Meghalaya has one Central Library, four District Libraries and Library run by voluntary effort. The Central Library has more than 10,000 registered members. It subscribes more than 70 journals and 25 newspapers.[71]

Mizoram

After the formation of Mizoram State, a library was established at the capital, Aizwal and two district Libraries at Lunglee and Saiha. At village level Young Mizo Associations and voluntary organization started village libraries. Mizoram Public Library Bill was presented before the Government in 1988.[72] The Mizoram Public Libraries Act came into force in 1993. Department of Art and Culture controls the Public library service here. There is a State Central Library, 3 sub- Divisional Libraries and 200 recognised Village Libraries are functioning in the State.

Tripura

Tripura got full-fledged statehood in 21st January 1972.

The Birch and State Central Library was taken over by the Government in 1953 was made State Central Library in 1973. The State provides public library service through State Central Library, District Libraries, Sub-Divisional Libraries and Block Libraries. These libraries are controlled by the Department of Higher Education.

Chandigarh

The Central State Library in the State was started in 1955 i.e., during the first Five Year Plan. The T.S. Central State Library has over 1.80 lakh books and over 44,000 members. This library has two branch libraries, two integrated library centers are reading room, one model village library and one mobile library.

Punjab

Various departments like Department of Education, Local Bodies, and Department of Public Relations control the public libraries in Punjab. The Directorate of Public Instruction controls the full-fledged Government Libraries. There is a State Central Library, one Town Library and 13 District Libraries are functioning in the state.

UNION TERRITORIES

Andaman Nicobar

The Hindu Library at Port Blair started in 1959 was converted into State Central Library in 1974. District Libraries are functioning in two districts. Andaman and Nicobar Library Association was formed in 1977 which prepared a Blue Print for a Public library system for the State. By the effort of the Association, the Government constituted Andaman and Nicobar Library Planning Committee in 1978.[73] At present there are 10 zonal Libraries, 11 Public Libraries, 8 Information Centres and a few libraries run by voluntary organizations.

Lakshadweep

The Central Library is located at Kavarathe.The entire territory was covered by public service. Here public libraries are controlled by social welfare Wing

Delhi

Delhi Library Association was formed in 1953. A library Bill was drafted in 1954 and submitted to the Delhi Administration. The Bill has provision for free library service throughout the State on statutory basis.

Pondicherry

The Education Department is now running 64 Branch Libraries in rural areas. All these libraries are functioning under the control of library development officer of the Government.

The Public Library and the Rural SC Women

Rural SC women are backward in all respects than their counter part urban centers. Lack of facilities to improve their knowledge regarding various aspects as well as the limited chances to come forward make them backward. Most of these women in rural areas are under the chains of traditionalism. They are confined in four walls of the kitchen. There is a famous dictum 'men for the field and women for the kitchen'. This was the case of the women for the past few centuries. But educational, technological, cultural, economic, social and political changes forced these deplorable section to respond strategically to the changing environment. But, it is not absolutely correct to say that they have broken the chains once they were under particularly regarding rural harijan women. This is mainly because of socio-cultural educational,ecnomic and political backwardness which is the result of hesitation to undergo education and other several reasons such as castiesm, domination of men, responsibility of family particularly kitchen work, vested interests of male folk, double standard of morality, traditionalism, customs etc. particularly in rural areas. Gradually, the state of women is changing due to the spread of education and other social reform movements. The increasing social status particulary education not only brings changes in the philosophy of life of these women but also provide new avenues of employment to them. Those who are educationally and economically independent demand more freedom in family affairs as well as other arenas of social life. In this regard, harijan libraries in villages can contribute a lot by the provision of educational materials and other extension activities.

Women are a significant group in the village. They have special needs in the domain of health and child care, food and nutrition, cooking, family planning and welfare, kitchen gardens, dairy development, handicrafts and cottage industries to supplement their family income.' [74] Library in a village is the best medium for the dissemination of knowledge regarding the above aspects.Harijan Women in a village may be often reluctant to go to a public library which serves all types of clienteles .In this situation, a library specially for these section helps them a lot as they can overcome the social stigma related to them. It is quite natural that women in a village are not in a position to behave freely as they are traditional bound. So, a public library specially for SC population catering the particular needs of them is highly essential.These libraries can do a lot to empower SC women in various ways.

'The housewives are by naturally dependent on information of every type to run their households. Their information need may thus be to assist their children's education, to prepare well balanced diet for the family members, to retain their health etc.' [75]Public libraries are the best resource centre for the distribution of literature regarding the above subjects. J. J. Thabali's study clearly indicates the need for women libraries. He says 'majority of the housewives depend on oral information handed down by their parents, in-laws, friends, neighbours as well as colleagues, to run their households. To some extent they also get information from the media and some of the housewives visit the library'[76]. Most of them depend relatives and friends for the information. The rural library has a pivotal role to satisfy the information needs of women. That is why P.N. Kaula puts 'rural library authorities ..... should take care of the book needs of..... women' [77] . when we think about SC women this comment is well suited.

Indian feminist leaders have realized that their efforts are meaningless unless it attempts to make a change in response to the demands of education and health care among the lives of 80 percent of women who are self-employed and their basic concerns are access to clean water, animal fodder and cooking fuel [78]. Harijan libraries in villages are essential to fulfil this goal of SC women. 'By defining women as primary domestic workers and the sexual and reproductive property of men and by assigning priority to man's paid employment, the society devalues educational attainment and economic and social contributions of women'[79]. This attitude is widely prevalent among rural population particularly among SC section which can be changed by harijan public library system . Through dissemination of necessary knowledge regarding various evils to devalue women, the attitude of SC women as a weaker section can be changed. Various programmes through village SC libraries can be conducted to empower women and help to lead a responsible and respectful life in the society. Library is the best medium to improve the status of women in family and society. Economic independence, self confidence and personal achievement motivation are a few tools that serve women well in negotiate their status in the family with their husbands and other family members. For this, education and information are important aspects. And Harijan libraries can play a very prominent role in educating and giving reliable information to enhance the status of SC women.

Rural SC women are suffered by several shortcomings, which include educational, social, political, economic and cultural, due to various reasons compared with urban women. Majority of these women are poor and away from opportunities needed for their development. To empower this section of the rural society, a well established harijan public library system is of high need. Harijan libraries in villages can contribute a lot positively to change their present status. Special SC libraries can provide knowledge and other extension activities to improve their status. Special SC libraries can be attracted by same women in the particular village as these are manned and run by the same category. Librarians and other authorities of these libraries are SC people and so they know the real problems and strengths of these women which help them to direct activities suitable to their overall development. To improve and empower them, libraries specially for SC population are a must as other general public libraries cannot take so much interest in these women's development.

But, unfortunately the Harijan Welfare Libraries in Kerala are not come to the desired expectation.

5. REVIEW OF PAST STUDIES

In developed countries, this problem has received attention. Some of the researches done in the field may briefly be mentioned as under:

Bertha T Hirschstein made a sociological study of the Aquilar Branch of the New York Public Library in 1933. This was a case study about the clientele, the library's activities and examination of the relevant literature. Some of the important conclusions reached in the study were the use of the library was directly proportional to the distance from the library and the delinquent boys read more fiction than other general readers.

Bernard Reuben Berelson made an analysis of the Role of Communications in determining Public Opinion in 1941[80]. He examined the effects of newspapers, magazines and radio on the public opinion. He found that the people accepted the arguments which supported their own views; and they were aware of the arguments emphasized by the communication media.

Jesse Hauk Shera[81] worked on the Foundations of the Public Library in New England, 1629-1855, reviewed the history of 'social and circulating libraries' and the economic, social and cultural climate of that period. He concluded that public library was born when the economic condition of the cities was strong enough to support it.

Sidney H Ditzion[82] studies the Social History of the American Public Library Movement in New England and the Middle States from 1850 to 1900. He found that the social, cultural and political background of the movement and the gradual transition from private to public libraries. He also traced the role of public library in mass education. He concluded that for the self- realization of the broad masses of the people, both the institution and methods were conceived.

Julia Elizabeth Sabine made a study of the Social and Cultural Background of New Jersey, the other Middle Atlantic States and the city of Newark as Antecedents of the Newark Public Library. She described that the early Newark settler's ideals of formal education and self-improvement, expansion of commerce and industry, Lyceum movement created urge for self-education and legislation for free education were the important contributing factors.

The Division of Research Techniques of the London School of Economics made a sample survey of the London Boroughs of Bermondsey, Tottenham and Wandsworth during 1951-52[83]. The study was to investigate the readership figures for the various classes of newspapers and periodicals and also their interest, content etc. on the extent of book-reading of any kind and on the characteristics and main sources of books read they read.

A few studies have been conducted in Britain and United States. This includes the study of Brian Groombridge[84] , Bryan Lukham[85], Barry Totterdell and Jean Bird[86] ,Joseph wheeler[87], Leon Carnovsky and Lowell Martin[88] and Bernard Berelson[89]. These studies were stimulating and helped to know the situation of libraries in those countries. These studies have only a limited value for the present investigation because of the drastic difference between the library situation in Asia and European and American library situation.

In 1979[90], Chin Studied the information needs of citizens of New England region. The study aimed to ascertain the information requirements of the general population, identify the source of information, explore the role of the library in citizen's information seeking process and investigate the use and non-use of libraries. It was explained in the study that libraries, at least, in New England, are not viewed as an important source provider by the information-seeking public. It seems that libraries are utilised by only a limited segment of society largely professionals and technical workers as well as students and housewives.

There was another study in 1990[91] on 'What Public Libraries Have to Offer, Collection Building in the Field of Women's Information' by Kain W. Schade Van Westrum. He found that the women's support groups frequently complained of the difficulty of locating information in public libraries because the subject is relatively new and material is scattered under several headings throughout the library.

Another interesting study was in 1991[92] by E.A. Chatman on 'Channels to a Large Social World : Older Women Staying in Contact with the Great Society'. The Study showed that the respondents were not revealed as users of the public library because they have in-house library and choosing to purchase reading materials and perceiving library items to be of little interest.

In India, on such an important problem little attentions has been paid and no significant work has been done. There are books on library science which are of professional nature and a few scholars have also worked on the utilitarian aspects of the library. But a few people have given interest to study the community problems, community interests and the educational needs which the library serves. The first sizable survey of a public library in Asia was done in respect of the Delhi Public Library in 1955[88]. This study was to find out how far it had met a social and cultural needs and how it had fitted into the social life of that city. Apart from the specific problems which may be peculiar to Delhi City and the socio-cultural variations, this study was evaluatory on nature. The project-evaluation was in terms of certain specific objectives which the Delhi Public Library was expected to fulfil.

Some other studies on Indian Villages have been conducted by M.N. Srinivas[94], A.H. Somjee[95], S.C. Dube[96] and the publications of Sussex[97] group on village studies which were helpful to know the problems of conducting village studies These studies were conducted in line with particular discipline and as such they were not of much importance in the present context.

M. Kumar and B.S. Biradar [98] conducted a study 'Uses of Mass Media and Public Library by the Rural Community' (1998). This was a questionnaire survey to assess the uses of mass media (newspaper, radio, T.V) compared with the use of public libraries by the people of Siganamane Gram Panchayat area of Shimoga Dist., Karnataka. The study revealed that a majority were not interested in the duration of the library opening hours. And also that the location of the library was as inconvenient.

K. Sarada[99] conducted another study in 1976 on 'Library Facilities for Women in Andhra Predesh Public Library system.'. The review covers three districts of Andhra Pradesh although the situation is considered to much the same in other districts. Enrolment of women in public libraries is extremely low, the reasons for which include the social and religions legacy of India. Special branch libraries for women are available but their number is totally inadequate. More mobile units equipped with motor vehicles, rather than cycle-rickshaws are necessary particularly in rural areas. Book selection is another problem with too little attention paid to such subjects as child care, hygiene and family planning.

L. Moore[100] conducted a study 'The Provision of Women's Reading Rooms in Public Libraries' (1993). It traces the history of the provision of separate reading rooms of separate reading rooms for women in public libraries from the 19th century, when a common view was that access to public libraries to educate women, distract them from household duties and undermine parental censorship and the gradual phasing out of women's reading rooms as society's views changed.

Some other recent studies conducted on this subject were of Dr. Shrinath Sahai, Dr. K. Sharda and Dr., S. S. Jagnayak. The hypotheses of study of Dr. Shrinath Sahai [101] was that there is a general apathy of the people towards library, there is a relation between the reader's personality and the nature and content of the literature they read. The readers in India still follow the traditional reading pattern and they have not yet developed taste for the modern scientific and technological subjects to a marked extent; library has a big role in moulding the reading pattern of the people, etc. It brings out social and economic background of the people using the library, and the extent to which they are representative cross section of the community in general. In more concrete term, this study explained the extent to which the library meets the educational and recreational needs of the people, the role it plays as a medium of mass communication and functions as a social institution providing fellow-feeling, imparting essence of discipline and effecting the social behaviour of the people.

Another study was of K Sarada (1982)[102] The objective of the study was to analyse the village community and its basic component groups, identification of the information needs of the village community, a descriptive account of the Branch library in the village, efficacy of the Branch library in meeting the information needs of the people, etc. It also focussed to analyse the Branch library in general and the village and not concentrating to the development of the women through women's library.

A very recent study was of S. S. Jagnayak[103] (1992), the objectives of the study was to find out the extent of the reading habit, educational attainment, agricultural development, economic development, social and political development and attitudinal change of the rural people. Here, the study concentrated on rural people and library in general and not particularly to the rural woman library and the development of rural woman through these libraries. But, the present study was fully concentrating on the role of women libraries in the socio-cultural, educational and economic development of rural women.

Another recent study was conducted by SS.Jagnayak on

'Role of Libraries in Socio-cultural,Economic and Educational Development among Rural Women' for ICSSR,New Delhi.This study was aimed to find out the socio-cultural,economic and educational development among rural women through Vanitha libraries in Kerala. The study clearly pointed out the development of women in social,cultural and educational fields except economic field.But this study was fully concentrated on women in general and not SC women.The present study is fully concentrated on SC women only and also through harijan libraries in Kerala.

Theoretical Basis of the Study

In general, there is no discrimination against women in Kerala in the matter of formal education. However, we find that compared to men, women do not make the best use of the libraries and their services for their continuing education. There are cultural inhibitions. In general, women above 20 do not visit libraries in person in rural areas. They get books through the male members or children. Similarly, they do not attend the seminars and discussions organized by these libraries. In other words the 'liberating influence' of the libraries are not being optimally utilized by the rural women folk. It is also a fact that men do not encourage women in this respect. Hence, gender discrimination and cultural inhibitions and practices will provide the theoretical back ground of the study.

6. THE PROBLEM

India is, generally a rural country and people residing in these areas are less advanced than the people in urban centres particularly the women population.And harijan women apart from the general women, are no doubt, suffering from several short comings since a few centuries and continuing these difficulties even today. Various institutions are important aids to development and as such harijan libraries are of highly needed in rural areas than in towns for their all-round development. Until and unless the information regarding social, cultural, economic, educational, political as well as health are made available and incorporated in the lives of these rural SC women, one cannot expect a progress that is lasting and secure. This can be done very efficiently by only a net work of harijan libraries in rural settings.

The functions of the public library is to assemble, preserve and make easily and freely available to all people the printed and other materials that will assist them to educate themselves continuously; keep pace with progress in all fields of knowledge, become better members of home and community, discharge social and political obligations; be more capable in their daily occupations, develop their creative and spiritual capacities; appreciate and enjoy works of art and literature; make such use of leisure time as will promote personal and social well being; and contribute to the growth of knowledge.[104]

The problem has been selected for several other reasons. The rural setting is a viable unit for research studies as well as such studies have become a valuable part of research investigations in social sciences. The effect and impact of harijan libraries on women and the interaction between women and library could be discerned and examined with greater accuracy in the village. For a state which enjoys high percentage of literacy and reading habit of women there is not better forum like library and its extension activities for contact with large number of women. Kerala is the land of libraries and a peculiar feature of these institutions are that they act as a cultural centre of the community at large. Besides, harijan women in rural areas are not coming forward in various areas of social life and harijan libraries help them in this regard. Even though various social reform movements have come forward to enhance their social status and succeeded to a certain extent. But to sustain and further all round development, harijan library service is of high need. Some harijan libraries are functioning in Kerala and this kind of a study will help a lot to find out whether they are working well or not and to assess short comings and also provide suggestions to improve their functioning. No systematic and scientific effort has been made so far to find out the part played by harijan libraries for the development of this section. So, a study like this will be helpful to find out the extent of its impact on women.

7. OBJECTIVES OF THE STUDY

1. To find out the extent of the reading habit of Scheduled Caste women.
2. To find out the educational development of the Scheduled Caste women.
3. To assess how far these libraries contributed to the socio-cultural development.
4. To examine the contribution of these libraries for the economic development of these women.
5. To investigate the extent of satisfaction of these women in getting relevant information from these libraries.

8. HYPOTHESES

The reading habit of Scheduled Caste women has been improved considerably due to these libraries.

These libraries have contributed much to the educational attainment of SC women.

These libraries have contributed to the attitudinal change of this section.

The libraries have contributed to a great extent to the socio-cultural development of the SC women.

These libraries have satisfied the information needs of the SC women to a considerable extent.

The income of the Scheduled Caste women has been improved due to the services of these libraries.

Concepts

Educational development Educational development for the present investigation is the increase of reading habit and consequent development in the personality of the individual.

Social developmentSocial development for our purpose is the increase of participation in social activities and consequent change in the attitudes towards social issues.

Cultural development Here, cultural development means increase in the attendance and participation in cultural activities and consequent improvement in the capabilities and habit of the individual.

Economic developmentIt is the increase in the income and production and the reduction in the expenses of the individual

Considerations for studying Sample Population

The population for this study consists of SC women who had access to Library and representing the rural SC population in Karalla. The focus was to identify harijan libraries and the selection was made in three districts in Kerala. The selection of the population to be surveyed, was based on the following factors:

Women belonged to the age group 15 years and above. The population groups selected conforms to the general SC population of the state.

The age and family structure of women surveyed was representative of the general SC population in Kerala.

50 % of the respondents should be members of the library.The other 50% consists of non-members.

Based on the above considerations of the samples, the variability due to other socio-economic indicators were minimized. All the parameters of social, cultural, educational and economic status to be studied were normalised to be dependent upon the library use and reading habits.

Sampling Design

On the basis of the preliminary study conducted in libraries in one of the harijan libraries simple random sampling design was adopted. 150 members and 75 non-members were selected from 5 libraries in the state. And thus total 225 respondents were selected and interviewed.

The respondents were selected from three districts via Thiruvananthapuram,Kollam and Pathanamthitta.The normal distribution of the age of the sample was used to stratify the sample into six categories of age groups.The lower limit for the population is taken as fifteen years and the upper limit is seventy five years.So the age wise distribution of the sample is as follows:

Age	*N*
7	
23	
45	
45	
22	
66-75	8
Total	150

Age is the parameter i.e. a common idicator in the population and the sample.Other strata like income and education are skewed in the library population. The control group is 75 non-members (50% of experimental group).The control group was 75 women obtained from scheduled caste women who are not members or users of any library. The age wise distribution of the control group is:

Age	*N*
4	
11	
22	
22	
12	
4	
Total	75

The justification for keeping the lower limit as fifteen years was that as individuals, economic dependence on the family might not reflect the socio-economic parameters. During selection of the sample only members who have completed two years in the library were selected in the study. Any socio-economic changes can be identified only during such a period.

The objective of choosing sample was to obtain observations that were representative of the parent population. The best known statistical tool is a simple random sample where each unit of observation had an equal chance of being included in any sample. In the proposed study the simple random sample was selected by random numbers generation from the membership numbers.It was achievrd by draw of lots method.

Unit of study

The unit of study was the rural harijan library with its circle of SC women readers. Therefore, attention was paid on the following aspects.

i. A brief history of the library.

ii. The present status of the library – facts and figures about eh library like the number of books, the category of books, the number of members, the number of daily visitors , the number of books issued daily., the number of working days per year, working hours, grant-in-aid amount, other sources of funds.

iii. Socio-cultural and extension activities etc.

iv. Whether the librarian has formal training in library management or not.

v. The organizational set up and the present office bearers.

vi. Bye-law etc.

Besides, there was a schedule for assessing the impact. Data was also collected from literature available in various libraries, Kerala Granthasala Sangham etc. authentic persons in the field were met and collected data through observation also. In sum, the study focused on library as a development institution in the rural areas and its impact on the SC women folk in respect of their socio-cultural, economic and educational development.

Quantitative Techniques.

The control group consisting of 75 SC women provided the bench-mark data regarding the socio-cultural status of women, who are not influenced by the institution of library. The experimental group which is being exposed intensively to the influence of the libraries to identify and measure the impact through statistical devices. An interview schedule consisting of questions related to the different types of impact with a four point scale attached to each question (nil/low/average/high) were used for collecting data from the selected respondents. The analysis was done to review the socio-economic background of the readers and its impact on reading pattern, reading habits, academic achievements ,change in the social and behavioral interaction, employment assistance income generating capacity and information on demand etc. of the harijan women. There was also questions to collect information about their reading habits- frequency, type of reading materials, intensity of reading, the utility of information acquired, whether they share the information with others in the family etc.

The data collected by the survey was computerized and analysed using SPSS Ver. 7.00 software. The Proforma were edited by the project Director and obvious inaccuracies were rectified before data entry. The errors in the data entry were eliminated by suitable programme validation and consistency checks. Quality control was maintained by cross checking the data input with the original proforma randomly. The analysis was done to review the socio-economic status and the impact of library on socio-cultural, educational and economic development of SC women. Based on available data, various hypotheses about the population were tested. The statistical analysis methods included computing the frequently tables. After identifying the distribution of data, cross-tabulation studies with correlated variable and multivariable analysis was done to establish possible causes of problems and the consequent effect on the population. Pearson's coefficient of correlation and regression index were evaluated to confirm the statistical significance of the result. Based on the trend of population behaviour the hypotheses made were subject to chi-square or students T-Test wherever applicable and p-values determined to validate the inferences of the study. The Project

Director correlated the statistical results with the observation during the survey and possible reasons were identified.

9. RESEARCH SETTING

The history of public library movement in Kerala is older than any other states in Indian Union. Kerala is the land of libraries. The attraction towards books, aptitude for reading and interest for book collection were part and parcel of well-to-do Keralites from ancient time onwards. The three constituent parts of Kerala viz. Travancore, Cochin and Malabar had different kinds of public libraries catering to the needs of the reading public in small way. In the later part of the 19th and beginning of the 20th century, these libraries were the centre of the activities of freedom movement. Under the auspices of these workers, what is called 'open University' by arranging services of lectures on topics of cultural interest pertaining to Malayalam which benefited for the socio-cultural educational and political development of the public.

The three former constituent parts of Kerala had their own history of public library movement. The Sate of Kerala had formed in two successive stages – merging of Travancore and Cochin in 1949 and Travancore–Cochin and Malabar in 1956. The public library development in Kerala had been compartmentalised into each of these areas.

The public library movement in Travancore emerged with the initiation of Trivandrum Public Library in 1829 which was started by the direct involvement of Col. Hans Sloan,[60] the founder of British Museum. In 1898, the government took over this library and opened for public use since 1899. It became State Central Library in 1958 and functioning under the Department of Education. Another major attempt in the library movement in Travancore started with the establishment of Suguna Poshini Library in 1880 which could not survive for more than two years. Another milestone in the development of public library was the founding of Kottayam Public Library in 1882 by Sir. T. Rama Rao.[61]

Some of the important public libraries in early time are the Jnana Pradayani Library, Neyyattinkara and the Mundenkavu Sankaravilasom Library at Chengannoor (1910), Y.M.C.A. Library at Keezhkara (1911), Sree Chithra Thrunal Library at Trivandrum and Raja Varma library at Oachira (1913), Lalithavilasaom Library at Padmanabhapuram and Kandiyoor Jnanapradayani Library at Mavelikkara (1916), and Bharathavilasam Library at Karapuzha (1919)[62]

Another boost to public library development in Travancore was the provision of grant-in-aid for libraries in 1917 under the condition that these libraries should provide free book service to the public[63]. The Travancore Educational Reforms Committee Report of 1932 helped the government to organise 78 libraries in rural areas attached to government primary schools[64]. Besides, a few libraries were existed with village uplift centres[65] and municipalities prior to 1949.

The first All Travancore Library Conference was organised by Jnanapradayani Library in 1925 followed by another conference of Sree Chithira Thirunal Library in 1933 which resulted in the formation of first library association known as All Travancore Library Association.

The library development in Cochin started with the establishment of Ernakulam Public Library (1869) followed-by Trichur Public Library (1873). The government of Cochin started number of rural libraries during the year 1926. Government of Cochin had a Department of public libraries to look after the library matters. In 1946, there were three types of libraries – public libraries (17), major rural libraries (5) and village libraries (224). A meeting was held under the chairmanship of T.K. Krishna Menon in 1949 which was an important event in the history of public library development in Cochin In the Malabar area, social and political workers started many reading rooms which turned to become libraries in course of time. In area.

Malabar, the movement was mainly initiated by Municipalities and other local bodies. The Calicut Public Library was established in 1890 by the Calicut Municipality.

From 1900 to 1956, the libraries in Malabar area were libraries organised by Municipalities and Panchayats, libraries organised by Local Library Authority (LLA) and libraries organised by voluntary effort. The Fourth All India Library Conference was held at Madras in 1927 which inspired to start an association called Samastha Kerala Pusthakalaya Samithi. Another conference called Malabar Vayanasala Sammelanum was held at Kozhikode in 1937 resulted in the formation of the Malabar Vyanasala Sangham in 1943, its name was changed into Kerala Granthalaya Sangham[66]

After 1956, when Malabar region was bifurcated into three small districts namely Palakkad, Kozhikode and Kannur, three local library authorities were created which established district central libraries, branch libraries and deposit centres throughout the districts[67]. At the time of formation of Kerala, the Malabar had 500 libraries in addition to the LLA libraries .

Kerala Granthasala Sangham

The year 1945 is a landmark in the history of public library development as the seed of Kerala Granthasala Sangham was sown. In 1947, the All Travancore Granthasala Sangham was registered under Travancore Company Act of 1939 which became the All Travancore-Cochin Granthasala Sangham in 1948 when the two states- Travancore and Cochin were integrated. With the formation of Kerala stae in 1956 with Malabar, the Sangham titled as Kerala Granthasala Sangham with the principle aim of establishing a network of libraries through out the state so as to enlighten and encourage the rural population in their social, cultural and educational persuits[68].

Sangham's initial contribution was the pressure on the government to hand over libraries attached to government primary schools in the Travancore area to the Sangham and with the co-operation of the local people. It established village libraries in all centres where these libraries existed. Besides, the Sangham got village uplift libraries in certain areas of Travancore and these were also re-organised to function as public libraries. All public libraries in Cochin area including those of government were handed over to Sangham. By 1956, the Sangham had about 1500 libraries. After the formation of Kerala state, the Sangham extended its activities to Malabar area also and got 500 libraries which were not covered by Madras Library Act. By the Act of 1989, the libraries under LLAs were also attached to the Sangham. Through the Sangham, the government distributes annual grants to libraries and presently these are graded into six i.e A to F. In 1977 , the government dismissed the Central Administrative Committee of the Sangham and power is given to a Central Board which affected the public library development of Kerala adversely for a period of 15 years. Public Library Act was passed in 1989 and constituted an apex body known as State Library Council through democratic way and got all power concerning public libraries of Kerala in 1994.

Kerala Public Libraries (Kerala Granthasala Sangham) Act

Many public library bills were presented during various governments in 1971 , 1974,1977,1985 and 1989 and last one only could complete the legislative process and became law. It was exactly on 16th May, 1989 and brought out Kerala Public Libraries (Kerala Granthasala Sangham) Rules in 1991. As a result of the provisions in the Act, there are 3 levels of body viz., the State Library Council, District Library Councils and Taluk Library Unions which should be organised through representatives elected from various affiliated libraries of the Sangham. The State Library Council has also ex-officio and nominated members but not having power to elect office bearers. The Act provides three types of libraries viz grant-in-aid libraries, public libraries to be established by State Library Council, District Library Councils and Taluk Library Unions, libraries functioned under government for the use of the public libraries run by local bodies.

10. THE HARIJAN WELFARE LIBRARIES IN KERALA

The government of Kerala started a number of Harijan welfare libraries in the state for the upliftment Harijan people under Harijan Welfare Department. But these libraries were not working well and the Sangham initiated its efforts to undertake these libraries for which the government formed a committee . The committee enquired the matter and after which transferred these libraries to the Sangham.

Director of Harijan welfare had written a letter dated 6-6-1968 numbered D.O.No.D3-26964/66 in which he had written to the Secretary, Kerala Grandhasala Sangham as follows:

The Committee has classified the libraries into three categories, those which could be amalgamated with neighbouring libraries recognized by the Grandhasala Sangham, those which could be transferred to the Grandhasala Sangham and run under its auspices independently, that is without any amalgamation and those which are to be revitalized or transferred to more suitable places where there are larger concentration of Scheduled Castes of this Department. There are three categories of libraries

The commitments now undertaken by this Department in regard to these libraries are: remunerations to the librarian at Rs.17/- per mensem.(Rs.7/- pay plus Rs.10/-)

Rs.5/-p.m.for purshase of journals and Rs.6/- towards contingencies i.e, a total of Rs.27/- per month ie: Rs.324/- per year. In some cases the buildings belong to the Department while in the remaining cases individuals free of rent donate the buildings.

In respect of categories II and I what the Department can do on amalgamation of the libraries or their transfer to the control of your Sangham is to pay the concerned libraries or your Sangham the above amount as an annual grant. This will be a temporary measure, which may have to be reviewed after sometime. The new agency will have to provide library facilities to the Harijans free. It will also have to entertain in its service the existing librarians at appropriate terms and conditions, which should not be less advantage than the present conditions of service.

Kindly let me no whether the libraries concerned and your Sangham would be prepared to take over the

Departmental libraries mentioned in categories I and II under the above terms.

As the III category, i.e. libraries which are to be revitalized or transferred to more suitable places, here also my personal opinion is that it would be better if the revitalization, transfer etc could be undertaken by your Sangham and the library facilities continued under its auspices subject to the conditions mentioned above in connection with categories I and II.

According to the government order of 1970 the harijan libraries were transferred to Kerala Grandhasala Sangham with suggestions to categorizing of the libraries into three groups as follows.

1. Libraries which could be amalgamated to the neighboring libraries recognized by the Kerala Grandhasala Sangham for efficient working,
2. Libraries that can be transferred to the control of the Grandhasala Sangham and run by it,and
3. Libraries that can be kept under the control of the Harijan Welfare Department but which are to be revitalized.

Rules for payment of grants to Kerala Grandhasala Sangham for conducting the libraries transferred from the Harijan Welfare Department.

1. The grandhasala Sangham should submit application for grant for the libraries to the Director of Harijan Welfare during the 1st week of April every year unless otherwise ordered.
2. The application for grant should be accompanied by a statement of expenditure anticipated by the Grandhasala Sangham in respect of the libraries transferred to the control of the Grandhasala Sangham from the Harijan Welfare Department.
3. The application for grant will be examined by the Director of Harijan Welfare and orders will be passed for payment of the grant to the Sangham.

4. On receipt of communication of the amount sanctioned towards grant,the Grandhasala Sangham should prepare a bill for the amount and forward the same to the Director of Harijan Welfare for counter signature and return for encashment by the Grandhasala Sangham.
5. If any portion of the grant remains undisbursed or unutilized at the end of the financial year,it should be remitted to the State funds under intimation to the Director of Harijan Welfare.
6. The Grandhasala Sangham should make available all books and records in respect of the grants received from the Harijan Welfare Department for inspection by any officer from Directorate of Harijan Welfare.
7. The GrandhasalaSangham should make available the books and records in respect of the grant for the purpose for which it is given.
8. The Grandhasala Sangham should prepare a statement of expenditure incurred for different items for each year to the Examiner of Local Fund Accounts within three months after the close of the year under intimation to the Director of Harijan Welfare.

The following table gives the number and districts where Harijan Welfare Libraries are existed in Kerala.

Trivandrum	-	4
Kollam	-	6
Pathanamthitta	-	9
Kottayam	-	1
Thrissur	-	1
		21

The following are the names and addresses of Harijan Welfare Libraries in Kerala.

1. The Harijan Welfare Library,
   Barton Hill, Trivandrum.

2. The Harijan Welfare Library,
Thiruvallur . P.O.,Thiruvalla,Pathanamthitta.
3. The Harijan Welfare Library,
Prakkulam,Kollam.
4. The Harijan Welfare Library,
Veliyam P.O.,Kottarakkara,Kollam.
5. The Harijan Welfare Library,
Kuttur,Thiruvalla,Pathanamthitta.
6. The Harijan Welfare Library,
Oachira.P.O.,Kollam.
7. The Harijan Welfare Library,
Pongar,Thrissur.
8. The Harijan Welfare Library,
Mezhuveli,Chengannur,Pathanamthitta.
9. The Harijan Welfare Library,
Aruviyodu,Vattappara.P.O.Trivandrum.
10. The Harijan Welfare Library,
Kallumoola P.O.,Mavelikkara,Kollam.
11. The Harijan Welfare Library,
Errath,Vadakkedathukavu.P.O.,Adoor,
Pathanamthitta.
12. The Harijan Welfare Library,
Puthukkulam,Malayalapuzha.P.O.,
Pathanamthitta.
13. The Harijan Welfare Library,
Chiranickal,Puthumala.P.O.,Prakkodu.P.O,.
Pathanamthitta.
14. The Harijan Welfare Library,
Vadakkadathukavu P.O.,Adoor, Pathanamthitta.
15. The Harijan Welfare Library,
Thekketheri.P.O.,Pattazhy,Pathanamthitta.

16. The Harijan Welfare Library,
    Mundackal,Kollam.
17. The Harijan Welfare Library,
    Ozhukkupara,Nednkolam,Kollam.
18. The Harijan Welfare Library,
    Orukunnu.P.O.,Edemon,Pathanamthitta.
19. The Harijan Welfare Library,
    Anayara.P.O.,Trivandrum.
20. The Harijan Welfare Library,
    Vallakadavu.P.O.,Trivandrum.
21. The Harijan Welfare Library,
    Payippadu,Changanachery,Kottayam.

From the above ,five libraries were selected via,one from Trivandrum namely Harijan Welfare Library, Aruviyodu, Vattappara, two from Kollam namely Harijan Weifare Library, Prakkulam and Nedunkolam and two from Pathanamthitta namely Harijan Welfare Library, Vadakkedathukavu and Puthumala, Adoor. All these libraries are located in rural areas.The following are the details of the libraries selected for the study.

The Harijan Welfare Library (Ambedkar Memorial Harijan Welfare Library) Aruviyodu, Vattappara, Trivandrum

History

Though this library was originated in 1948 its regular functioning was started in 1963 from its present location. It had no proper shelter in 1948 and so the District Welfare Officer of Harijan Welfare Department relocated the library to the present place in 1963.The exact place where it locates is Aruviyodu Harijan Colony formerly known as Mahatma Gandhi Harijan Colony in Aruviyodu, Vattappara, Trivandrum.A thatched hut was present in 20 cents of public land of colony in which the library existed.But it was taken away for the purpose of building community hall by giving promise of providing a part for it after the construction of the hall.The promise was given by the Harijan Welfare Officer of that time.But they did not provide a portion of the hall after its construction.Now it is functioning in a rented room of a house in the colony and the rent of Rs.100/- is given by the Librarin himself.A sports club and a tuition programme were associated with the library when it had a shed.A committee has been constituted by the Library Council in 1999and the committee meets once in a while.The library has no bye-law.

Details

* Working hours -8 to 10 am and 4 to 6 pm.Sunday is holiday.
* Members -Males – 22; Females – 60;
* Books -1000; News Paper -1(Mathrubhumi-Sponsored by the Librarian); Magazine -1(Grandhalokam of Kerala Grandhasala Sangham)
* Book Issue -2 persons/day(Average)
* Newspaper Readers -7 persons/day(Average)
* Income -No income(No subscription fee and grant)
* Salary of Librarian -Rs.2980/- from Harijan Welfare Department.

The library's functioning is not satisfactory at all. No new books are being purchased due to lack of funds. Librarian is a casual visitor. Local people are not interested in the library. A good number of localities are even not aware of the existence of the library. Women members are visiting the library very rarely.They are not interested in taking books due to the absence of new and needful ones. It is interesting to note that the people who belong to other parties and enemies of the family where the library locates are reluctant to visit the library. No supervision and monitoring on the part of apex body i.e., District or State Library Council.

Harijan Welfare Library, Prakkulam, Kollam

This library was started in 16-4-1963.The register number of the library is 5800/02.The first committee members are: P. Muraleedharan, K. Dhanapalan, P. Babu, Ruban, S. Pappachan,

P. Lakshmanan, V. Raghavan, M.N. Sivasankaran, N. Asokan. The following are the details of the library:

Total number of members (at the beginning) :

Males	-115
Females	-72
(in 2003)	
Males	-164
Females	-93
Total number of books	: 2011
History	: 526
Novel	: 462
General Knowledge	: 462
Agricultural	: 350
Stories	: 121
Daily visitors	: 50
Book issue/day	: 12

Cultural Activities : Volley Ball and Foot Ball.

The library's working is not satisfactory.

Harijan Welfare Library (Dr. Ramankutty Memorial Harijan Welfare Library), Nedumkolam, Kollam

History

It was started in 1957 .It was initiated under the auspices of Dr.Ramankutty.From the beginning onwards the library had a manuscript magazine and other cultural programmes associated with anniversary of the library. There was agriculture book corner connected with the library and got some books from Grandhasala Sangham. First it was situated in Punnamukku and then the library is transferred to Ozhukkupara in its own building. The building was constructed with the help of public. The library collected a number of books at the time of anniversaries and thus it has got sufficient books. The library has got a shelf and a few books from Scheduled Caste Development Department. The library has got Rs.7800/

- from Block as a part of people's planning programme which has been utilized for constructing a new building for the library during 97-98.

Details

Total Membership -356 (Males-175;Females-181)

Total Number of Books -1372(English-88;Hindi-85;Malayalam-1199)

Novel -300

Poetry -100

Story -250

Drama -50

Biography -50

General -622

Visitors/day -25

Book Distribution/day -8; Ladies/day -5

Cultual Activities -Carams, Volley ball and Chess

Working Hours -9-10 am;4-6 pm.

Working Days -365 days/year

Newspapers -Malayala Manorama, Kerala Kaumudi sponsored by Panchayath)

The library has a TV and other necessary furniture(sponsored by Panchayath)

The present secretary is Aji and president is Ramkumar.The library is registered in Panchayath. The women population to a certain extent is reluctant to visit the library due to the presence of antisocial elements of nearby. The library is not functioning well.

The Harijan Welfare Library, Chiranickal, Ezhamkulam, Pathanamthitta.

It was functioning at Ezhamkulam in a rented building. But there was no sufficient space in the building and therefore the present librarian constructed a new building in his own land which is used for library now.The concerned authorities gave sanction to the new building for the working of the library during the year 85-87 .The library has no bye-law. The library is getting a grant of Rs.3000/- per year from the Sangham. The amount is utilized for purchasing books(75%) and administration(25%).

Details

Total Number of books -2250(Majority are novels, stories, biographies and poems)

English -18

Malayalam -2232

Total Number of Members -246(Males-126; Females-120)

Visitors/day -15

Working Time -3 pm-8 pm.

Newspapers -Malayala Manorama

Total Committee Members -7(President-Janardana Kurup and Secretary-Sreedharan)

The library is not satisfactorily functioning. This is mainly due to the lack of proper supervision and monitoring on the part of concerned library councils. The librarian is a casual visitor and will got salary even if he is not properly engaged in his duties. That is why he is not discharging his duties efficiently.

The Harijan Welfare Library, Aereth, Vadakkedathukavu, Adoor, Pathanamthitta

This library was started in 1956 and is functioning in a rented building in the above place.

Total number of members -300(Males-215; Females-85)

Total number of books -8000

Visitors/day -25

Working time -4-8 pm

Total number of committee members -11

There is no bye-law for the library. This library is also not working effectively among SC population particularly among women.

11. ANALYSIS

The data collected for the present study consists of 225 samples (Schedule caste women), of which 150 were regular users of Harijan Welfare Libraries, and has completed a minimum of two years as members. 75 non-members were also selected so as to make a comparison between them, of the variables under study. The sample was selected keeping in mind aspects like providing due and adequate representation to all related and pertinent variables like age, spread among the different districts selected for study, etc.

Random sampling method has been used to select the sample for investigation. A random sample from a population is a sample which is formed in such a way that every member of the population has an equal chance of being selected and the selection of an individual does not influence the selection of the other.

There are a total of 25 Harijan Welfare Libraries in Kerala, which is enumerated in Table 1.

Table 1. District wise Break-up of Harijan Welfare Libraries in Kerala

No.	District	Number of Harijan Welfare Libraries
1	Thiruvananthapuram	5
2	Kollam	9
3	Pathanamthitta	8
4	Kottayam	1
5	Thrissur	1
6	Ernakulam	1
	Total	25

It may be noted that the three southern districts of Thiruvananthapuram, Kollam and Pathanamthitta are having 22 Libraries out of the total 25 in the state. A sample of 30 members each from five Harijan Welfare Libraries, selected from the above districts was used for the study. The age wise breakup of the sample selected for the study is presented in Table 2.

Table 2. Age-wise Breakup of Sample

Sl. No.	*Age (years)*	*Members*	*Non Members*
1.	15 to 25	7	4
2.	26 to 35	23	11
3.	36 to 45	45	22
4.	46 to 55	45	22
5.	56 to 65	22	12
6.	66 to 75	8	4
	Total	150	75

The marital status of the respondents is as per table 3.

Table 3. Marital Status of the Respondents

Status	*Members (N = 150)* *Non members (N=75)*
Married	99
Unmarried	20
Widow	23
Divorced	2
Separated	6
Total	150

The educational background of the respondents was also varied, and is presented in Table 4.

Table 4. Education-wise Breakup of the Respondents

Education	*Members (N = 150)* *Non members (N=75)*
Neo-literate	4
Primary	26
Upper Primary	41
High School	42
SSLC	18
Higher Secondary/PDC	6
Graduate	9
Technical	4
Total	150

The occupations of the respondents were spread over almost all sectors and the same is presented in Table 5.

Table 5. Occupation-wise Breakup of Respondents

Occupation	*Members (N = 150)* *Non members (N=75)*
Service	58
Cottage Industry	17
Construction	31
Agriculture/Fisheries	7
Domestic Jobs	34
Manufacturing	4
Total	150

The income-wise breakup of the respondents revealed that the respondents selected for the study pertained to almost all income groups. The income-wise distribution of the respondents is as per Table 6.

Table 6. Income-wise Distribution of Respondents

Annual Income (Rs.)	*Members (N = 150)* *Non members (N=75)*
< 20,000/-	79
20,001 to 40,000	53
40,001 to 60,000	10
60,001 to 80,000	4
80,000 <	4
Total	150

It may be observed that the respondents of the present study pertain to the cross section of the Harijan society and can thus be established that they are representative of the population.

The data collected were analyzed using various statistical techniques, and the analysis is presented in this section.

The following statistical techniques were used, for analyzing the data, and for testing the hypotheses formulated for the study, which is presented elsewhere in this report:

The t-test

The test of significance of the difference between means for large independent samples.

Correlation

Pearson product-moment method of correlation.

Analysis of Variance (ANOVA)

(Garrett, 1973)

1. The t-test: The Test of Significance of The Difference Between Means for Large Independent Samples:

The different variables were compared using t-test (test of significance for difference between means of large independent samples) to find out if there exists any difference in their attitude towards the library.

2. Correlation: Pearson Product-Moment Method of Correlation:

The statistical procedure used in interpreting correlation (r) is mentioned in the following sections.

a. The Significance of r

The correlation is interpreted only after its statistical significance of coefficient of correlation has been considered. This is done by deciding whether the obtained r exceeds the value 1 / N=1.96 for significance at 0.05 level and 1 / N=2.58, for significance at 0.01 level.

b. Verbal Interpretation of Correlations

The following classification for interpreting the various values of r's are given below:

r from .00 to +/- .20

denotes indifferent or negligible relationship.

r from +/- .20 to +/-.40

denotes low correlation; present but slight.

r from +/- .40 to +/- .70

denotes substantial or marked relationship.

r from +/- .70 to +/- 1.00

denotes high to very high relationship.

This classification can be accepted only as a general guideline for interpreting a coefficient or correlation.

3. ANALYSIS OF VARIANCE (ANOVA):

The usual univariate analysis of variance (ANOVA) as explained by Garrett (1973) was carried out for calculating the F-ratio. Here, instead of taking all the four variables under study together, a single variable is considered at a time.

It may be mentioned that ANOVA furnishes an overall test of significance of the difference among means of the different groups of subjects.

DESCIPTION OF TOOL - WELFARE INDEX

This is deduced from the responses of the interview schedule. Welfare Index is measured in terms of the four major component variables namely:

Educational Development,

Socio-cultural Development,

Economic Development, and

Efficiency in Providing Information

1. Educational Development:

The libraries are instruments for educational development. The items included under this variable were such that it could elicit information pertaining to this particular function of the library. A few items under this variable and the response of the respondents are presented in the following sections.

a. Do you think you have general academic improvement after joining the library?

The response to this item is presented in Table 7. It can be observed that majority of the respondents (95%) are of the opinion that they have improved their academic performance after joining the library, which indeed is significant.

Table 7. Table Showing Response to the Above Item (N=150)

Responses	*Number*	*Percentage*
Very Much	141	95.00
Much	1	00.66
Little	7	04.68
Low	1	00.66
Total	150	100.00

b. Do you think your general knowledge has improved after joining the library?

The results of this item as presented in Table 8 shows that 76 % of the respondents were of the opinion that they have improved their general knowledge 'very much' after joining the library. However 10.67 and 12.66 per cent opined that they gained 'little' or 'low' after joining the library.

Table 8. Table Showing Response to the Above Item (N=150)

Responses	*Number*	*Percentage*
Very Much	114	76.00
Much	1	00.66
Little	16	10.67
Low	19	12.66
Total	150	100.00

2. Socio cultural Development

Like any other libraries, Harijan Welfare Libraries too conduct different social services, which include lectures, seminars, debates, film shows, etc. The items included under this head attempts to elicit information as to whether the members derived any socio cultural development by using the services of the library. A few items and the responses are provided below:

a. Have you increased your social contacts after joining the library?

While a substantial number of the respondents (76%) were of the opinion that they increased 'very well' their social contacts, 17 per cent held the view that they were able to increase their social contacts only 'little' as a result of joining Harijan Welfare Libraries. The result of the responses pertaining to this item is presented in Table 9 below.

Table 9. Table Showing Response to the Above Item (N=150)

Responses	*Number*	*Percentage*
Very Well	114	76.00
Well	6	04.00
Little	26	17.33
Nil	4	02.67
Total	150	100.00

Do you think your awareness regarding developmental activities of the community has increased after joining the Library?

The result of the responses pertaining to this item is presented in Table 10 below.

Table 10. Table Showing Response to the Above Item (N=150)

Responses	*Number*	*Percentage*
Very Well	118	78.67
Well	12	08.00
Little	19	12.66
Nil	1	00.67
Total	150	100.00

It is observed that majority (78.67 per cent) of the respondents were of the opinion that they have increased their awareness regarding developmental activities of the community, very well. 12 per cent have increased well. Together those who responded 'very well' and 'well' constitute over 85 per cent which is a highly desirable quality.

3. Economic Development

The questions set under this item were desired to elicit information regarding availability of information regarding various government schemes, employment opportunities, availability of application forms, etc. A few items and their responses are provided here.

a. Do you get information about employment opportunities from the library?

The result of the responses pertaining to this item is presented in Table 11.

Table 11. Table Showing Response to the Above Item (N=150)

Responses	*Number*	*Percentage*
Very Well	7	04.67
Well	1	00.67
Little	10	06.66
Nil	132	88.00
Total	150	100.00

It is indeed a sad thing to note that a total of 94.66 percent of the respondents opined that they gained 'Nil' or 'Little' information about employment opportunities from the library. The libraries, particularly the Harijan Libraries should go a long way in this area and should provide the members with information that may help them in gaining suitable employment.

b. Have you got commercial information from the library that has benefited you financially?

The result of the responses pertaining to this item is presented in Table 12.

Table 12. Table Showing Response to the Above Item (N=150)

Responses	***Number***	***Percentage***
Very Well	12	08.00
Well	1	00.67
Little	5	03.33
Nil	132	88.00
Total	150	100.00

As in the patter set out in the item described above, over 90 per cent (91.33) opined that they were not able to gain commercial information from the library that has benefited you financially. This is also not a good state of affairs as regarding a library, set up for the purpose of emancipation of the downtrodden schedule caste persons.

4. Information awareness

Efficacy of the library in providing information to the members was included under this variable. The items set out under this variable were such that to elicit information regarding the efficacy to provide timely information. A few responses are described here.

a. Do you think that the collection of literature available in the library is adequate for your purpose?

It is significant to note that over 95 percent of the responded were of the opinion that the collection of literature available in the library is adequate for their purpose, which is highly encouraging. This literature if made user specific, it will be of great help to the community members in general, and women members in particular. The results pertaining to this item is presented in Table 13 below.

Table 13. Table Showing Response to the Above Item (N=150)

Responses	*Number*	*Percentage*
Very Well	136	95.34
Well	02	01.33
Little	12	03.33
Nil	00	00.00
Total	150	100.00

b. Do you get the latest literature from the library?

The result of the responses to this item is provided in Table 14. It is evident that a vast majority of the respondent (91.33 per cent) are of the opinion that they get the latest literature from the library. This is a matter worth appreciating, as the libraries are in a position to provide its members with the latest literature, which is sure to help the members in updating their information and knowledge.

Table 14. Table Showing Response to the Above Item (N=150)

Responses	*Number*	*Percentage*
Always	137	91.33
Sometimes	3	02.00
Rarely	10	06.67
Never	0	00.00
Total	150	100.00

All the four component variables are scored and the total of these variables is taken as the Index. Here Educational Development is the increase of reading habit and educational attainment of the subjects through different programmes of the library. Socio-cultural Development is associated with quality of life, standard of living, and welfare of the individual in particular and the society in general. It is also the enhanced participation in the social activities and efficacy through knowledge, information sharing, and consequent improvement in the quality of life, social habits and individual as well as collective abilities. Economic Development encompasses the overall progress in the standard of life of the members achieved by the utilization of the services of the respective libraries. .

Results of Analysis ofVariance (ANOVA) for the Variables Under Study.

As mentioned elsewhere in the present report, Analysis of variance (ANOVA) was conducted so as to have an insight, as to whether there exist significant differences for all the variables among the different groups, viz. age, marital status, education, occupation, etc. studied. The results obtained for Analysis of Variance (ANOVA) for the above mentioned variables are presented in the following pages.

Since all the F ratios (vide Table 15) were significant at 0.01 level, it is evident that the women members of Harijan Welfare Libraries of different age groups differ among themselves in all the variables under study. It can therefore be inferred that age factor exerts significant influence on the utilization of various welfare measures.

Table 15. Results of ANOVA for the five variables among Members of different age groups

(N = 150)

Variable	*Source*	*Sum of Squares*	*Df*	*Mean Squares*	*F*
Educational Development	Between Groups	2594.31	5	518.86	8.08*
	Within groups	9252.15	144	64.25	
	Total	11846.46	149		
Socio Cultural Development	Between Groups	670.95	5	134.19	3.32*
	Within Groups	5820.38	144	40.42	
	Total	6491.33	149		
Economic Development	Between Groups	733.19	5	147.64	15.93*
	Within Groups	1334.37	144	9.27	

	Total	2072.56	149		
Efficiency in Providing Information	Between Groups	308.36	5	61.67	2.84*
	Within Groups	3127.92	144	21.72	
	Total	3436.28	149		
Welfare Index	Between Groups	12769.75	5	2553.95	6.59*
	Within Groups	55840.42	144	387.78	
	Total	68610.16	149		

Note: * indicates that the F ratio is significant at 0.01 level.

ANOVA was done to find out if there existed any differences among the respondents based on their marital status for the variables studied, and the results are presented in Table 8. It is observed from the results that there was significant difference for only two variables. Only the first variable, viz, Educational Development had significant difference at 0.01 level, and the other variables did not have any significant difference.

Table 16. Results of ANOVA for the five variables among Members of different Marital Status (N = 150)

Variable	*Source*	*Sum of Squares*	*Df*	*Mean Squares*	*F*
Educational Development	Between Groups	1102.75	5	220.55	2.96*
	Within groups	10743.71	144	74.61	
	Total	11846.46	149		
Socio Cultural Development	Between Groups	199.41	5	39.88	0.91
	Within Groups	6291.93	144	43.69	
	Total	6491.34	149		
Economic Development	Between Groups	82.25	5	16.45	1.19
	Within Groups	1990.31	144	13.82	
	Total	2072.56	149		
Efficiency in Providing Information	Between Groups	109.70	5	21.94	0.[illegible]
	Within Groups	3326.58	144	23.10	
	Total	3436.28	149		
Welfare Index	Between Groups	2564.76	5	512.95	1.12
	Within Groups	66045.40	144	458.65	
	Total	68610.16	149		

Note: * indicates that the F ratio is significant at 0.01 level.

The results of ANOVA with respect to Education revealed that there existed significant differences among the respondents for all the variables studied. Table 9 presents the results of ANOVA with respect to education. It is worth noting that the difference for this variable is significantly very high for all the variables studies, which is in tune with a number of earlier studies in the area.

Table 17. Results of ANOVA for the five variables among Members of Various Educational Background (N = 150)

Variable	*Source*	*Sum of Squares*	*Df*	*Mean Squares*	*F*
Educational Development	Between Groups	4490.93	7	641.56	12.39*
	Within groups	7355.53	142	51.80	
	Total	11846.46	149		
Socio Cultural Development	Between Groups	1864.66	7	266.38	8.18*
	Within Groups	4626.68	142	32.58	
	Total	6491.34	149		
Economic Development	Between Groups	571.56	7	81.65	7.72*
	Within Groups	1501.00	142	10.57	
	Total	2072.56	149		
Efficiency in Providing Information	Between Groups	826.30	7	118.04	6.42*
	Within Groups	2609.97	142	18.38	
	Total	3436.27	149		
Welfare Index	Between Groups	25173.77	7	3596.25	11.76*
	Within Groups	43436.39	142	305.89	
	Total	68610.16	149		

Note: * indicates that the F ratio is significant at 0.01 level.

Results of t-test for the Variables Under Study.

As mentioned elsewhere, 150 members of Harijan Welfare Libraries were compared with 75 women Schedule caste non-members. All the variables were compared using t-test (test of significance for difference between means of large independent samples) to find out if there exists any difference, with respect to the various classes of members and non members. The results are discussed in the following sections.

Table 18. Data and Results of t-test for comparison of Members and Non members for the variable Welfare Index.

Sl. No	Group	N	Mean	SD	t Value
1	Members	150	72.16	21.46	4.68*
2.	Non Members	75	62.93	7.86	

Note: * indicates significance at 0.01 level.

The details in Table 18 shows that the mean values for Welfare Index obtained by Members and non Members were 72.16 and 62.93, and the Standard Deviation were 21.46 and 7.86 respectively. The t-value obtained was 4.68, which is significant at 0.01 level. This indicates that the members benefit significantly in various aspects of Welfare index compared to non members.

The test of significance for difference between means of the component variables were also found, for the comparison of members and non members and details are reported below.

1. Comparison of members and non members for the variable Educational Development.

The results of t-test for comparison of schedule caste women members and non members of Harijan Welfare Library, are presented in Table 19.

Table 19. Data and Resulsts of t-test for comparison of Members and Non members for the variable Educational Development.

Sl. No	Group	N	Mean	SD	t Value
1	Members	150	20.94	8.92	3.84*
2.	Non Members	75	17.51	4.48	

Note: * indicates significance at 0.01 level.

It is evident from Table 19 that the mean values for Educational Development obtained by Members and Non Members were 20.94 and 17.51, and the Standard Deviation were 8.92 and 4.48 respectively. The t-value obtained was 3.84 which is found to be significant at 0.01 level. This indicates that the members benefit significantly in the various aspects of Educational Development compared to non members of Harijan Welfare Libraries.

2. Comparison of members and non members for the variable Socio Cultural Development.

The results of t-test for comparison of members and non members of Harijan Welfare Library, for the variable Socio Cultural Development are presented in Table 20.

Table 20. Data and Resulsts of t-test for comparison of Members and Non members for the variable Socio Cultural Development.

Sl. No	Group	N	Mean	SD	t Value
1	Members	150	16.93	6.60	4.41*
2.	Non Members	75	14.25	2.44	

Note: * indicates significance at 0.01 level.

As given in Table 20, the mean values for Socio Cultural Development obtained by Members and non Members of Harijan Welfare Libraries were 16.93 and 14.25, and the Standard Deviation was 6.60 and 2.44 respectively. The t-value obtained was 4.4. This t-value is significant at 0.01 level. This means that the members benefit significantly in various aspects of Socio Cultural Development, by using the services provided by the library, compared to non members.

3. Comparison of members and non members for the variable Economic Development.

Table 21. Data and Results of t-test for comparison of Members and Non members for the variable Economic Development.

Sl. No	Group	N	Mean	SD	t Value
1	Members	150	23.61	3.73	1.69 NS
2.	Non Members	75	22.92	2.59	

Note: NS indicates that t value is not significant statistically.

It is evident from Table 21 there was no significant difference between the members and non-members of Harijan Welfare Libraries of the state with respect to the variable Economic Development (t-value = 1.69). This may be attributed to the fact that due to penetration of newspapers and other audio visual media the general population is aware of the economic policies and packages available to them is the economy. However, the mean value of members is marginally high at 23.61 as against 22.92 of non members. Similarly the Standard Deviation is also high for members (3.73) as compared to non members (2.59), thereby denoting that they have a better access to information pertaining to areas related to economic development.

4. Comparison of members and non members for the variable Information Awareness.

As enumerated in Table 22, the mean values were 10.65 and 8.25; and Standard deviation 4.88 and 1.53 for the variable Information Awareness, with members having higher values against Non member, which is consistent with the values of the other variables of the present study. The t-value (5.57) is significant at 0.01 level. The result denotes that members of Harijan Welfare Libraries have better Information Awareness as compared to non members of their community.

Table 22. Data and Results of t-test for comparison of Members and Non members for the variable Information Awareness.

Sl. No	*Group*	*N*	*Mean*	*SD*	*t Value*
1	Members	150	10.65	4.88	5.57*
2.	Non Members	75	8.25	1.53	

Note: * indicates significance at 0.01 level.

A comparison of the Mean values and Standard Deviation of members and non members of Harijan Welfare Libraries for all the four component variables and the Welfare Index is worth making, and the results are presented in Table 23.

Table 23. Comparison between Members and Non members for All the Variables

Variables	*Group*	*N*	*Mean*	*SD*
Educational	Members	150	20.94	8.92
Development	Non Members	75	17.51	4.48
Socio Cultural	Members	150	16.93	6.60
Development	Non Members	75	14.25	2.44
Economic	Members	150	23.61	3.73
Development	Non Members	75	22.92	2.59
Welfare Index	Members	150	72.16	21.46
	Non Members	75	62.93	7.86

It is evident from Table 23 that, the mean and standard deviation pertaining to women members of Harijan Welfare Libraries are higher as compared to non members, of the same community. This is an indication that members on whom the study was conducted benefit from using the services provided by the libraries. However, it is worth noting that the mean value is only marginally higher, which is an indication that the benefit derived by members is not as desired.

When the concept of Harijan Welfare Libraries was introduced it was considered that it would help in the all round development of the rural schedule caste people. It was also expected to fulfill the social and cultural needs of the community as a whole. The study has proved that, though the rural schedule caste women have not benefited fully from the services, provided by the Harijan Welfare Libraries, there is marginal difference in the level of development between members and non-members. If the community is to be emancipated and their full potential is to be utilized by them and the society, they should be made to wholeheartedly participate in the activities of the Library, and derive maximum benefits of such an institution.

Results of Correlation for the Variables Under Study.

The inter correlations among all the variables which were studied in the present investigation have been estimated using

Pearson r. The correlation coefficients are presented in Table 24.

It may be observed from Table 24 that the five variables namely, Educational Development, Socio cultural Development, Economic Development, Information Awareness and Welfare Index variable have positive and significant correlation among themselves. All the 10 correlation coefficients were found to be significant statistically at 0.01 level, with four of the coefficients having moderate relationship, and the remaining six indicating high to very high relationship.

Table 24. Co efficient of Correlation among the five variables

Sl.No	*Variable*	*1*	*2*	*3*	*4*	*5*
1	**Educational Development**	( )	.797*	.583*	.791*	.939*
2	**Socio cultural Development**	..	( )	..512*	.866*	.921*
3	**Economic Development**	..	..	( )	.560*	.699*
4	**Information awareness**	..	..	..	( )	.916*
5	**Welfare Index**	..	..	..	..	( )

Note: * indicates that the coefficient of correlation is significant at 0.01 level

The correlation between Economic Development and that of Educational Development, Socio cultural Development, and Information Awareness had moderate relationship. The other variables had high to very high relationship. This means that the all the variables investigated under the present study are related to one another. In other words the increase in one variable will automatically lead to the increase the other variable correlated. Further, it is also an established fact that Educational, Socio cultural, Economic development etc., of any society is interconnected and development in any of the said variable will invariable lead to the development in the other variables, thereby acting as a catalyst for transformation of the entire society. The present study done among schedule caste rural women is thus in conformity with a number of earlier studies in the field.

As a whole this investigation has brought to light certain facts about the utilization of Harijan Welfare Libraries by Schedule Caste women. It is worth noting that the members of the library a marginally high in the all the variables considered for this study, in comparison with non members. However, this definitely is not enough, if the concept of Harijan Welfare Libraries is to be a success, as desired by the Government. The number of members and those who use the facilities and services provided by the Libraries should increase, and this should ultimately lead to their well being and the resultant development of the society as a whole.

The summary and conclusions of the investigation are provided in the next section.

12. SUMMARY AND CONCLUSION

13. THE STUDY IN RETROSPECT

Libraries are social institutions created to work as a catalyst for social progress. The focus of the present study has been on the role played by Harijan Welfare Libraries among rural women towards their overall upliftment. The present study has been conducted with the object of finding out as to whether the concept of Harijan Welfare Libraries has helped in the overall development of the rural women belonging to the Schedule Castes. The study focused on the development aspects, particularly the socio-cultural, economic, educational, and information awareness.

The present study made use of the following variables:

Socio-cultural,

Economic,

Educational, and

Information awareness.

The total score of the said variables were taken as Welfare Index. The sample for the study consisted of 150 rural Schedule Caste women who have completed a minimum of two years of membership (experimental group), and 75 non members of Schedule caste (control group), of the three southern districts of Trivandrum, Kollam and Pathnamthitta, of Kerala State. Data were collected using an Interview Schedule having close ended questions. Personal data such as sex, age, income, qualification, occupation, etc, were also collected.

Statistical techniques like Analysis of Variance (ANOVA), t-test, Pearson Product-moment Method of Correlation, etc., were used for analyzing the data.

14. RESULTS AT A GLANCE

1. The results of ANOVA indicated that:

There existed significant difference between rural schedule caste women members of different age groups in all the variables studied.

There existed significant difference among members of different marital status, for all the variables compared.

There existed significant difference among member having different educational background, in all the variables under study.

2. The results of the t-test indicated that:

There existed significant difference in the comparison between members and non members for the variable 'Educational Development'.

There existed significant difference in the comparison between members and non members for the variable 'Socio-cultural Development'.

There existed significant difference in the comparison between members and non members for the variable 'Economic Development'.

There existed significant difference in the comparison between members and non members for the variable 'Infcrmation awareness'.

The variable 'Welfare Index', denoting the overall score also had significant difference among members and non-members.

3. **The comparison between mean and standard deviation for members and non-members revealed that:**

The women members of rural Harijan Libraries had higher mean scores than non-members in all the variables studied.

The standard deviation of members was also high as compared to that of non-members.

4. **The results of inter correlation obtained for the five variables indicated that:**

All the five variables namely, Educational Development, Socio cultural Development, Economic Development, Information Awareness and Welfare Index variable have positive and significant correlating among themselves.

15. TEST OF TENABILITY OF HYPOTHESIS

The results, as discussed above throw adequate light on the hypotheses formulated for the present study.

The hypotheses formulated for the study were:

The libraries have contributed much to the educational attainment of rural schedule caste women.

The libraries have contributed substantially to the attitudinal change of schedule caste women.

The libraries have contributed to a great extent, the socio-cultural development of the schedule caste women.

The libraries have satisfied the information needs of the schedule caste women to a considerable extent.

From the results it can be concluded that all the above hypotheses have been accepted partly. The libraries have contributed to a certain extent to the educational attainment of the rural schedule caste women, but have not contributed 'much' in the educational attainment.

Similarly, though the Harijan Welfare Libraries contributed towards the attitudinal change, the contribution is meager and not as desired. This is also the case of socio-cultural development. Though there has been development in the socio cultural field, the same is only to a certain extent, ant not to a 'great extent'. It is also evident that the libraries have not been able to satisfy the information needs of the schedule caste women to a 'considerable extent'. From the results it is established that the rural schedule caste women members were not able to gain economically from the use of the libraries, as the mean score for the variable is only marginally high from that of non-members, and much have to be done in this field.

As a whole it can be stated that though the Harijan Welfare Libraries have contributed towards the development of the women members, the contribution is not to the levels as desired by the pioneers who were instrumental in setting up this institution.

REFERENCE

1. Jefferson,G. Libraries and Society. London: James Clark and Co.Ltd., 1969,p.55
2. Gopalrao Ekbote Public Library System.Hyderabad : M/ S Ekbote Brothers, 1987, p.25
3. Singh,R.S.P. Glimses of Librarianship.NewDelhi: Janaki Prakashan, 1981, p.81
4. Jagnayak,S.S. Role of Libraries in Socio- Economic, Cultural and Educational Development among Rural People. New Delhi: Classical Publishing, 1997, p.48
5. Walford Ashworth Special Librarianship. London: Clive Bingley, 1979,p.6
6. Gopalarao Ekbote op.cit.,1987,p.23
7. Ibid, p.24
8. Banerjea,P.K. Reflections of University Libraries of India. Indian Librarian, 19, 1957, p.23-27
9. Ibid, p.24
10. Deshpande,K.S. National Policy and Programmes for University Libraries in India. Inamdar,N.B.et.al. NationalPolicy for University Libraries in India. New Delhi : Concept Publishing Company, 1989,p.3-16

11. Gopalarao Ekbote op.cit. p.251
12. Mukherji. A.K. Librarianship-its Philosophy and History. Bombay: Asia Publishing House, 1966,pp.53-133
13. Shera,J.H. Foundations of Public Library.Organisation of Public Library Movement in England. Chicago: University of Chicago Press, 1994, p.Introduction V
14. Ogburn,W.E. Library and New Social Order,Wilson Library Bulletin. New York: H.W.Wilson and Co., 1934,p.443
15. Patrick R. Penland Community and Library .Encyclopedia of Library and Information Science. New York : Marchel Dekker Inc.,1968, p.483
16. Adimorah, E.N.O. An analysis of progress made by Public Libraries as Socio Institutions in Nigeria. UNESCO journal of Information Science, librarianship and archives administration, Vol.V, No.3,. Paris: UNESCO, 1983, p.162
17. Kaila,D.R. A Report on role of Cultural Institutions in adult Education, Education Commission. New Delhi: Govt. of India, 1965, p.15
18. Harrison, K.C. Library and Community. London : Andre Deustch Ltd., 1962,p.15
19. Shera, J.H. Sociological Foundations of Librarianship. Bombay: Asia Publishing House,1970,p.44-52
20. Trehan,G.L. Modern Public Library Movement and Services in India. Chandigarh: Library Literature House, 1982,p.105
21. Gopinathan Menon,A.G. Adoption behavior of small farmers in relation to their attitude towards Agricultural Innovation. Trivandrum, Dept. of Sociology, Unpublished PhD Thesis, 1982,p.16
22. Soul Ross Development, Canadian Journal of Development Studies. Canada: University of Ottawa, 1986

23. Seetharamu,A.S. Education and Rural development. New Delhi: Ashish Publishing House, 1980,p.23.
24. Sant Ram Bhatia Librarian and Libraies.Jaipur: Sri Sanmati Pustakaya Trust,1973,p.34
25. Viswanathan,C.G. Public Librraies Operations and Services. Lucknow : Print House,1985,p.2
26. Library Associations, Public Libraries aims and Objectives, Library Associations Record. London : London and home Countries,1971,p.7
27. Singh,R.S.P. Glimpses of Librarianship. New Delhi, Janaki Prakasan, 1981, p.38-32
28. Mittal,S.R. Organising a Village Library. NewDelhi: National Council of Education Research and Training, 1964,p.1
29. Homby,A.S. Oxford's advanced Learner's Dictionary of Current English. Britain : The English Language Book Society and Oxford University Press, 1974,p.280
30. Emile Durkheim Education and Society. New York, 1965, p.28
31. Robert J. Stalcup Sociology and education. Ohio: Charles E. Merrii Publishing Company,1968 p.29
32. Padma Ramachandran Libraries as Catalysts of change.Trivandrum:Government of Kerala,1974,p.105
33. Trehan,G.L. A Developing Society and its Library needs. Twenty-eight All India library conference-seminar papers. Delhi: The Indian Library association, 1982, p.18
34. Mittal,R.I. Library Administration-theory and Practice. Delhi: Meropolitan Books Co., 1983,p.2
35. Mangal,S.K. Educational Psychology.Ludhiana: Prakash Brothers,1985.,p.117
36. Ganguli,B.N. Gandhi in Social Development, Social Development essays in honour of Smt. Durgabhai Deshmukh. NewDelhi: Sterling publishers,1977,p.156

37. Nittal V. Ratnam and Bhaskara Rao, B. The measurement of social development in areas. New Delhi : New man Group of Publishers,1982,p.8
38. Owens R. The state Government and libraries, XXVI, All India Library Conference-Seminar Papers. New Delhi: Indian Library Association, 1980, p.28
39. Peter J.McCormick Identifying the libraries Public community. The Library as a community information centre papers. Illinois: Illinois I Library School, 1957,p.57
40. Williams Raymond P. Culture. Glasgow: William Collins Sons and co Ltd., 1981, p.13
41. Ronald C. Benge Libraries and Cultural change. London: Clive Begley Ltd., 1970, p.240
42. Robert J.Benge Op.ct, 1968,p.8
43. Baby Mookhan Samuhikajeevithathil Granthasalakalude Panke, Granthalokam. Trivandrum: Kerala Granthasalasangham, 1973,p.23
44. Jhingan,M.C. The Economic of Development and Planning. New Delhi: Vikas Publishing House Pvt. Ltd., 1976, pp.4-6
45. Ibid., p.6
46. Jagat Bihari Library Services for a Developing Society, XXVI th Library Conference-seminar Papers. New Delhi: Indian Library Association, 1980,0.23
47. Adimoral,E.N.O A analysis of progress made by Public Libraries as social institutions in Nigeria., Unesco Journal of Information science. Paris; Unesco, 1983,p.162
48. Dipak Kumar Barua Ancient Indian Libraries.The modern Review-April & July.Jullunder: Modern Town,1963,p.284
49. Kaila D.R. Public library development in India. Trivandrum Public Library Platinum jubilee souvenir-1974. Trivandrum: Government of Kerala,1974,p.21
50. Ibid, pp.23-24

51. Trehan,G.L. Modern Public Library. Chandigarh:Library and Literature house,1983,p.42
52. Trehan,G.L. Op.cit,1983,p.99
53. Trehan,G.L. Op.cit,1983,p.144
54. Krishan Kumar 1985,op.cit, p.85
55. Krishan Kumar 1985,op.cit, p.85
56. Ibid, p.86
57. Ibid, p.86
58. Raman Nair Public Library development. New Delhi: Ess Ess Publications, 1983, p.21-22
59. Thomas V.K. Op.cit., 1997,p.27-28
60. Trehan,G.L. Op.cit, 1997, p.29
61. Thomas V.K. Op.cit. 1997, p.29
62. Ibid,p.29
63. Ibid,p.30
64. Ibid,p.31
65. Thengamom Kerala Grandhasala Sangham, Kerala Grandhasala Sangham Rajatha jubilee souvanir. Trivandrum: Kerala Grandhasala Sangham,1971,p.21
66. Vasudeva Menon,T Library Movement in Kerala, Library Movement in India. Delhi: Delhi Library Association, 1997.
67. Thomas,V.K. Op.cit,1997,p.30
68. Bhargava ,G.D. and Nigam,B.S. Madhya pradesh needs library legislation, In Library movement. and library development in India. 30th all India conference papers.C.P.Vasisth(ed.). Delhi: Indian Library association, 1994,p.52-60
69. Raman Nair Op.cit. pp.27-28
70. Singh,R.S.P. Public library development in Bihar, Granthana, Indian Journal of library studies, 2(2), 1991, p.193-204
71. Thomas,V.K. Op. cit., 1993,p.26

72. Raman Nair Op.Cit., 1993,pp.26
73. Ibid,p.28
74. Sarada,K. Rural library Services in India. New Delhi, Ess , Ess Publications,1986,p.128
75. Thabah,J.J. Information needs and information seeking behaviour of housewives,Library herald,Vol.39 (142). Delhi, 2001,p.65
76. Ibid,p.70
77. Kaula,P.N. Op.cit.,p.190
78. Elizabeth Bumiller May you be the mother of a hundred sons. A journal among the women in India. New York, Raindom House,1990
79. Sarala R. Murgai Motivation to manage: A compararative study between male and female library and information science students in United states of America and India, 50 years of Indian Librarianship,Ed. By G.devaraja. New Delhi: Ess Ess Publications, 1999, p.286
80. Bernard Reuben Berelson Library's Public. New York: Columbia University,1949
81. Sse Hauk Shera Foundations of the Public library: Origins of the Public library in New England. Chicago: University of Chicago press, 1949.
82. Ydney H. Ditizon Arsenals of a Democratic culture. A social history of the American public library movement in New England and the middle states from 1850-1900. Chicago: American library association, 1947
83. Stuart Reading habits in three London boroughs, Journal of documentation,vol.8(4),1952,pp.34-39
84. Brian Groombridge The Londner and Hislibrary. London, 1965
85. Bryan Luckham The library in society: a study of the public library in an urban setting. London,1971
86. Barry Totterdell and Jean Bird The effective library report of the Hillingdon project on Public Library effectiveness. Margaret Redfern (ed.), London, 1976

87. Joseph L. Wheeler. The library and the community. Chicago,1924
88. Leon Carnovosky and Lowell martin(eds.) The library in the community. Chicago,1944
89. Bernard Berelson The library's public: a report of the public library inquiry. Newyork,1949
90. Ching-chin chen Citizen's information needs: a regional investigation. Robert D. Stuart (ed.) Information needs of the 80's. London: jain press, 1982
91. Kain W. Schade Van Westurn What public libraries have to offer: collection building in the field of women's information. Biblithek En Samenleving, 18(10), 1990
92. Chatman,E.A. Channels to a larger social world: older women staying in contact with the great society. Library and information scince research.(3),1991
93. Frank M.Gardner. Delhi public library: an evaluation report. Paris:Unesco, 1957
94. Srinivas,M.N. India's Villages. Bombay,1960
95. Somjee,A.H. Democracy and political change in village India. Delhi,1971
96. Dube,S.C. Indian Village. London,1955
97. Biplab Das Gupta (ed.) Village studies in the third world. Delhi,1978
98 Kumar,M and biradar,B.S. Use of mass media and public library by the rural community: a study, annals of library scene and documentation.,44(3), 1998
99 Sarada,S. Library facilities for women in Andra Pradesh Public library system. Indian Librraian,3(1),1976
100 Moore,L The provision of women's reading room in Public libraries. Library History,995 & 6), 1993
101 Srinath Shahi Library and Community. New Delhi: Today and tommorow's printers and publishers,1973
102 Sarada Op.cit. p1.
103 Jagnayak, S.S. Op.cit.,1997

104 Jagnayak, S.S. Role of libraries in soci-culture, economic and educational development among rural women. New Delhi: Unpublished report,2002

105 Gerald W.Johnson Role of public library, Public library service. Chicago,American association.

106 Menon,V.K.N. The Trivandrum Public library. Trivandrum: Trivandrum Public Library planinum jubilee suvanir,1974,p.15

107 Koya Pakkar Some major libraries in Kerala, Trivandrum: Trivandrum Public Library planinum jubilee suvanir,1974,p.118

108 Sivadasan Pillai, K. A.,Ed. Kerala Grandhasala Sangham (1940-80), Trivandrum,1981,p.2

109 Issac,K.A. Library movement in Kerala. Timeless fellowship,1973,p.46

110 Velupillai,t.K. Travancore state manual, Vol.2,Trivandrum: Government pres,1958,p.4

111 Vettoor Raman Nair Kerala Grandhasala Sangham pravarthanacharithavum khadanayum (Kerala Grandhasala Sangham –history and constitution Trivandrum: Kerala Grandhasala directory,1964,p.53

112 Krishna Kurup Malabar grandhasala prasthanam (Library movement in Malabar), Granthalokaam,9(4). Trivandrum: Kerala grandhasala sangham, 1957,p.197

113 Krishna kumar 9Ed.) XXXVI All India Library conference. New Delhi: Indian Library association,1980

114 Vasudeva Menon,T. Library movement in Kerala, Library movement in India. Delhi: Delhi Library association, 1958, p. 98

4

Academic Status of Librarians in the Universities in Kerala: An Analytical Study

Dr. Dineshan Koovakkai

0. INTRODUCTION

The role of libraries in higher education has been emphasised often by education commissions, educationalists, professionals and scholars. In a university, the standard of study, teaching and research depends heavily on the strength of library collection and services. Library is regarded as the heart of the university. Exposure to libraries is inevitable for the academic community to set in motion the cultural revolution of a nation. It was, however, only after the inception of the University Grants Commission (UGC) that the libraries and librarians began to be recognised as inevitable parts of teaching and learning. The UGC is keen in providing financial support for the development of academic libraries and maintaining high quality library staff. Provision of academic status to librarians is a venture in this regard.

1. ACADEMIC STATUS FOR LIBRARIANS

The academic status of librarians has been a matter of discussion in library literature and seminars for the last several years. It is an approved fact that in the independent learning system of the present day, librarians occupy a prominent place in imparting knowledge to the students. By assisting the learners to acquire knowledge, librarians perform the duty of a teacher who makes the task of acquiring knowledge simple.

However, it is difficult to say whether librarians have academic status in our country. Khanna (1994) is of the view that in Indian society; at least, the librarian is looked upon as a caretaker of books or a book lifter.

Association of College and Research Libraries (ACRL) viewed the academic status of librarians as " the formal recognition in writing, by an institution's authorities, of librarians as members of the instructional and research staff. The recognition may take the form of assigned faculty ranks and titles, of equivalent rank and titles, according to institutional custom" (Status of college and university librarians, 1959).

Though various commissions and committees recommended academic status to librarians in India, it was only in 1961 that the UGC brought the academic librarians on par with teachers following the recommendations of Ranganathan Committee. Though this status had been denied later, it was restored in 1980.

2. KERALA SCENE

It was only in 1990 that the Government of Kerala decided to implement the UGC scheme to university and college librarians with effect from 1.1.1986 following the decision of the Government of India to give financial assistance to state governments to implement the UGC scheme accepting Mehrotra Committee Report. This decision of the Government of Kerala placed the librarians, though a limited group, on par with teachers. The revised pay and designation as per the UGC scheme are shown in Table 1.

Table 1. Revised Pay Scales of Librarians in Universities with effect from 1.1.1986

Existing Designation and Scale of Pay	***Revised Designation and Scale of Pay***
Assistant Librarian Gr. II (1150- 2270)	Assistant Librarian / Documentation Officer(2200- 4000)
Assistant Librarian Gr. I(1500- 2685)	Assistant Librarian / Documentation Officer (Senior Scale)(3000- 5000)
Deputy Librarian(1950- 2950)	Assistant Librarian / Documentation Officer (Selection Grade) (3700- 5700)Deputy Librarian (3700- 5700)
University Librarian (2450- 3600 / 2250- 3350)	University Librarian(4500- 7300)

It is evident from the table that Assistant Librarians and above are given the financial status equal to that of the teaching faculty in universities. The scale of pay of Assistant Librarian / Documentation Officer (2200- 4000) is the same as that of Lecturer in universities, of Assistant Librarian / Documentation Officer (Senior Scale) (3000- 5000) is equal to that of Lecturer (Senior Scale), of Assistant Librarian / Documentation Officer (Selection Grade) and Deputy Librarian (3700- 5700) is equal to that of Reader and of University Librarian (4500- 7300) is equal to that of Professor. This parity is maintained in the subsequent revision with effect from 1.1.1996 also. The new scale of pay and equivalent grades in teaching faculty are shown in Table 2.

Table 2. Pay Scale and Designation with effect from 1.1.1996

Designation	*Scale of Pay*	*Equivalent Grade in Teaching Faculty*
Assistant Librarian / Documentation Officer	(8000-13500)	Lecturer
Assistant Librarian / Documentation Officer (Senior Scale)	(10, 000-15, 200)	Lecturer (Senior Scale)
Assistant Librarian / Documentation Officer (Selection Grade)	(12, 000- 18, 300)	Lecturer (Selection Grade)
Deputy Librarian	(12, 000- 18, 300)	Reader
University Librarian	(16, 400- 22, 400)	Professor

Table 2 reveals that the academic status of librarians who come under the UGC scheme is maintained in the 1996 revision also.

3. GROUPS BENEFITED

Though the implementation of the UGC scheme has given academic status to the librarians in universities in Kerala, it is confined to a group of librarians. The categories benefited are Assistant Librarians / Documentation officers, Deputy Librarians and University Librarians. The Government has also given relaxation in qualification to these categories denying the benefits to a majority who have even more qualifications.

4. GROUPS DENIED

Those who have been denied the UGC scale in universities in Kerala form the majority of the library professionals. Those who work in the categories such as Junior Librarian / Reference Assistant, Professional Assistant Gr. I / Technical Assistant and Professional Assistant Gr. II / Library assistant are excluded from the scheme. It is a fact that in the university library system in Kerala, the majority of the juniors are more qualified than the senior staff who get all the benefits of the UGC scheme.

5. IMPACTS

The implementation of the UGC scheme, which gave academic status to the librarians in the universities in Kerala has far reaching effects. It has both positive and negative impacts. The most important among them are discussed here.

5.1. Positive Impacts

Though limited to a few, the positive impacts of the implementation of the UGC scheme to librarians cannot be discarded. The positive impacts include monetary benefit, career advancement opportunities and job satisfaction at least to a group of librarians.

5.1.1. Monetary Benefit

It is apparent from comparing the pre- revised and revised scales that there was a doubling of pay in the first phase and more than three fold increase in the subsequent revision. More over, due to the delay in implementation, those who were benefited from the UGC scheme could bag a few lakhs in lump sum by way of arrears.

5.1.2. Career Advancement Opportunities

Career advancement opportunity is an important benefit gained by the librarians from the UGC scheme. According to the career advancement facility as per the 1986 revision, every Assistant Librarian who has completed 8 years of service and participated in two refresher courses will be placed in the Senior Scale and those who are in the Senior Scale will be promoted as Deputy Librarian if they have 8 years of service in the Senior Scale and have obtained Ph.D. degree. Those who have no Ph.D. degree will be placed in the Selection Grade with the scale of pay equal to that of Deputy Librarian.

These opportunities are retained in the subsequent revision of 1996 also. However, as per this revision, librarians have not been given opportunity equal to that of teachers.

5.1.3. Job Satisfaction

One of the most significant impacts of the implementation of the UGC scheme to librarians is the high level of job satisfaction of librarians coming under the scheme. The study conducted by Dineshan Koovakkai (1996) revealed that the level of job satisfaction is higher among the groups having UGC scale. The study brought out that among the library professionals working in the universities in Kerala only 48 percent have job satisfaction. However, a comparison between the level of job satisfaction of those who come under the UGC scheme and that of others shows that 68.97 percent of the UGC group are satisfied while only 39.44 percent of the non-UGC group are satisfied. Table 3 shows this.

Table 3. Percentage of Satisfied Library Professionals in Different Categories

Category	*Sample Size*	*Number of Satisfied Professionals*	*Percentage*
UGC Group	29	20	68.97
Non-UGC Group	71	28	39.44

6. NEGATIVE IMPACTS

The positive impacts mentioned above are limited to a group of senior professionals who come under the UGC scheme. The negative impacts, however, have much more implications as they affect the overall atmosphere of the university library system in Kerala. Some of the most important negative impacts are discussed below.

6.1. Rift between Senior and Junior Professionals

Limiting the benefits of the UGC scheme to a group of librarians in universities in Kerala caused a rift between the 'haves and have nots'. The rift is an out come of the feeling that the juniors who have equal or even higher qualifications than the seniors and performing almost same duties are denied the benefits of UGC scheme. This has resulted in the worsening of the library atmosphere as well as service.

6.2. Threat of Open Recruitment

The Kerala Government order implementing the UGC scheme stipulates 25 percent open recruitment to the cadre of

Assistant Librarian. The vacancies have to be filled in the ratio 3:1 by promotion and open recruitment. By this order, every second post in 4 vacancies should be filled by open recruitment. Though the figure is not so high, the neglected fact is that most of the seniors who get the post of Assistant Librarian by promotion will retire within five or six years. Open recruitment has to be made for 25 percent of these retirement vacancies also. It is a fact that those who get the post by open recruitment will be young and in due course there will be no scope for even the qualified junior staff for any promotion. Also there is no guarantee that qualified juniors will get these posts when they compete with outsiders. Even at present no library professional in universities in Kerala will have even the opportunity to apply for the post of University Librarian, as they cannot obtain the minimum service of 18 years as Assistant Librarian prescribed by the UGC for applying for the post. A library professional in the universities in Kerala will become an Assistant Librarian in the present situation at the age of 45 or 50.

6.3. Confusion

The problem of open recruitment has created confusion in the universities in Kerala. As a result of this confusion some of the universities in Kerala have even stopped giving the UGC scale to the newly promoted Assistant Librarians. The qualification for promotion also is a matter of controversy, which delays the amendment of the university statutes. All these have resulted into a number of legal battles.

7. CONCLUSION

An analysis of the situation in university libraries in Kerala after the implementation of the UGC scheme shows that the disparity of income and opportunity between the seniors and the juniors have resulted into the generation of a feeling among the junior professionals that they are degraded and neglected. A professional below the rank of Assistant Librarian is not even regarded as a 'professional'. This has resulted into the deterioration in the quality of library services and worsening of the library atmosphere.

REFERENCES

1. Datta, N. (1989). Academic status for university and college librarians in India. Delhi: Indian Bibliographies Bureaux.
2. Dev Raj Singh (1991). Academic status for university and college librarians: an appraisal. *Library Herald*, 30 (1), 20-29.
3. Dineshan Koovakkai (1996). A study of job satisfaction among the library professionals in the universities in Kerala. University of Calicut. Unpublished MLISc dissertation.
4. Dineshan Koovakkai and Parameswaran, M. (2005). Human resource development issues in university libraries in Kerala in the context of e-resources and services. Paper presented in the KLA National Seminar, Trivandrum.
5. Jain, M. K. (1999). Library manual: a practical approach to management. Delhi: Shipra.
6. Jalaja, V. and Dineshan Koovakkai (2000). Librarianship in the modern age: is librarian's identity at stake? In Baby et al. ed. Changing trends in library and information science. New Delhi: Ess Ess, 31-37.
7. Khanna, J. K. (1994). Library and society. 2nd ed. New Delhi: Ess Ess.
8. Mangala, P. B. (1992). University libraries and librarians in India: an overview. *CLIS Observer*, 9 (3&4), 57-70.
9. Status of college and university librarians (1959). *College and Research Libraries*, 20, 400.
10. Ushadevi, S. P. (1999). University and college libraries. New Delhi: Ess Ess.

5
Bibliometric Analysis of the Journal 'AMBIO'

B. Mini Devi

0. INTRODUCTION

Environmental crisis which is confronting the world, will profoundly alter the future destiny of our planet. Interest in the environment has grown a great deal since the early 1970s, initially mainly among scientists but more recently increasingly among the general public and politicians. The general public has woken upto the possible environmental impacts and now each and every individual of our planet are aware of the environmental issues. The acid rain, ozone depletion, climate change, loss of biodiversity, toxic and hazardous products and water, pollution of rivers, depletion of freshwater resources are serious threats to our environment.

The UNEP global environment outlook 2000 report highlights two critical themes at the opening of the third millennium.

a. The global human ecosystem is threatened by grave imbalances in productivity and in the distribution of good and services. A significant proportion of humanity still lives in dire poverty, and projected trends are for increasing divergence between those who benefit from economic and technological development and those who do not.

b. The world is undergoing accelerating change, with internationally co-ordinated environmental stewardship lagging behind economic and social development.

Air pollution by green house gases is already starting to cause global warming. One of the most serious environmental problem today is the continued destruction of tropical rain forests. Many species of plants and animals are under threat because their natural habitats are being destroyed.

The recent interest in the environmental problems reflects a growing awareness that the future of the planet at its sake. Global environmental research is increasingly being focused on culturally induced environment at change as awareness grows about. Many of the themes that are capturing widespread attention and interest include desertification, deforestation, acid deposition, stratospheric ozone depletion, climate change etc. Hence the subject environmental science has broadened from subject-specific disciplinary towards multidisciplinary and interdisciplinary research. The two biggest global research programmes are the International Geosphere – Biosphere programme (IGB) and the Human Dimension of Global Change Programme (HDGCP).

1. AMBIO

AMBIO is a journal of the human environment, international in scope publishing original research articles, reports and comments on developments and issues in environmental research, policy and related activities, including environmental management, sustainable technology and use of natural resource, monthly publishing from Sweden.

2. OBJECTIVES OF THE STUDY.

The objectives of the study are:

1. To examine the types of documents cited;
2. To assess the year-wise trend of cited documents;
3. To find out the proportion of English and Foreign languages;
4. To analyse the subject dispersion in citations;
5. To prepare a rank list of cited journals;
6. To study the self-citation pattern in the journals;

7. To study the authorship collaboration.

3. HYPOTHESES

The hypothesis of the study are:

1. Journal citation is more than book citation.
2. Self-citation is less in environmental science.
3. Author collaboration is more in environmental science.

4. METHODOLOGY

The following methods were adopted for the collection of data.

4.1 Literature survey

To know about similar studies made in the topic extensive literature survey was conducted. For literature survey, primary sources such as journals, Ph.D thesis and dissertations were consulted. The secondary sourcs such as LISA PLUS (CD-ROM Version), Indian Library Science Abstract (ILSA) were consulted.

4.2 Data Collection

For the collection of data, all the issues of the journal AMBIO, from 2000-2004 was collected. The articles and citations published during the above year was entered into a data sheet having the variables needed for the study. Then the data was analysed using SAS software.

4.3 Bibliometric Analysis

Bibliometric analysis is the application of mathematical and statistical methods to books and other records of communication. In otherwords it is the quantitative treatment of the properties of bibliographic unit.

5. LIMITATIONS OF THE STUDY

The study is confined only the period from 2000-2004 to the literature published in the journal 'AMBIO'. However the findings reflect the general implications for the scientists working in the field of environmental science.

6. ANALYSIS

The data collected were systematically analysed and nferences drawn as detailed below :

6.1 Types of documents cited

The environmental scientists had interested mostly in journal and book articles. Out of the total 8034 citations, 72.98% were journal articles and 11.55% belonged to book category. The conference proceedings occupied third position ie. 8.863% followed by reports having 2.61% of citations. The dissertations / thesis covered 2.3%, newsletters 1.3% and indexing and abstracting periodicals about 0.31%. The analysis of the types of document cited are provided in the Table 1.

Table 1. Types of Document cited

Types of document	*Total number of citations*	*% from total citations*	*Cumulative of citation*
Journals	5863	72.98	-
Books	928	11.55	84.53
Conference proceedings	712	8.86	93.39
Reports	210	2.61	96
Dissertations/theses	184	2.3	98.3
Newsletters	112	1.39	99.69
Indexing and abstracting periodicals	25	0.31	100
	8034	100	

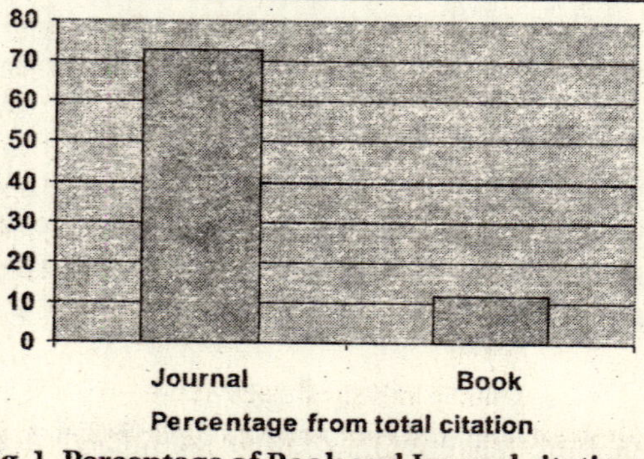

Fig 1. Percentage of Book and Journal citations.

From the analysis, it is noticed that journal articles were cited more than books. As journal articles are original, nascent product of scientific research, environmental scientists are more interested in referring them. The hypothesis is significantly proved by the outcome of the study. Today in environmental science field also e-journals established a dominant position and research results are published in them without any delay and the information is pushed to the laptop of every scientists. After giving importance to journals and books, environmental scientists give preference to conference proceedings because it act as stage where scientists announce the world about their research results before they are published as articles in journals.

6.2 Year-wise trend of cited documents

From the year 2000 to 2004, there is an increase in the number of citation of all types of documents. Of these, journals are cited more than any other type of documents. The details of percentage of type of document cited are provided in the Table 2.

Table 2. Types of documents cited during various years.

Year	*Journals (% from total citation of the year)*	*Books (% from total citation of the year)*	*Conference proceedings (% from total citation of the year)*	*Reports (% from total citation of the year)*	*Dissetation /thesis (% from total citation of the year)*	*News letters (% from total citation of the year)*	*Indexing &abstracting periodicals (% from total citation of the year)*
2000	603 (76.23)	91 (11.5)	48 (6.06)	22 (2.78)	15 (1.9)	9 (1.14)	3 (0.38)
2001	958 (77.2)	131 (10.6)	83 (6.68)	34 (2.73)	21 (1.69)	12 (0.96)	2 (0.16)
2002	1020 (72.24)	158 (11.19)	113 (8)	59 (4.18)	39 (2.76)	18 (1.27)	5 (0.35)
2003	1452 (72.63)	210 (10.5)	218 (10.9)	41 (2.05)	47 (2.35)	24 (1.2)	7 (0.35)
2004	1830 (70.63)	338 (13.05)	250 (9.65)	54 (2.08)	62 (2.39)	49 (1.89)	8 (0.31)

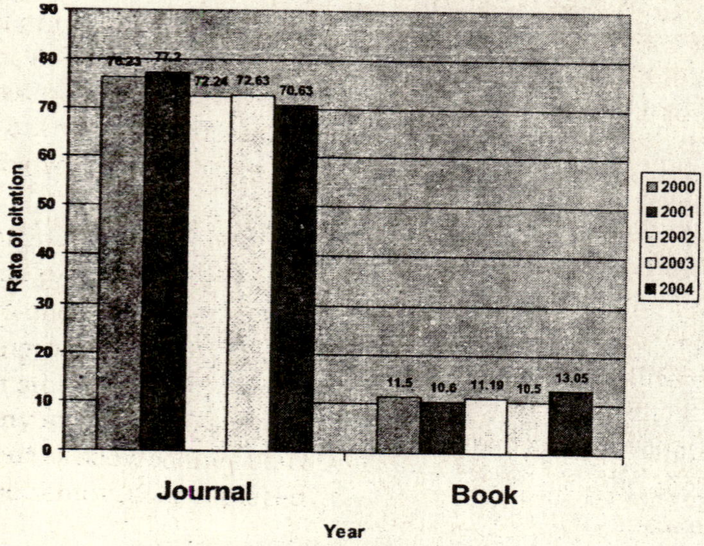

Fig. 2. Trend of Book & Journal citation.

The percentage of year-wise trend of journal and book citations (Fig. 2) indicates the wide acceptance of journals among the researches in environmental sciences.

6.3 Language of cited documents

Out of the total 8034 citations, 7910 (98.46%) were documents published in English language, 97(1.21%) citations were documents in foreign languages and 27 (0.33%) were documents published in foreign language that were translated into English. The analysis of language of cited documents are provided in the Table 3.

Table 3. Language of cited documents.

No.	*Languages*	*Total number of citations*	*% from total citations*	*Cumulative percentage*
1	English	7910	98.46	-
2.	Foreign language	97	1.21	99.67
3.	Foreign language translated into English	27	0.33	100
		8034		

From the analysis it is clear that English is still the common language of communication among researchers in environmental science. The documents written in regional languages was very less when compared to English language.

6.4 Subject dispersion in citations.

Out of the total 8034 citations, documents on 'Atmospheric Pollution' (15.55%) were cited maximum number of times followed by 'Toxicology' (12.6%), 'Public Health & Safety' (11.3%), 'Ecology' (10.5%), 'Forestry' (7.56%), 'Chemical Pollution' (6.71%), 'Medicine' (6.45%), 'Biotechnology' (6.31%), 'Waste Management' (5%), 'Conservation' (4.27%), 'Marine Pollution' (3.4%), 'Environmental Law' (2.99%), 'Desertification' (2.71%) and 'Biology' (2.4%). The subject 'Water Resources' got minimum number of citations (2.3%). The details of subject dispersion in citations are given in the Table 4. From the analysis, it is indicated that the trend of research is towards the applied branches of environmental science than pure branches.

Table 4. Dispersion of subjects in citations.

Sl. No.	*Subject*	*Number of references*	*Cumulative number of references*	*%*	*Cumulative %*
1.	Atmospheric Pollution	1249	-	15.55	-
2.	Toxicology	1012	2261	12.6	28.15
3.	Public health & safety	908	3169	11.3	39.45
4.	Ecology	843	4012	10.5	49.95
5.	Forestry	607	4619	7.56	57.51
6.	Chemical Pollution	539	5158	6.71	64.22
7.	Medicine	518	5676	6.45	70.67
8.	Biotechnology	507	6183	6.31	76.98
9.	Waste Management	402	6585	5.00	81.98
10.	Conservation	343	6928	4.27	86.25
11.	Marine Pollution	271	7199	3.4	89.65
12.	Environmental Law	240	7439	2.99	92.64
13.	Desertification	218	7657	2.71	95.35

14.	Biology	193	7850	2.4	97.75
15.	Water Resources	184	8034	2.3	100.05
		8034			

6.5 Rank list of cited journals

An alphabetical list of cited journals is prepared by sorting data collected from citations of the source journal "AMBIO" from 2000 to 2004 taken as sample for the study. This list consists of 248 journals with their abbreviated names and citations received by each journal. From this list most cited journals are searched and ranked by the decreasing order of citations. Thus a list of 15 core journals ranked according to the number of citations is prepared. These journals form the core journals in environmental science consulted by research workers all over the world. This list is helpful for the acquisition of periodicals in libraries specializing environmental science within the constrained budget and escalating price of journals. The journal 'International Journal of Environment and Pollution' got Ist rank among the core journals.

6.5 Rank list of most cited journals

From the rank list of most cited journals, the first 15 journals were selected as core journals as shown in the Table 5.

Table 5. Rank list of cited journals

Sl. No.	*Name of Journal*	*No. of times cited*	*Rank*
1.	International Journal of Environment and Pollution	939	I
2.	Environmental Conservation	877	II
3.	Management of Environmental Quality	617	III
4.	Global Ecology and Biogeography	512	IV
5.	Environment International	480	V
6.	Environmental Geochemistry and Health	414	VI
7.	Journal of Environment & Development	391	VII
8.	Natural Areas Journal	201	VIII
9.	Journal of Environmental Policy & Planning	154	IX

10.	Renewable Resources Journal	133	X
11.	Journal of Environmental Quality	124	XI
12.	World Resource Review	113	XII
13.	Boreal Environment Research	110	XIII
14.	Applied Environmental Education and Communication	108	XIV
15.	Water, Air and Soil Pollution		XV

6.6 Rate of self-citations

The analysis of self-citations in the first nine core journals revealed that out of the total 4585 citations, 240 (5.23%) were self-citations. Among the journals, 'International Journal of Environment and Pollution' had got maximum number of self-citations (32.5%) and 'Journal of Environmental Policy and Planning' had got minimum number of self-citations (0.83%). The journal 'Environmental Conversation' had got 22.5% of self-citations followed by 'Management of Environmental Quality' (12.93%), 'Global Ecology and Biogeography' (10.42%), 'Environment International' (8.33%), 'Environmental Geochemistry and Health' (7.5%), 'Journal of Environment and Development' (3.75%), and 'Natural Areas Journal' (1.25%). The percentage of self-citations in the individual journals are provided in the Table 6. From the analysis it is evident that in environmental science few researches are based on the previous works. The analysis of the study on the basis of hypothesis II is significantly positive.

Table 6. Self-citation in different journals.

Rank	Journals	No. of self-citations	% from total self citations	% from total citations of the individual journal
1.	International Journal of Environment and Pollution	78	32.5	8.3
2.	Environmental Conservation	54	22.5	6.15
3.	Management of Environmental Quality	31	12.92	5.02
4.	Global Ecology and Biogeography	25	10.42	4.88
5.	Environment International	20	8.33	4.16
6.	Environmental Geochemistry and Health	18	7.5	4.35
7.	Journal of Environment & Development	9	3.75	2.3
8.	Natural Areas Journal	3	1.25	1.49
9.	Journal of Environmental Policy and Planning	2	0.83	1.29
	Total	240	100	5.23

7.7 Year wise trend of self-citations

The year wise trend of the growth of self-citations was in an increasing order from the year 2001 to 2004. The maximum self-citations were reported in the year 2000(19) and maximum in 2004 (78). The growth of the number of self-citations during 2001, 2002 and 2003 were 44, 46 and 53 respectively. From the analysis it is observed that when the number of citations increase there was a corresponding increase in the number of self-citations. The year-wise trend of self-citations are provided in the Table 7.

Table 7. Year-wise trend of self-citations

Year	*No. of self citations*	*% from total self-citations*	*% from total citations of the individual years.*
2000	19	7.92	2.96
2001	44	18.33	5.18
2002	46	19.17	5.41
2003	53	22.08	5.10
2004	78	32.5	6.54
	240	100	5.23

The comparison of the percentage of self-citations from total self-citations with that from total citations of the individual year (Fig. 7) indicated the same growth pattern.

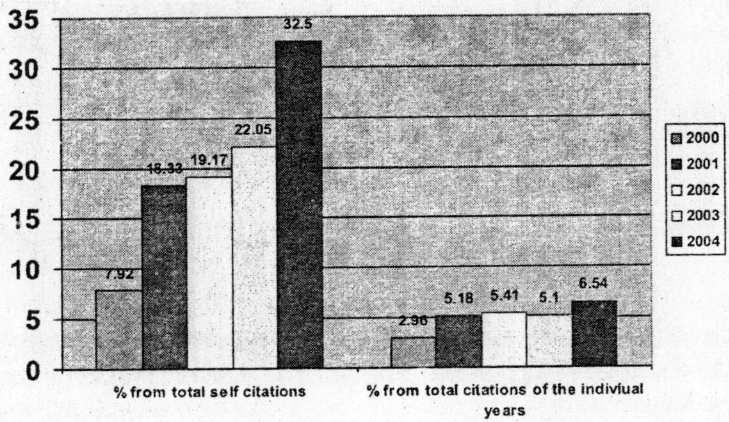

Fig. 3. Year wise trend of self-citations.

8 Self-citing articles in different journals

Out of the total 1048 articles of the nine core journals, 116 (11.07%) were self-citing articles. The 'International Journal of Environment and Pollution' bagged highest number of self-citing articles ie. 41 (35.34%) and the 'Journal of Environmental Policy and Planning' had lowest number of self-citing articles ie. 2(1.72%). The number of self-citing articles in different journals are presented in the Table 8.

The journal 'Management of Environmental Quality' had 22(18.96%) self-citing articles followed by 'Environmental Conservation' 17 (14.66%), 'Environmental Geochemistry and Health' 10 (8.62%), 'Environment International' 9(7.76%), 'Journal of Environment and Development' 8 (6.9%), 'Global Ecology and Biogeography' 4 (3.45%), 'Natural Areas Journal' 3 (2.59%).

Table 8. Self-citing articles in different journals

Rank	*Journals*	*No. of self-citing articles*	*% from total self-citing articles*	*% from total articles of the specific journal*
1.	International Journal of Environment and Pollution	41	35.34	13.14
2.	Management of Environmental Quality	22	18.96	10.47
3.	Environmental Conservation	17	14.66	14.16
4.	Environmental Geochemistry and Health	10	8.62	9.61
5.	Environment International	9	7.76	9.18
6.	Journal of Environment & Development	8	6.9	10.12
7.	Global Ecology and Biogeography	4	3.45	6.55
8.	Natural Areas Journal	3	2.59	5.76
9.	Journal of Environmental Policy and Planning	2	1.72	16.66
	Total	116	100	11.07

A comparative analysis of the percentage of self-citing articles from total self-citing articles and from total citations of the individual journals (Fig. 8) indicated that individual journals had a different percentage of self-citation than that of the percentage from total self-citations.

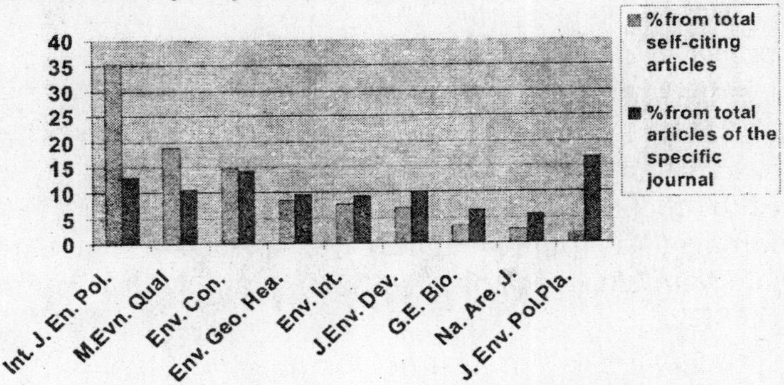

Fig. 4. Percentage of self-citing articles in different journals.

9. Self-citing articles during 2001-2004

From the analysis, it is observed that there was an increasing rate in the growth of self-citing articles. The year 2000 showed a minimum (7.76%) rate of self-citing articles where as maximum (45.52%) rate of self-citing articles was found in the year 2004. The rate of self-citing articles in the year 2001 was 11 (9.48%) followed by 20(17.24%) in the year 2002 and 29 (25%) in the year 2003. The year-wise distribution of self-citing articles are presented in the Table 9.

When a comparison is made between the self-citing articles from total self-citing articles with the total articles of specific years, it is observed that the growth pattern is almost similar (Fig. 6.9). If there is an increase in the percentage from total self-citing articles, there is a simultaneous increase in the percentage from total articles of the specific years.

Table 9. Self-citing articles during different years.

Year	*No. of articles containing self citations*	*% from total self-citing articles*	*% from total articles of the year.*
2000	9	7.76	9.89
2001	11	9.48	10.78
2002	20	17.24	9.95
2003	29	25.00	9.29
2004	47	45.52	13.74
	116	100	11.07

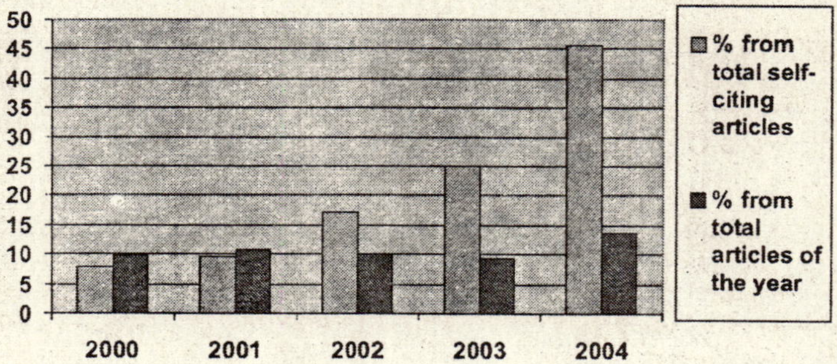

Fig. 5. Year-wise trend of self-citing articles

10. Self-citation habit of Indian and foreign authors.

Out of the total 1048 articles, the self-citing articles by authors of Indian origin were 99 (9.45%) and those by foreign authors were 17 (1.62%). The self-citation habits of Indian and foreign authors are presented in Table 10.

From the study it is evident that articles by Indian environmental scientists had more self-citations (85.34%) than articles by the foreign authors (14.66%). This may be due to the fact that more number of Indian authors like to self-cite than by foreign authors. Hence the self-citation habit is common among Indian authors.

Table 10. Self-citation habit of Indian and foreign authors

Authors	*No. of self-citing articles*	*% from self citing articles*	*% from total articles*
Indian authors	99	85.34	9.45
Foreign authors	17	14.66	1.62
Total	116	100	

11. Categories of authors

Out of the total 8034 citations, 93.5% were works by personal authors and 4.46% were works by corporate bodies. Anonymous works contribute about 2.04% of the citations. The various categories of authors in citations are presented in the Table 11.

Table 11. Categories of authors in citations.

Sl. No.	*Authors*	*Number of citations*	*% from total citations*	*Cumulative %*
1.	Personal authors	7512	93.5	-
2.	Corporate body	358	4.46	97.96
3.	Anonymous works	164	2.04	100
		8034	100	

Fig. 6. Categories of authors in citations

12. Collaborative authors of Publications

Among the 2042 citing articles published during 2000 to 2004, there were 15.39% of articles were written by single authors, 84.16% belonged to co-authors and 8 articles were not having the name of authors. The degree of collaboration of authors was high among environmental scientists. The value of group coefficient (g_p) was

Table 12. Value of group co-effecient for collaborative authors of publications.

Number of authors article	*Number of publications*	*% from total publication*	*Value of g_p = Nm/(Ns + Nm)*
Number of personal author publications	2034		
Number of single author publications	313 (Ns)	15.39	
Number of co-author publications	1721 (Nm)	84.61	0.85
Two authors publications	518	25.47	0.62
Three authors publications	439	21.58	0.58
More than three authors publications	764	37.56	0.71

The value of group co-effecient for collaborative authors for publications are presented in the Table 12. The degree of collaboration among co-authors was maximum (0.71) in articles written by more than three persons and minimum (0.58) in three author articles. In two-authors publications the value of 'g_p' was 0.62. Thus the analysis revealed that collaborated works are numerous in Environmental Science field ie. researchers and scientists from different subject field contribute to the tansdisciplinary nature of Environmental Sciences.

13. Collaborative authors of citations.

The analysis of citation with regard to collaborative trend indicated that the maximum number of citations (80.4%) were contributed by co-authors. The minimum number of citations (19.6%) were contributed by single authors. The value of group coefficient for citations (g_c) was 0.8. Among the collaborated works, the value of 'g_c' was maximum (0.69) in more than three authored citations. The study on collaborative authors of citations supports the validity of the hypothesis III. The value of group co-efficient for collaborative authors of citations are presented in the Table 13.

Table 13. Value of group co-efficient for collaborative authors of citations.

Number of authors per citation	*Number of citations*	*Percentage from total personal author citation*	*Value of $g_c = Nm/(Ns + Nm)$*
Total no. of personal author citations	7512		
Number of single authored citations	1472 (Ns)	19.6	
Number of co-authored citations	6040 (Nm)	80.4	0.8
Two authored citations	1710	22.76	0.54
Three authored citations	1059	14.09	0.42
Moe than three-authored citations	3271	43.54	0.69

7. FINDINGS

1) Journal citation is more (72.98%) than book (11.55%) citation. With the introduction of e-journals and other services provided by various publishers time and price are not barriers of communication between the researcher and the user community.

   After journal and book citations, citations from conference proceedings (8.86%) dominate Environmental Science field. This indication is a clear cut evidence that researchers give conference proceedings to almost the same credit to journal articles.

2) Year-wise trend of cited documents ie. Journals, books, conference proceedings, reports, theses/dissertations, news letters and indexing & abstracting periodicals showed a tremendous increase in the rate of citations from the year 2000 to 2004. Increase in citation indicate the increased research activities and publication of original research articles.

3) English language is the dominant language of communication among researchers and scientists. Authors from non-english speaking countries also write in English to get a wide exposition of their articles.

4) Majority of citations are on the topic 'Atmospheric Pollution' indicating research in this field is very active. It is also seen that research on applied fields are more than on fundamental areas such as Biology. Research on toxicology, forestry, waste management and conservation of environment are given priority by researchers. The contributions from various subjects gave Environmental Science to a subject having transdisciplinary nature.

5) The 'International Journal of Environment and Pollution' is the core journal in the field of Environmental Science. The core journal list can be used by the librarians and policy makers of institutions in the field of Environmental Science. Research workers and scientists in the field can be made aware of core journals relevant to their studies from the rank list of journals.

6) The self-citation rate of the first nine core journals was about 5.23% and the study revealed that few researchers are based on the previous works. The 'International Journal of Environment and Pollution' contained maximum number (32.5%) of self-citations. The year 2004 reported maximum number (32.5%) of self-citations. The articles by Indian authors had more self-citations (85.34%) than articles by foreign authors.

7) Multiple authorship is dominant in environmental science like other science fields. Among the co-author publications, the degree of collaboration was maximum (0.71) in more than three-authored publications and minimum (0.58) in three authorised publications. Regarding the collaborative author citations, the degree of collaboration is maximum (0.69) in more than three-authored citations and minimum (0.42) in three-

authored citations. As a transdisciplinary subject Environmental Science articles and citations include authors from both pure and applied subject fields.

CONCLUSION

The bibliometric analysis of articles and citations published in the journal AMBIO brings out many finding of wide applications to researchers and libraries specializing environmental sciences. These findings can be taken as guidelines for researchers in selecting information sources for their study.

REFERENCES

1. Fairthorne, Robert A. Empirical hyperbolic distribution for bibliometric discription and production. Journal of Documentation. 25: 1969. p. 319.
2. Kundu A.K. Self-citation by Indian Library scientists. Annals of Library Science and Documentation. 28: 1981.pp.1-4; 39-41.
3. Mahapatra, M. and Musib, S.K. Subject dispersion studies in agricultural economics. Libri. 34(4): 1984.pp.341-349.
4. Pritchard, A. Statistical Bibliography or bibliometrics. Journal of Documentation. 25:1969. p. 348.
5. Smith, Linda. Citation analysis. Library Trends. 30(1): 1981.pp.83-106.
6. Sridhar, M.S. A study of co-authorship and collaborative research among Indian space technologists. Research and Development Management. 15(3): 1985.pp. 243-249.
7. Subramanyam, K. Bibliometric studies of research collaboration : a review. Journal of Information Science. 6. 1983. pp. 33-38.
8. Swanson, Don R. Two medical literatures that are logically but not bibliographically connected. Journal of the American Society for Information Science. 38(4): 1987.p.230.
9. Taglia – Cozzo, R. Self-citations in scientific literature. Journal of Documentation. 33: 1977.pp.251-265.

6
Emerging Technologies for Hi-Tech Libraries

Dr. M Bavakutty
Dr. Mohamed Haneefa K

0. INTRODUCTION

The rapid application of information and communication technologies (ICT) in libraries and information centers has changed the modes and methods of information handling. Libraries throughout the world are using more and more information and communication technologies for their operations and services. The application of ICT has become an indicator of a library's efficiency in their services and operations. The explosive growth of information and widespread reliance on digital information resources necessitated the need to device and use new technologies for the storage, retrieval and dissemination of information. Spectacular, exciting, and promising developments are taking place in Information and Communication Technologies. Emerging technologies has provided the means and methods of managing and organizing information through the improved capabilities of locating, collecting, storing, processing, organizing and disseminating information.

1. WIRELESS NETWORKING IN LIBRARIES

Wireless networking helps library users to access digital information resources without connecting physically, and library system administrators can set up or extend networks without installing or moving wires. Mobility is the most attractive feature of wireless networking. It is more flexible than wired networking. It provides all the functionality of wired networking, without the physical constraints of the wire. In the 1980's the Federal Communications Commission (FCC) proposed the 802.11 as the IEEE standard for wireless networks (1).

Wireless networking can be used to access the library network, library resources and Internet without plug in by wires and cables. Wireless networking will allow users with devices like laptops, notebooks, simputers, PDAs, tablet PCs, etc. to move freely in the library while remaining connected to the library network. Wireless networking is an excellent solution for libraries with historic buildings or older buildings where the installation of wired networking is either impossible or very expensive. Libraries can be saved from the constant wiring and rewiring by installing wireless networks. Libraries can also save space by wireless networking. Installation of wireless network is very easy as there are no wires and its components can be set up anywhere in the library. Wireless networking makes it easy to move computers and other devices without the need to reconfigure the network.

1.1. The Benefits of Wireless Networking in Libraries

Here are some of the benefits of wireless networking in libraries (2).

* A library wireless network provides access to multiple computers, databases, the Internet and library OPAC throughout the library or outside the library.
* It provides faster access to information for library users, resulting in better service and improved user satisfaction, location independent access for network administrators for easier on-site-trouble-shooting and support.
* Using laptop computers library users can access electronic media and also be physically near whatever printed material they want.
* Sharing of peripherals, files, multimedia resources and databases are easier.

* Improved database access.
* Simplified network configuration.
* Wireless networking permit quick connectivity to the network.
* Wireless networking is an excellent solution for libraries with historic buildings or older buildings, which make the installation of wired networking either impossible or very expensive.

1.2. Issues to Consider for Installing Wireless Networks in Libraries

There are some issues to be considered while installing wireless networks in libraries (2).

* It should be simple to install, set up, use and manage.
* It should be reliable and easy to expand as the library network grows.
* It should be compatible with other network devices.
* It should be built by reputable, experienced companies that know the complexities of wireless networking.
* It should be backed by easily accessible, sound technical support.
* Interference in wireless environment should be avoided.
* Wireless technologies should meet the prescribed standards for safety.

1.3. Wireless Internet Access in Libraries

Wireless technology allows users to access the Internet without the constraints of cables, data lines, phone jacks, or even walls. When connected to library wireless network, users can use their laptops, notebooks, simputers, handheld devices, or web-enabled pagers or phones to check e-mail or to surf the web without a physical connection. Each device connected to a wireless library network allows users to e-mail, or surf the Internet. Notebook computers and simputers are becoming more affordable and portable. Users can use this facility for reading E-mails and newsgroups, accessing online library catalogues, searching information through web, and live online reference.

1.4. SMS in Libraries

Short Messaging Service or SMS can be applied in libraries for sending information to library users. Messages like the status of a loaned item, reservation information, overdue notice, reminders and major events can be sent through this service. SMS is convenient and cost effective for a number of reasons. Messages can be received while making voice calls. A single message can be up to 160 characters of text in length. It is not sent directly from sender to recipient, but always via an SMS Centre. The sender of the message can receive a return message back notifying that the message has been delivered or not. To use SMS, users need a subscription to a mobile telephone network that supports SMS and a mobile phone that supports SMS· Users should have the knowledge of how to send or read a short message using mobile phone. The most common devices used with SMS are digital cell phones equipped with one-way receive capability.

1.5. Wireless Technologies for Libraries

Wireless networks use high-frequency electromagnetic waves, either infrared (IR) or radio frequency (RF) to transmit information from one point to another without relying on any physical connections. RF is expected to be of more practical use in library networking than IR, because it is not limited by line-of-sight transmission; radio waves travel through wall and windows. Data and voice traffic is superimposed or modulated, onto the radio waves or carriers, and extracted at the receiving end. Multiple radio carriers can exist in the same space at the same time without interfering with each other by transmitting at different frequencies. There are a large number of different technologies that can be used in wireless library network applications. Following are some of the technologies for wireless networking.

1.5.1. Bluetooth

Bluetooth is a global de facto standard for wireless

connectivity and is based on a low-cost, low-power, short-range radio link for mobile devices and for Wide Area Network/Local Area Network access points. It offers fast and reliable transmissions of both voice and data over the globally available 2.4 GHz ISM (Industrial, Scientific and Medical) band. Bluetooth will enable users to connect to a wide range of computing and telecommunication devices without the need to buy, carry, or connect cables. And because Bluetooth utilizes a radio-based link, it doesn't require a line-of-sight connection in order to communicate. When two Bluetooth equipped devices come within 10 metres of each other, they can establish a connection.

Bluetooth uses a radio link to connect devices instead of a cable and it can handle raw data of 1 Mbps with a peak asymmetric asynchronous throughput of 721 Kbps or three symmetric voice channels of 64 Kbps. Bluetooth has sufficient in built encryption and authentication. In addition, a frequency-hopping scheme with 1600 hops per second is also employed. Bluetooth eliminates the need for numerous cable attachments for connecting practically any kind of communication devices. The range of each radio is approximately 10 metres, but it can be extended to around 100 metres with an optional amplifier. Up to eight devices can be connected together wirelessly in a network called a 'piconet'. A master unit is the device in a piconet whose clock and frequency hopping sequence are used to synchronise all other devices in the piconet. There is one master unit per piconet. Slaveunits are all devices in a piconet that are not the master. The slaves receive frequency-hopping sequences from the master and rely on the master's clock for the timing of the piconet. Up to 10 piconets can come together to form a 'scatternet' resulting in a total of 80 devices that are able to communicate through the network.

1.5.2. Infrared

IrDA is a wireless technology that uses infrared, a faster wave frequency that is closer to visible light. It is a cable replacement technology similar to Bluetooth wireless technology. It has a short transmission range, 15 feet to 5 metres. Two devices must have an almost direct line-of-sight to connect. It transmits data in a point-to-point configuration. IrDA technologies did not develop with interoperability and industry standardization as a primary goal, as did Bluetooth.

1.5.3. HiPeRLAN Technology

High Performance Radio Local Area Network type 2 (HIPERLAN/2) provides high-speed multimedia communications between different broadband core networks and mobile terminals. HIPERLAN/2 relies on cellular networking topology combined with and ad hoc networking capability. It supports two basic modes of operation: centralised mode and direct mode. The centralised mode is used in the cellular networking topology where each radio cell is controlled by an access point covering a certain geographical area. In this mode, a mobile terminal communicates with other mobile terminals or with the core network via an access point. The direct mode is used in the ad hoc networking topology, where a radio cell covers the whole serving area.

1.5.4. Wireless LAN

A Wireless Local Area Network (WLAN) is a flexible data communication system implemented as an extension to, or as an alternative for, a wired LAN. It uses a high speed, radio-frequency (RF) network access technology to transmit data. It links computers to each other or to networks for shared access and Internet based information. The Institute of Electrical and Electronic Engineers (IEEE) established the 802.11b standard for wireless networks, and the Wireless Compatibility Ethernet Alliance (WECA), assures that Wireless LAN products are interoperable from manufacturer to manufacturer (3). Following are some of the benefits of Wireless LAN.

1.5.4.1. Mobility

Wireless LAN systems can provide LAN users with access to real-time information anywhere in their organization. This mobility supports productivity and service opportunities not possible with wired networks.

1.5.4.2. Simplicity

Users need very little information to take advantage of wireless LANs. Because the wireless nature of a wireless LAN is transparent to a user's NOS, applications work the same as they do on wired LANs.

1.5.4.3. Installation Speed

Installing a wireless LAN system can be fast and easy. Therefore it can eliminate the need to pull cable through walls and ceilings. Since only the access points of wireless LANs require cabling, network managers are saved from pulling cables for wireless LAN end users. Lack of cabling also makes moves, adds, and changes trivial operations on wireless LANs. The portable nature of wireless LANs lets network managers pre-configure and troubleshoot entire networks before installing them at remote locations.

1.5.4.4. Installation Flexibility

Wireless technology allows the network to go where wire cannot go.

1.5.4.5. Reduced Cost

While the initial investment required for wireless LAN hardware can be higher than the cost of wired LAN hardware, overall installation expenses and life-cycle costs can be significantly lower. Long-term cost benefits are greatest in dynamic environments requiring frequent moves and changes.

1.5.4.6. Scalability

Wireless networks can be designed to be extremely simple or quite complex. Wireless networks can support large numbers of nodes and/or large physical areas by adding access points to extend coverage.

2. MOBILE TECHNOLOGIES

Mobile technologies provide wide coverage to access information from networks. There are several mobile technologies. Here are some of the most used mobile technologies.

2.1. WAP

Wireless Application Protocol (WAP) is a protocol for wireless access to information resources and services from mobile devices. It is the de-facto-standard for the presentation and delivery of wireless information on mobile devices. WAP can be used to access Internet without a PC or modem. Mobile devices contain specifically designed WAP enabled microbrowser to display the information from Internet. Microbrowser is software built into a wireless device that allows users to access and display specially formatted Internet content. But in order to display the information on the screen of mobile devices, websites should be written in specifically designed Wireless Markup Language (WML). WML is based on Extensible Markup Language (XML) and created to address the display, bandwidth and memory limitations of mobile and wireless devices. WML supports text and images and manages navigation and command execution. Websites written in Hypertext Markup Language (HTML) should be transferred to WML. The WAP gateway facilitates the delivery of WML contents to wireless devices. WAP technology can be used to send information to users' mobile devices. It can be used to provide reference services for specific information.

2.2. GPRS

The General Packet Radio Service (GPRS) is a service that allows mobile phones to be used for sending and receiving data over an Internet Protocol based network. GPRS enables wireless access to Internet, enabling users to access E-mail and other Internet applications using mobile phones. As in Internet, GPRS data is also handled as a series of "packets" that can be routed over several paths through the network. GPRS enables any service that is used over the Internet like File Transfer Protocol (FTP), web browsing, chat, E-mail, and telnet. It allows information to be transmitted more quickly and efficiently and facilitates instant connections whereby information can be sent or received immediately as the need arises. To use GPRS, users need a mobile phone or terminal that supports GPRS and a subscription to a mobile telephone network that supports

GPRS. Users should know how to send and receive GPRS information using the mobile devices.

2.3. UMTS

Universal Mobile Telecommunications System (UMTS) uses ATM based switching network architecture. UMTS aims to provide services for mobile and fixed subscribers by common call processing procedures. It will provide at least 144 kbps for full mobility, 384 kbps for limited mobility and 2048 mbps for low mobility applications (4). It can deliver low-cost, high-capacity mobile communications offering data rates up to 2Mbit/sec with global roaming and other advanced capabilities. UMTS can deliver pictures, graphics, video communications and other wide-band information as well as voice and data. It will extend the capability of mobile technologies by providing increased capacity, data capability and a far greater range of services using an innovative radio access scheme and an enhanced network.

3. PUSH TECHNOLOGY

Information, web sites and applications can be sent via the Internet straight to people's computers with a variety of technologies collectively known as push. Push technology is the software that automates the delivery of information to individuals. In contrast, the World Wide Web is a 'pull' environment where users go to the web for information. For retrieving information from the Internet, push technology scans several basic "channels", or content providers as sources for its customised desktop bulletins. In 'push' environment, information is send to the user through a web browser, e-mail, or even voice mail or a pager (5).

The more sophisticated push applications, used increasingly at the institutional level or within the corporate enterprise environment, enable information professionals and end-users to create relational profiles and receive relevant information from multiple sources. Push technology can also streamline the delivery of targeted information to a variety of users from a corporate Intranet. Lastly, and most recently, push technology has been used to automatically update software. Handled properly, push can become one of the information professional's most valuable tools.

4. SMART CARD

Similar in look and size to a credit card, a smart card has an embedded microprocessor or memory chip, or both, instead of magnetic strip commonly found on credit and debit cards. It provides not only memory capacity, but computational capacity as well. The self-containment of smart card makes it resistant to attack, as it does not need to depend upon potentially vulnerable external resources. This technology will have several applications in identification, authentication, access control, healthcare, finance, administration, etc. Application of smart card in library delivers increased efficiency by providing a means of regularly updating the library's inventory and maintaining an accurate control of borrowing records.

5. RFID TECHNOLOGY

RFID stands for Radio Frequency Identification, use radio waves to uniquely identify an object by transmitting a stored code from a chip to a reader (6). It is a form of automatic identification and data capture technology. It has a combination of radio frequency and microchip technology. It stores and retrieves data from computer chips using radio frequency transmission. It does not require line of sight contact and it can be used anywhere that needed a unique identification. It is an emerging, more effective, convenient, and cost efficient technology in library automation and security. It has been around libraries for more than two decades. Libraries began using this technology in the late 1990s (7). Several libraries around the world, especially in U.S., Canada, and Singapore are using this technology for library functions.

RFID technology has many advantages. As far as a library or information center is concerned it will increase the speed of charging and discharging of documents, RFID tags can detect and read much faster and it can read several documents at the same time. Library users can charge several documents simultaneously using special self-charging stations and return documents in the special boxes or book-drops making circulation faster and easier. Library staff can relive from repetitive and clerical tasks and they can concentrate on more demanding personalised information services. RFID can sort documents automatically and library staff can shelve documents very easily. Library staff can use portable hand held readers for electronic inventorying by passing them rapidly along the shelves to read all the documents. There is no need of handling each document individually. They can report the lost, hidden or unordered documents more easily using these portable readers.

RFID tags have greater storage capacity and can hold large amount of information about a document. Its microchips are read/write with update flexibility. It can be used for status control as well as for security checks. It can be placed anywhere in the documents since it does not need a line of sight contact. For example it can be placed inside the documents and this will provide protection to the tags from damage or destruction during rough handling of documents. The tags can stand up in harsh environments. Several tags can read simultaneously even through the hard document covers.

Security is a major concern in an electronic environment. RFID will provide improved security without staff intervention. Its tags have an advanced security bit and it will detect uncharged documents while passing through the security gate. The tags have an interface between the readers in the exit and the circulation system to detect and identify items moving through the exit. The same tag can be used for detecting materials and also for security.

RFID technology has few drawbacks. As far as the libraries in developing country like India is concerned, cost is a major concern. For implementing and maintaining RFID system, a substantial amount is needed. It may cost around $50,000 for a library with 40,000 documents. A comprehensive RFID system for 100,000 documents with self-charging station, book-drop unit and automatic book sorting system ranges from $100,000 to $200,000(8). But recent advancements in hardware and software have boosted the potential of this technology and shortly libraries are going to implement RFID technology for their functions.

Another drawback is that the radio waves cannot pass through metal and liquid at certain frequencies. But this is not a major drawback, that RFID is far better than the barcode technology. Lack of standard is another disadvantage of RFID. This may be due to the limited use of RFID technology. A uniform standard is necessary to bring interoperability to libraries using RFID. This condition may change and RFID readers can read any tags. It is also possible to compromise an RFID system by placing two items against one another to cancel out the signals.

6. INSTITUTIONAL REPOSITORIES

Institutional repositories are created to organize, manage and preserve the digital resources of the institutions like its intellectual output, institutional assets, etc. Repositories in universities and scientific research institutions may include reprints of journal articles, technical reports, standards, research data, theses, dissertations, important print and image collections, teaching and learning materials, and materials documenting the history of the institution. The increased demand for information in science and technology will probably increase the pressure on scientific institutions and universities to create repositories. Institutional repositories now represent potentially rich sources of digital information, data, images, and valuable research results. These types of repositories provide services to its users who want archive research, historic and creative materials. Librarians and information professionals have a major role in building these repositories, they can fulfill this as an expert by locating, organizing, preserving, and providing access to resources.

The main purposes of institutional repositories are to collect, organize and preserve the intellectual output of the parent institutions. They may be limited to a specific field, one institution, or a consortium of several institutions. Forming a consortium reduces costs for each member institution through resource sharing while expanding access to digital materials. Institutions have their own policies and procedures in managing, organizing and dealing with access to the resources of repositories. Some materials in the repositories may have restrictions for accessing and some other materials may be restricted to special category of users.

Each institution has their own policies, procedures and architecture in establishing the repositories and this will depend on the context, scope and purpose of the repositories. Creation, maintenance and sustainability of repositories are major issues that involve the long-term commitment of money by management. Information resources, software, and accessibility of repositories can change. Information professionals need to know the consequences of changes in hardware, software, and standards and be able to adjust accordingly.

7. THE SEMANTIC WEB

The Semantic Web is the representation of data on the World Wide Web. It is a collaborative effort led by W3C with participation from a large number of researchers and industrial partners. It is based on the Resource Description Framework (RDF), which integrates a variety of applications using XML for syntax and URIs for naming (9). The Semantic Web is an extension of the current web in which information is given well-defined meaning, better enabling computers and people to work in cooperation (10).

Electronic data that is hidden away in HTML documents is sometimes useful in some contexts. The electronic data in this form is very difficult to use, because there is no method or system for publishing data in such a way as it can be easily processed by anyone. The Semantic Web allow this information to be surfaced in the form of data, and it will allow people to generate files which explain the relationship between different sets of data. The Semantic Web facilitates the discovery of information by providing the enabling standards and technologies for allowing communities to express data in ways in which it can more easily be integrated, merged and effectively searched.

The current web provides a useful and powerful foundation for the Semantic Web. The principal technologies of the Semantic Web fit into a set of layered specifications. The current components of that framework are the RDF Core Model, the RDF Schema language and the Web Ontology language. These languages all build on the foundation of URIs, XML, and XML namespaces (11). The Semantic Web builds on technologies like XML that provide for a standardized representation for data and for the conceptual structures behind that data to support a variety of new information management and data integration applications. There are many commercial, not-for profit, and academic organizations from all over the world working with W3C on creating the Semantic Web. The Semantic Web technology integrates existing work such as web technology, knowledge representation technology, and digital libraries. The Semantic Web is all about data integration, and much richer ways of organizing things based on contextual relationships. Various communities have already adopted these technologies for supporting their various metadata requirements. To information professional, this translates into greater access, more accurate and timely information, and reduced costs. The development of metadata in digital library and the systematic organization of digital resources were very influential in the original standards and technologies for supporting the Semantic Web.

8. CONCLUSION

The emergence of new and innovative information and communication technologies enables libraries and information centers to handle library operations and services more efficiently and effectively. Wireless technologies offer cost-effective access to digital information and provide connection to a wide range of computing and telecommunications devices without the need to buy, carry, or connect cables. In the future it will be the major technology for digital exchange of information. The application of wireless technologies in libraries like Wireless networking, Wireless Internet, Wireless OPAC, SMS, etc. will provide easy access to databases, Internet, online catalogue, and other digital information. RFID technology is an emerging, more effective, convenient, and cost efficient technology in library automation and security. It will change the electronic environment of libraries. It will provide improved speed and ease of use in document handling. It will increase the productivity and library staff can concentrate on more productive and personalised information services. Library professionals should try to develop a common standard for RFID for its successful use. Librarians and information professionals have a major role in building institutional repositories, they can help in creating and managing repositories as an expert by locating, organizing, preserving, and providing access to resources.

REFERENCES

1. Mohamed Haneefa, K & Bavakutty, M. (2001) **Wireless Networking in Libraries: A Conceptual Introduction.** IN: Library Co-operation in a Networked World: Papers presented in the National Seminar held at the University of Calicut, 25-26 May 2001, edited by M. Bavakutty 132-145. New Delhi: Ess Ess Publications.
2. Mohamed Haneefa, K. (2004) **Application of Wireless Technologies in Libraries.** IN: Road Map to New Generation of Libraries Using Emerging Technologies: Paper presented in the Second International CALIBER 2004, February 11-13, 2004, ed. By T A V Murthy and others, Ahmedabad: INFLIBNET. p. 367.
3. Bhartiya, Chandra Shekhar. (2001) Wireless LANs a Cost Benefit Analysis. **Information Technology**, 10 (7), p-80.
4. Kush, Ashwani & Chauhan, R.K. (2003) Wirelss Media: A

New Paradigm. **DESIDOC Bulletin of Information Technology**, 23 (3), p. 4.

5. Premchand, Cmde & Jubali, Praveen M. (2000) IT training requirements for the year 2000 and beyond. **DESIDOC Bulletin of Information Technology**, 20 (1-2), p. 63.

6. Jones, Peter. et al. (2004) Radio Frequency Identification in the UK: Opportunities and Challenges. **International Journal of Retail & Distribution Management** [Internet] 32(3), pp.164-171. Available from: *<http://juno.emeraldinsight.com/vl=3706277/cl=47/nw=1/rpsv/~1081/v32n3/s4/p164>* [Accessed October 4th 2004].

7. Kern, Christian. (2004) Radio-Frequency-Identification for Security and Media Circulation in Libraries. **The Electronic Library** [Internet] 22 (4), pp.317-324. Available from: *<http://juno.emeraldinsight.com/vl=3706277/cl=47/nw=1/rpsv/~1091/v22n4/s2/p317>* [Accessed October 4th 2004].

8. Indira Koneru. (2004) **RFID technology: a revolution in library management.** IN: Proceedings of the Second International CALIBER on Road Map to New Generation of Libraries using Emerging Technologies, Feb. 11-13, New Delhi. Ahmedabad, INFLIBNET Centre, p. 414.

9. W3C Technology and Society Domain. **Semantic Web** [Internet] Available from: *<http://www.w3.org/2001/sw/* > [Accessed May 21st 2005].

10. Berners-Lee, Tim., Hendler, James & Lassila, Ora. (2001) The Semantic Web: A New Form of Web Content that is Meaningful to Computers will Unleash a Revolution of New Possibilities. **Scientific American** [Internet] May, Available from: *<http://www.sciam.com article.cfm?articleID=00048144-10D2-1C70-84A9809EC588EF21>* [Accessed May 21st 2005].

11. Semantic Web Activity Statement. [Internet] Available from: *<http://www.w3.org/2001/sw/Activity>* [Accessed May 21st 2005].

7

User Education in College Libraries of Kerala In The I.T Era: An Analytical Study

Dr. Ambili K.S

Dr. Adarsh N Gokul

0. INTRODUCTION

Technological advancements coupled with information revolution has given rise to tremendous capacity to man to record, encode, reproduce, repackage and disseminate information and has brought out significant changes in learning and teaching strategies and in educational system as a whole all over the world. It is high time for us to adopt these changes into our stream and provide necessary user education facilities for efficient and optimum use of libraries to enrich the learning, teaching and research. A Librarian's duty does not end with the collection of fairly worth and specialized books (print and electronic), CD-ROMs and subscription of online and print journals but only starts with its procurement. Librarian should create intimate group of readers who infuse life into a library by intelligent information organization and provide personalized reliable content delivery tailored to individual needs along with user education in the present networked digital environment.

1. DEFINITION OF KEY TERMS

User education

UNESCO defines[2] user education as any effort or programme, which will guide and instruct existing and potential users, individually or collectively with objective of facilitating: a. the recognition of their own information needs; b. the formalization of their needs; c. the effective and efficient use of information service; and d. the assessment of these services.

Information Technology

UNESCO defines Information technology (IT) as "scientific, technological and engineering disciplines and management techniques used in information handling and processing, their application, computers and their interaction with men and machines, and associated social, economical and cultural matters"[3]. Darton and Giacoletto (1992) defines IT as systematic study of artifacts that can be used to give form or description to facts in order to provide meaning or support for decision making, and artifacts that can be used the organisation, processing, communication and application of information[4].

2. OBJECTIVES OF THE STUDY

The study was conducted to examine the existing user education programmes for various categories of users in college libraries of Kerala; to examine the need for user education for various categories of users in the present IT era; to assess its organization, methods and the equipments used for teaching; and to envisage and suggest uniform user education programmes at Undergraduate and Post graduate level in the present IT scenario.

3. HYPOTHESES

Hypotheses formulated are that most of the college libraries in Kerala are not conducting any user education programme in their colleges; the existing user education prevailing in some of the colleges are not based on scientific lines; and there is no uniformity, evaluation and constant revision in the existing user education programme.

4. METHODOLOGY

The methodologies used for collecting data are

Questionnaire and Interview. Under this study a well-structured questionnaire given as appendix were distributed to a sample of 27 library professionals including nine professional college librarians from Kerala. Out of these 20 form persons attending to the VIth refresher course in library science of U.G.C Academic Staff College of University of Kerala. The questionnaire was so framed as to gather information on the following points such as name and status of the college, provision of IT facilities such as Internet and CD search, organization of library orientation lectures, availability of courses offered for technical writing/ user education, helpfulness of the course, areas of instruction needed and type of instruction, opinion regarding uniformity in user education course and suggestions and comments on implementation of user education at various levels in the present IT scenario.

5. SIGNIFICANCE OF THE STUDY

To the extend of knowledge of the investigator no study has been undertaken so far to examine the existing user education and to redesign it in the Information technology era. The advancement in information technology, the information explosion, and the complexities of publications, emergence and growth of bibliographic tools, automation of library operations and introduction of sophisticated information services necessitates orientation programmes geared to the requirements of different groups of users for the maximum utilization of its resources and also from relevant centers outside. This study will be helpful in assessing the present user education programme and its need in the college libraries, to induct it into course curricula for effective and economic use of information at the least cost for lifelong education.

Why and how of user education in the present information technology scenario-a brief description UNESCO Guide has stated the importance of user education in the preface as users of information are an integral part of and the final link in the information transfer chain, they are the raison d'etra' of every instrument made for bettering the storage, processing and retrieval of information. In every country from the least developed to the most advanced certain amount of scientific and technological information – locally produced or of international origin is stored in some fashion for the benefit of users. Unless these users know how to find relevant information available to them, the information 'Machinery' falls short of its main goal.[5] A library is rather like a laboratory where books are the apparatus. Just as in a laboratory, it is difficult to use the apparatus without instruction.[6] According to Harper the equipment of the library will not be finished until it shall have upon its staff, men and women whose entire work shall not be the care of books, not the cataloguing of books, but giving instruction concerning their use.[7]

Information is Power and the socio-economic developments of a country mainly depend upon the development and transfer of information on science and technology. The user is an important component in an information system. Though the fact that the user study is a precondition for efficient library service was realized in western countries half a century ago, it is still a recent phenomenon in India and is rarely practiced. To claim an efficient and effective information service in this networked digital environment, the Librarian should carry out user education after ascertaining the information requirements – user needs, use pattern and use behavior of his library users from time to time.

To obtain relevant information economically and pin pointedly the teacher, the researcher, and students have to be acquainted with different components and services of library. Uncoordinated information networks, poor telecommunication facilities and shortage of well qualified trained professionals in handling digital information and IT gadgets and user education programmes are crucial problems facing information services in the third world countries. Information explosion, increased rate of publications in electronic form and the multidisciplinary nature of subjects, further complicates the effective coordination and integration of information. A specialized information requirement of users makes libraries not only to switch over to the modern techniques of information storage and retrieval but also to devise modern methods and programmes of user education.

Computer networks have increased dramatically over the past few years, and have spectacular increase in respect of speed and data capacity. The Internet imagined as the electronic mobile library in the cyberspace providing info map of global resource centre has accelerated the process of data communication. The Internet offers seamless access to variety of information sources of valuable resource centers scattered in different parts of the world as well as exposes their resources for the users dispersed worldwide. Librarians need to be proactive and must train users to exploit the full potential of modern gadgets and Internet sources. User education is indispensable to get information at the fingertips of students, scientists, research scholars and teachers in spite of geographical location.

Mews argues that training in the use of information should be part of all students' education. She stresses the need for instruction in the use of libraries and information services as a continuous process, which should cover use of the catalogue, abstracts, bibliographies and reference books and detailed instruction in methods of searching and formulation of clear requests at the post-graduate level.[8] Ministry of Education, China recommended three levels of user education based on the users educational background. The first level is library orientation for freshmen; the second courses of bibliographic instruction for juniors and seniors; and the third is more sophisticated user education involving the sorting and summarizing of documentation and the studying and analyzing of information for all graduate students.[9]

Tiefel opines that 'broadly defined, library user education (also called library instruction) teaches users how to make the most effective use of the library system'. At Ohio State University, user education encompasses all activities undertaken to help students become efficient users of information – i.e., how to identify the information needs and then how to find, evaluate, and select the best information to meet that need. Activities to achieve that goal include orientation sessions, workshops, handouts and course-related and course integrated instruction. According to him the term 'library user education' has more recently been broadened to include the concept of information literacy.[10] Green, and Gilbert argues that "Information literacy will be essential for the growing cadre of knowledge workers in the 21st century".[11]

The Think Tank II report on bibliographic instruction defined information literacy as encompassing the entire world of information and seeking to prepare people to pursue the concept of lifelong learning. Information literacy extends its objectives to teaching information-seeking skills to all ages and at all times. It prepares people to use information effectively in a situation. There are no boundaries for information any where in any format. Information literacy may be defined as the ability to access and evaluate information effectively for problem solving and decision-making. Information literate people know how to be life long learners in an information society.[12]

The above views indicate that user education is a continuous process, which has to be performed for all user groups. To ensure that users are equipped with efficient methods of accessing, evaluating information from a variety of sources and tailored to their needs, training can be organized based on level of difficulty to find information and or users educational background.

User education strategies are the subject of much lively discussion and development in foreign countries. User education stands as a link between the user, information and the librarian. Librarian introduces his library and the library without walls, the cyberspace and its resources and services especially WWW the lifeblood of Internet, tips on searching for information and on scientific writing through user education. The key factors in user education configuration are the users, information sources and tools and the librarian. Hence while designing the user education programme one has to study the users their approaches to information, their information needs and their use pattern, the librarians ways and means and methods to link the user with appropriate information expeditiously and his methods in educating and orienting the users to access the right information.[13] Recent changes in the University teaching methods, composition and size of the student community, recognition of the importance of study skills, efficiency and quality monitoring and pressure on staff time demand this change in delivering user education. The quality of user education provision by libraries is crucial and hence several national initiatives such as EDUCATE (End user Courses in Information Access through Technology) have been established to enhance user education provision and to share scarce resources. User education should be directed towards designing programmes for all categories of users depending upon their information requirements while it has to be integrated into the course curricula of undergraduate and postgraduate students. [14] New methods and skills with media mix have to be developed to make user education more appealing effective and meaningful.

6. MAJOR FINDINGS

Major Findings and inferences that have evolved out of the study are summed up below which can be used for design and development of User Education Programme on scientific lines.

1. Internet and CD search service the study revealed that only 59.26 per cent college libraries provide Internet facility. All the Professional colleges under study other than Law College, Trivandrum provides Internet facility. Only 74.07 per cent college libraries provide CD search facility. While cent percent Professional college libraries provide CD search facility only 61.11 per cent other college libraries provide it.

   Lack of fund for Internet subscription renewal is the main lacuna for not providing this facility in Government colleges. Some sort of payment from users is essential for the perfect maintenance of computer systems and Internet facility in the long run if the institution is not collecting separate library fee to maintain the financial sustainability. At the same time one system may be retained as free of charge on first come first served basis for use for poor students who cannot afford to pay for it. As Internet is provided by 88.89 per cent Professional colleges and 44.44 other colleges, it is essential to teach the use of Internet to the user category by including it in the user education course curriculum. A consortium among colleges for procurement of CD-ROMs and journals can reduce the cost to many lakhs and hence UGC should establish a CD-ROM network access facility among college and University libraries without violating the IPR at the earliest.

2. Library Orientation It is seen that only 25.93 per cent libraries give orientation to teachers while orientation is given to undergraduates and postgraduates by 55.56 per cent and 51.85 per cent libraries respectively. Orientation programme, the initiation of freshman in the use of library can be given either individually or in groups during the admission time of various courses. Orientation comprises of lecture/teaching about library membership/privileges, the rules and regulations of library, method of consulting the library catalogue and locating the required materials from the shelf/databases and its use. In the present age it also include teaching of use of Internet, GD and database search at different levels. The low rate of orientation in the case of teachers may be under the presumption that they are prominent in the general procedures followed in libraries and in handling IT tools. But it is also essential to arrange at least one-day workshop or include IT application in libraries in the refresher courses for the continuous updation of knowledge in recent technologies and techniques by the teachers. For students this has to be integrated into the course curricula.

3. Teaching aids used for user education. The librarians were asked to indicate the teaching aids used for user education. Analysis shows that none of the respondents use Slide projector while OHP and LCD are used by only 18.52 and 11.11 per cent respectively for handling classes in User Education. Though LCD is a powerful teaching aid to present the matter through power point presentation only a negligible percent use this facility. This points to the need of a workshop in handling sophisticated methods for those who handle user education course, as they have to teach the preparation and presentation of power point slides to the students.

4. Technical writing/user education Course User education course is conducted by 3.33 per cent professional colleges libraries which are constituent colleges of Kerala Agricultural University as they follow library oriented teaching. 88.89 per cent answered negatively and all of them recommend the course as very useful. It is high time to integrate user education course into undergraduate programme to improve the general standards of students.

5. Course Teacher of User Education Professionally qualified librarian or Assistant Librarian is actively associated with teaching of this course either independently or jointly with other specialists in the three colleges where course is conducted.

6. Preferred areas needed for user Education On asking to indicate the preferred areas for user instruction the first preferred area is CD search (cent percent) and the second and third preference goes to bibliographic tools and their rules (92.59 percent) and internet search (88.89 percent) respectively. Other areas in the order of preference are latest software (85.19 percent), collection (81.48 percent), fundamentals of computer (70.37 percent), classification (62.96 percent) and cataloguing (55.55 percent). Hence a well structured user education course incorporating all these topics is the need of the hour.

7. Order of preference of course. The order of preference of librarians regarding methods of library instruction are credit course (cent percent), introductory lecture (88.89 percent), printed guide (85.19 percent), informal programmed lecture/orientation (77.78 percent) and occasional get together (18.52 percent). On interviewing all are convinced of the need for giving curriculum integrated credit course to students and recommend for the same.

8. Opinion on uniform course content for user education All college librarians of professional as well as other colleges agree for a uniform course content for user education for undergraduate level while only 55.56 percent professional colleges and 27.78 percent other colleges agree for uniform course at P.G level on having same subject back ground. All though there is a credit course in three colleges of Kerala Agricultural University under this study for P.G., there is no uniformity in course content. Further all though they are conducting scientific report writing course for P.G. the Asst. librarians are of the opinion to conduct this course at Under Graduate level itself as the students have to submit project report at the end of the internship of the course.

7. MAJOR RECOMMENDATIONS

I. It is recommended to have the user education programme by integrating it in the course curricula of undergraduate and post graduate programme (compulsory for P G, if not taken up the course with in three years / during previous course) and to conduct at central library of the university / concerned colleges on having sufficient facilities.

II. UGC/ Government have to take immediate steps to integrate the user education course as a component of the Academic course curricula of all UG and PG programmes / Refresher course for teachers according to the degree of intention required considering the present IT scenario

III University Library Consultative Group (ULCG) has to be constituted consisting of Administrators, librarians and other subject specialists to finalize the course outline of user education course at state level. A project on user education package has to be taken up for the preparation of effective common multimedia courseware modules - online as well as print- for all colleges for various categories with provision for local variation to avoid duplication of effort, men and material.

IV. UGC/ Government has to take immediate steps to publish a "Handbook for user education", for the standardization of the course.

V. An Assistant/Associate Professor qualified as per UGC norms in Library and Information Science has to be entrusted with teaching of user education course for various categories of users with the help of guest lecturers from other faculties. Librarian, Deputy Librarian having prescribed qualifications as per UGC norms associated with the teaching the course both at undergraduate and postgraduate level has to be recognized as teachers.

VI. A Standing Committee on user education has to be constituted to conduct utility survey, to ensure centralized, a more co-ordinated User Education Programme and to review, revise and propose new initiatives in the areas according to recent developments.

VII. College libraries have to be strengthened and networking among college and central libraries as well as web publishing is essential to conduct the on line user education programme and to meet the information requirements of users.

VIII. With a view of imparting formal user education at university level UGC has to specially train such

Librarians and DLIS has to well train the students of librarianship in information empowerment during their M. Phil. programme by integrating these topics in their course curriculum.

8. CONCLUSION

The era of globalization has made it imperative to improve the standards and quality of education. Common package of User Education is essential to strengthen and sustain the quality and integrity of education and improving transferability and marketability of students nationally and internationally. UGC has to take initiatives for assessment and to integrate user education programme into the course curriculum to achieve life long perpetual education, to improve the level of efficiency of manpower and to achieve the real goals of education. The curriculum integrated IT based User Education can bridge the information access gap between the 'haves' and 'have-nots' and can boost the academic caliber of our students, teachers, scientists and technologists to a great extent, which is the need of the hour.

REFERENCES

1. Sehgal, R.L. User education in computer based libraries. New Delhi: Ess Ess Publications, 1998, p.2.
2. UNESCO: Final report of UNISIST Seminar on the education and training of scientific and technological information. 18-21 October 1976, Rome, Paris, UNESCO, 1977.
3. William, James. Information technology: a state of the art report, ***In*** Information Technology, ed. by Allent Kent and T. J. Galwin. New york: Marcel Dekker, 1982, p. 342-458.
4. Darton, Geoffrey and Giacolctto. Information in the Enterprise: it's more than technology. New Delhi: Prentice Hall of India Pvt. Ltd., 1992.
5. Guskin, Alan E. et.al. The academic library as a teaching library: a role for the 1980's. *Library Trends,* 1979, p.285.
6. University of Bradford. Know your library. Bradford, University of Bradford, 1972. p.15.
7. Harper, W.R. The trend of university and college education in the United States. *North American Review,*

174, 1902, p.458.

8. Mews, Hazel. Reader instruction in Colleges and Universities: an introductory handbook. London: Clive Bingley, 1972.
9. Fang, P. and Callision, Daniel. User education in academic libraries of China. *International Library Review*, 22, 1990,pp. 95-103.
10. Tiefel, Virginia M. Library user education: examining its past, projecting its future. *Library trends*, fall, 1995, pp. 319-320.
11. Green, K.C and Gilbert, S.W. Myths, Realities and new necessities: academic productivity and technology. Academe, 81(1), 1995, pp.19-25.
12. Rader, H.B and Coons, W. Information literacy: one response to the new decade *in* B. Baker and M.E. Litzinger, Ed. The evolving educational mission of the library, Chicago, American Library Association, pp.109-127.
13. Ambili.K.S. Design and Development of User Education Programme based on Information Needs of Users in the Kerala Agricultural University Library Information System (Ph.D. Thesis). Thiruvananthapuram, University of Kerala, 2004. p.7.
14. ibid. p.7.

APPENDIX

Questionnaire for the survey of User Education in the College Libraries of Kerala in the Information Technology Era

Note: Please tick mark/write number where box is provided and write wherever necessary.

1. Name and Address of the college

   i. whether Professional

      Yes ☐ No ☐

2. Does Your Library provide

   (i) Internet Facility

      Yes ☐ No ☐

   (ii) CD search Facility

      Yes ☐ No ☐

3. Are you organizing library orientation lectures

   i For teachers

      Yes ☐ No ☐

   ii For undergraduate students

      Yes ☐ No ☐

   iii For Post Graduates

      Yes ☐ No ☐

   a) If yes what are the equipments used

      i OHP

      ii Slide projector

      iii LCD

      vi Other

4. Is there any regular course for technical writing/ user education in your college for students.

      Yes ☐ No ☐

(i) If yes, mention the course title *(Please attach a copy of the course content)*

(ii) Is the course compulsory/optional at

i Undergraduate level

ii Masters Level

iii Ph.D. level

5. Who teaches the course?

Librarian Deputy Librarian

Asst. Librarian Others specify

6. Do you think that instruction of some kind will be helpful to users?

Yes ☐ No ☐

If yes, kindly mark the areas where you find the instruction is needed in the order of priority (indicate the order of priority by number 1,2,3.etc.)

i. Collection
ii. Classification
iii. Cataloguing
iv. Bibliographic tools and their rules
v. CD search
vi. Internet search
vii. Fundamentals of Computer
viii. Latest software
ix. Any other areas (specify)

7. What type of instruction would you prefer?

Introductory lecture Printed guide

Informal programmed lecture/orientation

Occasional get together

Credit course

Other type (Please specify)

8. Do you welcome the idea of uniform user education course and textbook at

i. Undergraduate level

Yes ☐ No ☐

ii. Post graduate level

Yes ☐ No ☐

9. Have you ever conducted surveys on user education programme. If yes, please attach your findings briefly stating the methodologies adopted.
10. Please give your suggestions and comments on implementation of user education in the present IT scenario.

8

Library and Information Science Literature in Malayalam : A Bibliometric Study

Dimple Gopi

0. INTRODUCTION

A subject arises widening the horizons of knowledge further. The transformation of a subject into a discipline is an incessant process. A subject becomes a discipline only when a lot of literature is produced in it and academic institutions offer it as a course of study. It becomes widely discussed and a lot of literatures in the form of journals, books, reports etc. emerge and then the subject acquires the status of a discipline. Proliferation of literature is surely the sign of developing profession.

Library and information science as a discipline owes very much to the contributions made by Melvil Dewey. Dewey's system of classification for the organization of knowledge in libraries; his founding of first professional periodical library Journal and then his setting up the first library education school- all these happened in the year 1876 which is a golden year in the annals of librarianship. The contributions by Melvil Dewey helped in promoting the publication of library literature world over; a rough estimate of library and Information Science journals at international level exceeds 15,000 annually.

The beginning of library science literature in India dates

back to the 19th century, when John Mac Farlane, the then librarian of the Imperial Library, Calcutta (now called National Library), published his book "Library Administration" in 1898. The first library periodical in English language "Library Miscellany" made a beginning in1912 from Baroda. All these publications were in English language. The latest statistics of library and information science articles produced in English language from India is about 13,961.

The Indian languages have taken a back seat as far as the production of literature in library and information science field is concerned. Almost all the library schools in India use English as the medium of instruction. Naturally much of the research literature is produced in English in India also. This does not mean that there is no Library and Information Science literature in regional languages. But few attempts have been made to document them. There is an urgent need for bibliographic control and analysis of literature in regional languages.

Malayalam is an important regional language spoken by the people of Kerala. There are a umpteen number of contributions in Malayalam also in the library and information science field. But this literature is scattered over books, journal articles in books, reports, seminar papers newspapers, etc. Since there is no bibliographic control of the literature produced it goes unnoticed and the literary output becomes a national wastage. As Frohmann has observed that "just as a command of geography aids navigation, a good representation of the structural characteristics of a discipline helps both the researcher and the scholar to identify the issues and problems in the field.

There has been no attempt so far to comprehensively analyze the Library and Information Science literature in Malayalam. By this study both a comprehensive collection of literature and the analysis of literature is aimed at.

1. OBJECTIVES

The main objective of the study is the compilation of a bibliography of library and information science literature in

Malayalam and its bibliometric analysis.

The specific objectives are:

i) To examine the growth pattern of library and information science literature in Malayalam.

ii) To identify the different types of Library and Information Science documents in Malayalam and assess their quantity.

iii) To examine the chronological distribution of literature.

iv) To identify whether the contributions are more from the side of librarians or library science teachers.

v) To trace the authorship characteristics of the publications like

   a) Authorship pattern

   b) Gender wise distribution of authors.

   c) Geographical distribution of authors.

   d) Productivity of authors.

vi) To rank the journals according to their productivity.

vii) To rank the major publishers of Library and Information Science books.

viii) To rank the newspapers according to the productivity.

ix) To identify subject areas covered by the books and articles.

x) To locate the areas where the publications are lacking.

2. METHODOLOGY

The following methodology was adopted for the study

Compilation of the Bibliography of library and information science literature in Malayalam.

For the compilation of the bibliography the "Malayalam Granthasoochi" volumes 1-7 was consulted. This bibliography contains information about books produced in the library and information field. The information was noted down in 5" x 3" cards.

By scanning some periodicals like Granthalokam and Vijnanakairali which often contains Library and Information Science articles the names of writers were collected and they were approached either personally or through correspondence to provide bibliographs of their works. Altogether 50 persons were contacted and 18 persons responded with the list. But 2 persons would not provided the list since they do not maintain copies of their publications.

In order to make the list comprehensive 'Kerala Index', an indexing periodical which indexes almost all the journals and newspapers procured by the Kerala University library was also scanned from (1987-1999).

Vijnanakairali and Granthalokam are general periodicals but they often contain articles in the field of library and information Science. These two publications were also scanned to fill in the gaps.

3. BIBLIOMETRIC ANALYSIS

After gathering all the information the following bibliometric analysis was done.The analysis of the growth pattern of Library and Information Science literature in Malayalam

i) Analysis of the various types of Library and Information Science documents in Malayalam and their quantitative assessment.

ii) Analysis of the contributions.

iii) Analysis of the authorship characteristics.

iv) Analysis of the subjects covered by the books, journal articles, newspaper articles etc.

4. RELEVANCE

Although much literature is produced in the field of library and information field in Malayalam there has been no effort to control this literature. The Library and Information Science literature is scattered in journals, books and newspaper but all these have never been organized. Consequently no bibliography has ever been produced in the field, although the bibliography compiled may not be comprehensive in all aspects it is a pioneering effort in the collection of library and information science literature in Malayalam.

The analysis of the contribution is sure to reveal the strenghts and weaknesses in the field of library and Information science literature. The areas left out uncovered by the authors can be identified. By making comparisons with similar studies in other languages productivity of authors can also be accessed.

5. LIMITATIONS

a) Due to lack of time all the journals and newspapers could not be scanned.

b) Many of the authors who have not responded could not be contacted again due to paucity of time.

6. FINDINGS AND CONCLUSIONS

The main purpose of the study was the compilation of a bibliography of Library and Information Science literature in Malayalam and its bibliometric analysis. After collecting the details of the publication, the following analysis were carried out.

i) The growth pattern of library and information science literature in Malayalam.

ii) The quantity of different types of library and information science documents in Malayalam.

iii) The chronological distribution of literature.

iv) The share of contributions of librarians, library science teachers and non-professionals.

v) The authorship characteristics of the publications like.

vi) Authorship pattern.

vii) Gender wise distribution of authors.

viii) Geographical distribution of authors and

ix) Productivity of authors.

x) Ranking of journals according to their productivity.

xi) The major publishers of Library and Information Science books.

xii) Ranking the newspapers on the basis of productivity.

xiii) Major subject areas covered by the books and articles.

xiv) Areas where publications are lacking.

7. FINDINGS

7.1 Form of Publications

The study revealed, that articles published far exceed the total number of books and souvenirs. The total number of books and souvenirs come up to 53. Bibliographies are also included in this. There is one seminar paper published in the book form.

There is an upward trend registered over the years. But small fluctuations are also visible.

7.2 Chronological distribution of literature

In the case of books the earliest one was published in the year 1947 by Karunakaran Nair "Granthalaya Deepika". The year 1989-90 is the most productive period. More than half the number of books were produced during the period 1960-80. The earliest articles produced in books date back to 1948. Journal articles differ from the rest because the years 1991-99 are the most productive year. Newspaper articles also register an upward trend over the years.

7.3 Category of major contributors

Of the total number of literature produced about 154 are contributed by librarians. 92 are by library science teachers. But considering the fact that there are more than 1000 professional and 15 library science teacher within the state, the relative contribution of library professionals is abysmally low.

7.4 Authorship Characteristics

When the authorship pattern was analysed, it was found that about 98.47% of the publications are authored by single persons. This is quite natural because single author publications dominate in Library and Information Science even in the case of English publications where collaborative research publications appear. If this is so, one cannot expect more collaborative publications in Malayalam where original research works do not appear.

7.5 Gender Distribution

As far as the gender distribution is concerned contribution by females is very low. It is a fact that ladies constitute more than half of the work force in libraries of Kerala. This is also visible in the case of collaborate authorship. The male and female collaborative authorship is very low.

7.6 Geographical Distribution

The geographical distribution of the authors revealed that the contribution of Thiruvananthapuram is high. This is quite natural because the first Department of Library and Information Science in the state and many libraries of repute are located here. Kozhikode ranks second followed by Kottayam.

7.7 Productivity of Authors

When the productivity was analyzed it was found that K.M. Govi is the most productive author in terms of the number of articles in journals and newspapers. As far as articles in books are concerned K.M. Lenin comes second. The peculiarity here is that all his articles have come in a single book "Keralathile Granthasala Prasthanam (Library Movement in Kerala)" of which he is one of the editors. K.P. Vijay Kumar also shares the second position with K.M. Lenin. His contributions are all articles.

7.8 Major Publishers

Sahitya Pravarthaka Sahakarana Sandhom (SPCS) and Kerala Sahitya Academy are the leading publishers in the field. SPCS ever since its inception in 1945 has strived to produce qualitative books in the Malayalam language.

7.9 Major journals and newspapers

The major journals in the case of L & IS in Malayalam are 'Granthalokam' which accounts for about 61% of the literature produced. 'Granthalokam' is the official organ of the State Library Council. 'Mathrubhumi', the Malayalam newspaper ranks first in terms of the number of articles published.

7.10 Areas covered by the publications

Subject analysis shows that 20.66% of the journal articles in library and information deal with general aspects of libraries. In the case of books there is a dearth of publications in the subject fields like library network, classification, copy right, library movement and documentation.

7.11 Subject areas not covered in the publications

In the study the main subject areas not included in the L & IS publications in Malayalam were located. This was done using the subject headings in LISA. It was found out that important area in library marketing, library cooperation, library management etc. were lacking as subjects. Newly developing areas are also not represented like information technology and its application in libraries, information retrieval systems, information work, information centers, online cataloguing etc. Other areas not included are library buildings, library standards; research in libraries, user studies user education, statistical methods in librarianship, library association.

8. CONCLUSION

Library and Information science literature produced in Malayalam- books and journal articles is highly inadequate. As far we are concerned many of them were published decades back and needs complete revamping. Except one or two there are no suitable books, which can be used by students of certificate course in Library Science. There are three agencies in the state the State Central Library and the Kerala State Library Council and CACEE, University of Kerala that conduct certificate course and the students are permitted to answer the questions in either English or Malayalam. But absence of textbooks in Malayalam prevents many from answering in the mother tongue. It is high time that the State Library Council (SLC) comes forward and initiates steps to bring out books in Malayalam. Similarly the State Institute of Languages (SIL) can also encourage prospective authors to come forward with quality books in Malayalam. Considering the fact that except one or two, nobody has written books in the different branches of Library and Information Science, it is imperative on the part of the teachers of L&IS to give proposals to SIL or SLC for this cause.

As observed in the study, a major part of the articles in journals or books or newspapers were on library movement in the state or the problems faced by the libraries. A concerted attempt to enrich the Library and Information Science literature in Malayalam is woefully lacking from the part of library professionals. Similarly, it is a pity that while many Indian languages have journals exclusively devoted to Library and Information Science, a well developed language like Malayalam does not possess one in t his category. Here also the SLC has to come forward to seek the collaboration of a professional association of librarians to start such a venture. Such a journal can go a long way in enriching the Library and Information Science literature in Malayalam.

REFERENCES

1. ALAN, Prichard. Statistical bibliography or bibilometrics.Journal of Documentation; 25, 1969.p.348-49
2. ANAND, J.K Bibliometric studies of Library and information science journals: a review of related literature. Journal of Library and information science; 22(2), June December 1997.
3. DEVARAJAN, G. Library science literature in Malayalam: a survey and analysis. Herald of Library Science; 26(1-2) 1987.
4. FORHMANN, B.A Bibliometric analysis of the literature of cataloguing and classification. Library Research; 4, 1982.p.356.

9

Library Management Software in India : A Comparative Assessment of Leading Packages

K. Ravindran Asari

0. INTRODUCTION

Library automation as a trend started in India only during the mid 1980s, when the US and European countries completed automation of all types of libraries. In India the trend was initiated by special libraries and initially confined to larger special libraries attached to national research institutions. University libraries joined the fray only during the 1990s, when the University Grants Commission established an inter university center with the name 'Information and Library Network. (INFLIBNET), exclusively for enhancing access to information to the academic community by modernization, networking and nationwide information resources mobilization.

1. AUTOMATION CONSIDERATIONS

In this era of digital prominence, efficient library management is possible only by adopting state-of-the-art information technology practices. Actually, library is the most appropriate place for using computers and computer programs because the definition of a modern computer and that of a library are the same. Computer is a machine to store, process and disseminate information. Library also shares the same definition. The main objective of the digital technology is to make the communication process transparent and flexible. Libraries exist for providing the right information to the right user at right time. This can be achieved in this digital era only by automating all its operations. Library automation offers many opportunities to improve service to its patrons. Among other benefits, it makes materials easier for patrons locate the needed materials. It also help the staff to better serve the users by facilitating a multitude of staff tasks such as acquisition, cataloguing, circulation, reference, CAS, SDI and retrospective search services.

2. GENERATIONS OF LIBRARY SOFTWARE

Computers and programming languages are categorized into different generations based on the level of sophistication attained during the course of their evolution. The earliest library automation programs did not address all the functions and routines of a library. They could carry out one or two functions like circulation, and periodicals control. The library automation programs gradually evolved and now reached the stage of providing client-server computing. An analysis of the features of the LMS will enable us to categorize them into four different generations.

The first generation LMS were module based. There were separate modules for circulation, periodicals subscription, cataloguing, etc., without any integration between modules. Most such packages were created to run on specific hardware and software platforms.

The Second generation LMS could be run on different platforms and they functioned under UNIX or DOS operating systems. They were either command driven or menu driven.

The third generation LMS are characterized by their fully integrated nature based on relational database structures and data interchange between LMS is possible because they conform to international bibliographic formats like ISO 2709, MARC21or CCF. The third generation LMS can be operated using GUI, can accommodate infinite number of records and can support hundreds of terminals.

The fourth generation LMS have all the features of the third generation computers and possess additional features like client-server architecture and can facilitate access to other servers over the Internet. Unicode compliant multilingual database management and e-mail features are the added features.

Most of the LMS now available in India belong to the third generation with some features of the fourth generation. Let us examine the features of LMS, which are commonly used in Indian libraries.

3. LIBRARY MANAGEMENT SOFTWARE IN INDIA

Initially library automations were taken up in larger institutions and they developed their own software for it. But the concept of automation became familiar among the librarians in India with the introduction of CDS/ISIS – the software which was developed by UNESCO and freely distributed throughout the world. CDS/ISIS is a menu-driven generalized information storage and retrieval system designed specifically for the structured non-numerical databases. CDS/ISIS is not a LMS. Modules for circulation and periodical control can be developed as extensions of CDS/ISIS. It was an inappropriate decision of NISSAT to introduce CDS/ISIS in the country, as automation software because majority of the librarians who were trained in CDS/ISIS were not familiar with any programming language. Expecting them to develop Pascal interfaces to use with CDS/ISIS was hard to materialize.

The authorities of institutions, which sent librarians for training in CDS/ISIS, also expected that their librarians who returned after the training with a free copy of CDS/ISIS would automate their libraries very easily without much expense. In some libraries no follow up actions were taken while in some libraries bibliographic databases were created using CDS/ISIS. The only advantage of the trainings was that librarians became familiar with database structure many could create databases.

Out of nearly 20,000 librarians trained on CDS/ISIS only a very few, who had programming background could develop their own LMS. For example, DESIDOC developed DLMS (Defense Library Management System), INSDOC came with CATMAN (Catalogue Management) and SANJAY was developed by DESIDOC under NISSAT project by augmenting CDS/ISIS (Version 2.3) for library management activities. For SANJAY a Windows version called WINSANJAY was developed in 2003. None of these CDS/ISIS based LMS have been used extensively in Indian libraries.

Now hundreds of LMS are used in Indian libraries. Some of these are developed locally by individuals and small companies, who are not familiar with library routines and data, interchange formats such as MARC21 or ISO2709. The price of these LMS varies from Rupees 5000 to 20,000.

Of all the packages known in India, Alice for WINDOWS, LIBSYS and SOUL are the three commonly used LMS in India. The author has working experience with these packages in three different libraries, namely, the Sree Sankaracharya Sanskrit University, Kalady, Mahatma Gandhi University Library, Kottayam and The State Central Library, Kerala, Trivandrum. A comparative assessment of the features of these LMS is attempted in this article.

S. No.	*Name of the LMS*	*Name of Library using the LMS*
1	Alice for Windows (Softlink Alice)	Sree Sankaracharya Sanskrit University, Kalady, Kerala
2	SOUL (Software for University Libraries)	Mahatma Gandhi University Library, Kottayam, Kerala
3	LibSys	State Central Library, Thiruvananthapuram, Kerala

4. ALICE FOR WINDOWS (SOFTLINK ALICE)

The name of the software is changed to **Softlink Alice.** This is an international software package developed by Softlink International. This is marketed worldwide through a number of agencies based in America, Australia, Britain, Iceland, India, Malaysia, New Zealand and Singapore. In India it is marketed by Softlink Asia, Pvt. Ltd. New Delhi. Recently Softlink International decided to call the software **Softlink Alice** to maintain consistency in nomenclature because the software was known by different names in different countries. The main features of Softlink Alice are as follows:

It has four distinct versions – Public library version, Special library version, Academic library version and School library version.

The package is modular and modules are grouped into three sets as under:Standard Set: Includes Management, Reports & Utilities, Circulation and OPAC.

* **Advanced Set:** In addition to standard set it includes Acquisition, Periodicals Journal Indexing, Multimedia and Web Inquiry
* **Special Set:** In addition to Standard & Advanced set it includes Reservation,

Other features of this software include interlibrary loan, Patron self-checking, rapid retrospective conversion, multilingual features, self-circulation and union catalogue.

The LMS is backed by a number of support services which include onsite training programs, continued R & D, feedback system through user groups and free newsletters

Besides traditional library materials, it can be used to manage slides, audio & videocassettes, paper clippings, maps, charts, electronic documents and www sites. Location of documents in library could also be seen with the help of the library map. It is possible to maintain consistency in recording items through the use of authority files. It has elaborate provision for the creation of authority files, which ensure consistency and avoid typing the same entry again and again. The total record strength of Alice is 9.9 million.

It supports a total of eleven search criteria to search the database from any machine (UNIX/MAC/Apple etc.) through Internet or Intranet. It helps to generate customized reports in addition to 800 preformatted reports available with standard set. It supports bar coding. Features unique to this LMS are that it provides data protection functions, rapid retro-conversion facility and online tutorial & help system.

Instances of break down are very rare in Softlink Alice. Of the three LMS compared Softlink Alice is trouble free and librarians can use this package with confidence.

5. LIBSYS

LIBSYS is perhaps the first software of Indian origin, which supported comprehensive automation. Until the mid 1990s this was the only comprehensive automation package available in India. LIBSYS is a fully integrated multi-user library system based on client-server model and supports open system architecture, web-based access and GUI. This indigenous LMS is designed and developed by LibSys Corporation, New Delhi. LIBSYS was first developed under UNIX and later modified to suit Windows platform. Now Windows and Linex versions are available. LIBSYS has seven basic modules – Acquisition; Cataloguing; Circulation; Serials; OPAC; Web-OPAC and Article indexing.

The major advantages of using LIBSYS are as follows:

* Based on client-server model and TCP/IP for communication and networking
* Provides ANSI Z39.50 complaint web access for making the server accessible through Internet/Intranet.
* Supports web OPAC for access of bibliographic databases through Internet/Intranet
* Supports standard bibliographic formats like USMARC, UKMARC, CCF and UNIMARC.
* Images and multimedia interfaces can be used with LIBSYS search engine
* Supports barcode generation for membership card production and circulation

Offers SDI, CAS, fine calculation and e-mail reminders.

Some of the disadvantages of LibSys are:

Under the retrospective conversion option, data entry can be completed only through four windows.

The records in the database cannot be browsed from the beginning or from a desired point.

The record formats are predetermined and customization is not possible

The program stops very frequently when run certain modules

Help messages are very few and detailed user manual is not provided

Cost is the highest.

6. SOUL

With the development of SOUL (Software for University Libraries) INFLIBNET removed a long-standing hurdle in library automation. Library automation particularly automation of large public libraries and university libraries was slow because a suitable software was not available at affordable cost. Although LibSys and Softlink Alice were available, they were very costly and smaller libraries could not afford to purchase them. The development of SOUL by INFLIBNET filled the void. During the initial discussions, INFLIBNET collaborated with DESIDOC in developing SOUL. INFLIBNET decided to develop a state-of-the art, user-friendly, Window based system, which will contain all the features/ facilities available with other LMS in the market, particularly LibSys and Alice for Windows. Finally INFLIBNET came out with a LMS called 'SOUL'. The package was first demonstrated in February 1999 during CALIBER-99 at Nagpur. SOUL uses MSSQL, on Windows NT operating system as backend to store & retrieve data. SOUL has six modules – Acquisition; Cataloguing; Circulation; Serial Control; OPAC and Administration. The modules have further been divided into sub-modules to take care of various functions normally handled by the university libraries. Main features of SOUL are:

* Windows based system.
* Follows Client-server architecture.
* Uses MS-SQL as RDBMS to organize & query data
* Multi-user software with no limitation for simultaneous access
* Supports bibliographic standards like CCF, AACR II, MARC21 and ISO 2709 for export & import facility
* User friendly OPAC with web access facility
* Provides facility to create, view & print records in regional languages using CDAC's regional language utility.
* Supports LAN & WAN environment
* Affordable cost

There are a few disadvantages also with the system:

* As a measure of security a hardware lock is also provided with every installation and installation is not possible in systems with only universal ports and the hardware lock can be fixed only on parallel ports.
* The installation procedure is very cumbersome and involves a number of steps, which can be achieved only by trained staff.
* Backup and restoration of backup are possible in the same server where the software is in operation.
* Frequency of software interruption is very high.
* SOUL is constantly revised, but so far the software has not been stabilized.

The forgoing description of the three LMS reveals that, except some trivial differences, the three packages are almost identical. The essential features of these LMS are tabulated on next page.

The data provided in the table reveal that all the three LMS compared here have identical features and they belong to the third generation LMS. However the degree of reliability of each feature varies between systems. With regard to certain services Softlink Alice is superior to the other two. In the case

Sl. No.	*Features/Requirements*	*Alice for Windows*	*LibSys*	*SOUL*
1	Common routines like acquisition, cataloguing, circulation, serials control, OPAC, Retro-conversion	Yes	Yes	Yes
2	Customized record format	No	No	No
3	Data exchange facility	Yes	Yes	Yes
4	Article indexing	Yes	Yes	No
5	Standard Reports	Yes	Yes	Yes
6	Reservation	Yes	Yes	Yes
7.	Interlibrary loan	Yes	Yes	Yes
8	Multilingual Support	Yes	No	Yes
9	Union catalogue creation	Yes	No	Yes
10	Web OPAC	Yes	Yes	Yes
11	Creation of authority files	Yes	Yes	Yes
12	User self service	Yes	No	No
13	Online user orientation	Yes	No	No
14	Annual maintenance contract	Yes	Yes	Yes
15	Software updates	Yes	Yes	Yes
16	User group and Newsletter	Yes	No	No

of SOUL software, the installation procedure should be made simple. Although the software is less costly, the use of MS-SQL as the back end makes every customer invest Rs. 60,000 towards cost of MS-SQL.

Any LMS are application software, which requires some system software and hardware support for proper functioning. Thus the selection of LMS should be done on the basis of careful analysis of the basic hardware and software requirements for the package. The essential backend software and minimum hardware requirements for the selected packages are given below:

The features like, data storage techniques, programming language(s) used in the development of software, database structure, file organization etc. must also be taken into consideration for the comparative study because these factors will determine very important issues of maintenance, up-gradation and customization in future These features of the selected packages are also given in the table below:

7. HARDWARE & SOFTWARE REQUIREMENTS AND INTRINSIC FEATURES OF SELECTED LMS

Sl. No.	*LMS*	*Programming language*	*Data storage technique*	*Software requirement*	*Hardware requirement*
1	Alice for Windows	C++	Relational model	Windows 98 and above	Pentium I Processor32 MB RAM2.1 GB HDSVGA (640 X 480 X 256) CDROM Drive (48X)Sound Card
2	LIBSYS	C and Java	B Tree & Inverted file	ServerWIN NT/ SCO UNIX LINUX/ UNIXWARENovell Client WIN 95/98/ NTOrX-Windows	ServerPentium II16 MB RAM 640MB HD Client PC-AT 4868 MB RAM

3	SOUL	Java	Relational model	ServerWIN NTMSSQL Server (6.5)Client WIN 95	ServerPentium II64 MB RAM1.2 GB HD 32X CDROM DriveEthernet Card(10/100 MBPS)Client - Pentium I32 MB RAM1.2 GB HDEthernet Card(10/100 MBPS)

8. AFTER INSTALLATION SERVICE

Automation of any library can be successful only if the software used for the same is reliable and its uninterrupted service is ensured. This depends on the care and servicing of the software by the supplier. For Softlink Alice, although online service is provided, if there is a major maintenance work a service personnel has to come from Delhi. The same is the case with LIBSYS. With regard to SOUL, elaborate arrangements are being made for proper servicing. There are now four coordinating centers under the leadership of eminent librarians to look after SOUL installations through out the country. The annual maintenance charge for SOUL is only Rs. 1,500.00, while the same for Softlink Alice and LIBSYS are Rs. 30,000.00 and Rs. 45,000.00 respectively.

9. CONCLUSION

This study is based on the author's experience of using these three LMS. Once it was a monopoly of one or two firms to develop and supply LMS to libraries. Only because LibSys had no competitor during the early period, it gained popularity in major libraries. Now we have a choice of several LMS. But the selection of right LMS is always a difficult task for library managers. The present need, long term requirements, hardware & software requirements, financial resources of the library and customer support from software developers must be kept in view at the time of selection of any LMS. SOUL being a software developed by INFLIBNET, the cost as well as the annual maintenance charge could kept the minimum.

The prices of LibSys and Softlink Alice are very high. The price of LibSys is about Rs. 4,50,000 and that of Softlink Alice is Rs.3,00,000. At the same time the price of SOUL, which possess identical qualities is priced at Rs.50000.00. In other words, just for the service charges paid to the LibSys Corporation annually, we can purchase a copy of SOUL. Also of attraction is the subsidized rate offered for subsequent copies. If an institution purchase more than one copy of SOUL, Rs. 50,000 need be paid for the first copy. Subsequent copies are sold for Rs. 20,000 only. This is an added attraction.

LibSys and Softlink Alice cost very and they demand very high recurring cost, which is very much unbearable to libraries having strained budget allocations.

Now multilingual capability is achieved using C-DAC's fonts in Indian languages. It will be ideal if LMS can introduce Unicode compliant multilingual capability. The next dimension of library automation is converting the collection to the digital format. The ultimate goal of library automation should be linking every record in the computerized catalogue with the original text, which will be available in the digital format.

REFERENCES

1. Partha Sarathi Mukhopadhyay. Progress of Library Management Software: An Indian Scenario. http://drtc.isibang.ac.in
2. Website of INFLIBNET http://www.inflibnet.ac.in Website of Softlink Asia http://softlink.com.au LibSys Promotion Brochure, LibSys Corporation, New Delhi, 2003
3. Suku, J. and Mini G. Pillai. Automation of University Libraries in Kerala: Status, Problems and Prospects. J. Acad. Librarianship, 31(2), 2005: 151-159.
4. Breeding, Marshall. A new look at large-scale automation systems. Computers in Libraries, 19 (8) 1999: 36-40.
5. Safady, William. Introduction to Automation for Libraries, 4th Ed. Chicago: ALA, 1999.

10

Nitya Archives: Digital Library Software Using CDS/ISIS

K.H. Hussain

0. INTRODUCTION

Nitya Archives is a digital library/archives solution which combines high-level text compaction techniques and sophisticated free text search and retrieval procedure. The most outstanding aspect of Nitya is that any piece of information that may be graphics, sound or video, from millions of documents stored in this archival system can be searched and retrieved within seconds

Nitya Interfaces world's two best programs - CDS\ISIS by UNESCO and Adobe Acrobat. CDS\ISIS is the most used documentation package in the world and Adobe Acrobat is considered to be the defacto among e-Paper solutions.

Nitya has got two components. One is a collection of PDF documents created by scanning and using major e-publishing solutions. Second is a database describing the electronic documents using CDS/ISIS.

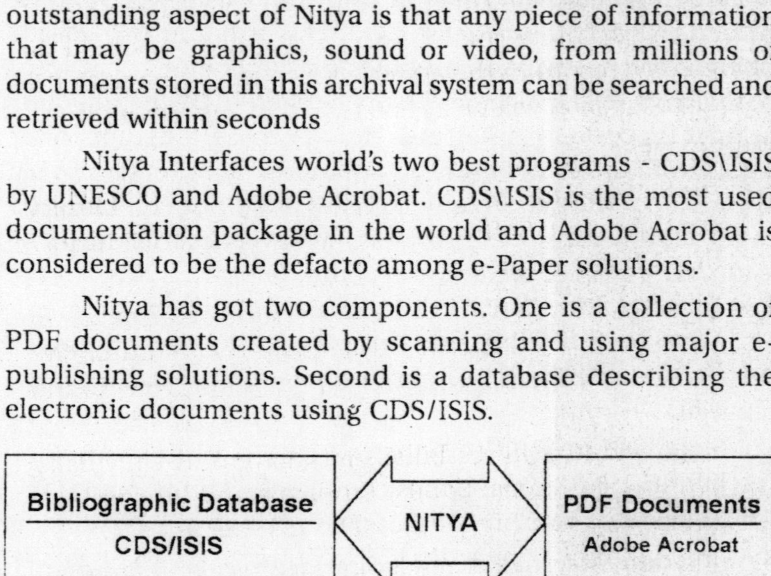

CDS/ISIS has been selected as Nitya's database engine after considering various aspects of this package. Among them

the most important aspect is that CDS/ISIS is the very popular documentation package in the world. In India it has been widely distributed and taught, under the initiative of NISSAT of Government of India. It has become part of the curriculum of library science education. It is the cost effective yet most powerful solution for electronic cataloguing. It is designed after 'integrated database' concept, which is ideal for bibliographic databases. It is faster in search and retrieval compared to modern RDBMS like ACCESS, Foxpro, Oracle, etc.

Library and documentation science principles have played a vital role in designing the structure of CDS/ISIS. 'Repeatable fields' is an example. Availability of four different 'indexing techniques' and 'Inverted file' contributes to its speed of retrieval. Boolean and Proximity operators, right truncation, etc. makes CDS/ISIS the best choice for creating bibliographic databases.

Though it has become the most known and loved package by librarian's community in India, it is now slowly retreating from the library automation field. This is because it doesn't provide any readymade modules for circulation, periodical control, etc. Many libraries have migrated to costly programs offered by commercial firms. Though these programs offer integrated and networked solutions for total library automation, they lack many facilities and flexibilities offered by CDS/ISIS. Some of the libraries have even returned to CDS/ISIS after a brief encounter with other programs. NISSAT has developed 'WinSanjay', a CDS\ISIS based total library program. So now again CDS/ISIS has become the most power full library software that can handle library automation or full text digital library development.

Since CDS\ISIS being Nitya's DBMS, complex queries can be formulated using Boolean and Proximity operators. Nitya has simplified traditional query syntax of CDS\ISIS by developing more popular WINSPIRS query syntax. Search is very fast for even million records. Nitya always presents Index Categories and Dictionary terms on which queries can be built up.

Nitya's approach to archiving is determined by unique characteristics of the collection. Nitya believes that building up a digital library of paper clipping is different from that of research reports. So Nitya is specifically designed and programmed for different collections, main difference being reflected in Index Categories.

Since CDS\ISIS offers four different indexing techniques searchable words/phrases for Index Categories can be precisely preplanned and generated. This will facilitate the relevancy in retrieval.

Nitya's information retrieval process goes through 4 distinct steps.

1. Search starts from a word or phrase.
2. Presents search results with minimum reference
3. Minimum reference can be blown up to detailed reference
4. From detailed reference full text is opened

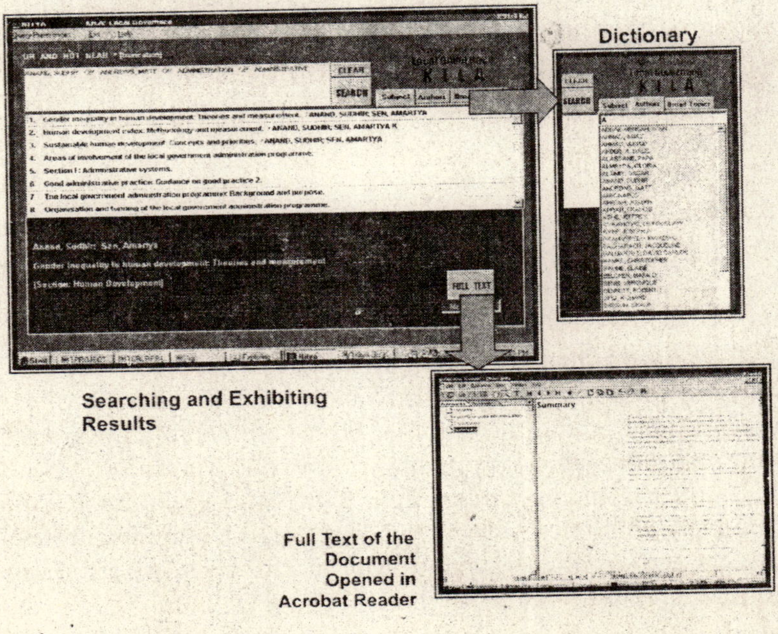

The following Figure using screens from a Nitya Archive Prototype developed for Kerala Institute of Local Administration (KILA) illustrates Nitya's information retrieval process.

Thus user gets chances to skip over unnecessary hits by looking minimum /detailed references. This reduces information gathering time.

Nitya can keep the archives in many CDs or Hard disk or CD server. Its installation and configuration is simple and takes hardly a minute. Once an archive is set up, new documents can be added and search system can be updated at any time.

Nitya is launched and supported by Centre for Informatics Research and Development (CIRD) a not for profit organization functioning under Government of India Act XXI of 1860. CIRD team for Nitya consists of library professionals having years of expertise in documentation and automation. So design and performance of Nitya is based on sound documentation principles. For example, long documents having thousands of pages are split up to many documents but keeping its integrity. This is achieved by applying cataloguing and classification principles. (eg. Working Plan archive. Each chapters are separate documents having unique class numbers which when sorted gives the full working plan)

Nitya Archives is now availble for English and Malaylam Scripts. Development is going on to make search and retrieval in other Indian vernacular languages. This will facilitate archiving of local historical records and manuscripts in palm leaves and other materials available in Inda.

Nitya is ideal for archiving and publishing in CD as well as for web publishing. Nitya is conceived as a flexible archival system. Documentation methods, dictionary building and query methods are to be changed depending upon the nature of materials and collection. As the archival and retrieval of Theses, Conference proceeding, Manuscripts in palm leaves, etc. are different from each other, CIRD plans to program different Nitya's according to the need and vision of participating museums, libraries and archives. CIRD plans to extend Nitya application to Indian languages too. Already techniques have been developed to search in Malayalam - the regional language of Kerala especially in its original scripts in which most of our ancient documents and publications that arose before 1950 are available.

REFERENCES

1. Centre for Informatics Research and Development. Nitya Archives: A Users Manual. Cochin, the Author, 2004.
2. Hussain, K.H and Ravindran Asari, K. Nithya Archives for Developing digital Libraries. In Advances in Library and Information Science: digital Librariesby Ojha, D.C and Kothari, D.V. Jodhpur, Scientific publishers, 2005.
3. Hussain, K.H, Raman Nair. R and Raveendran Asari, K. Importance of search and retrieval CD-ROM full text publishing: Experiments using PDF documents and 'Nitya' archival system. (Co-Author) Information Studies 8(3) (July 2002): 173-180.
4. Raman Nair, R. Developing Digital Libraries: Need for Proper Strategies. In Advances in Library and Information Science, V5: Digital Library. Jodhpur, Scientific Publishers, 2005.
5. Ravindran Asari, K. Nitya Archives: a solution for Organizing Digitized Content in Agriculture. In Agricultural Information systems: VISION 2020. Thrissur, IASLIC Study Circle, 2000.
6. Ravindran Asari, K *et al* Nitya Archives: Innovative Blending Techniques for Selective Access to Information fom digitally Organized Text. Proceedings of the National Conference on Information Management in e-Libraries, February 2002. IIT, Kharagpur.

11
Digitization of Indigenous Materials: Problems and Solutions in the Context of Kerala University

Dr. R. Raman Nair

0. INTRODUCTION

The problem of our Information Infrastructures is lack of information in the system. The systems let it be academic or other may provide you information from elsewhere without any limitation, which is made possible by the power of current communication technology. But what they lack is information relevant to us, valuable to us, generated by us, in our language or that of the common man in a way in which it s accessible. Take the example of the Information Systems existing in our educational and research institutions as well as departments of the State. Networks will be there. Sophisticated computers, communication lines or v-sats and high tech professionals will be there. Facility to access information from world wide sources will be there and some times every system in the institution will have connection to Internet. But none of these systems and connectivity is going to provide you very valuable information generated by that institution, in that region espcially records in local language and script or the information available only at that institution which is sought from all over the world or from the department itself. The systems may provide you access to any document in Library of Congress or a village library in U.K. But not any document from your organization or State. Take for example our Latest edition of Gazetteer of Kerala. Can we get it from Internet or any campus networks in Kerala? No. But if we want to read a similar publication on any region of U.K. we can go to the Internet Terminal in our organization or to any Internet cafe in our Panchayat if it has already been put up there as promised some five years back. Within seconds the Gazetteer or book on a region of United Kingdom will open in the terminal in front of you. But is it for this purpose we have established the information infrasructure of which that access terminals forms part?. If not where is the problem and how we can put up our content in such systems. This is the problem addressed by this paper.

1. KNOWLEDGE COLLECTIONS IN AND AROUND KERALA UNIVERSITY

This study is prepared in the context of the Libraries and Information Systems of Kerala University and a few institutions around it. The Kerala University Central Library, the Campus Central Library at Karyavattom, the departmental libraries, the Manuscript Library, the University Publications Division and various other collections under its control as well as institutions and departments associating with the University possess many rare and important documents generated in the university system or in the region during the last century. But these important sources of information are yet to be digitized. So none of them are available through Internet or online even in the university's campus network. Even more than a thousand very important reference sources on Kerala published by the State government is not yet availble online.

The present library systems in higher education and specialized institutions in all advanced countries are automated systems with digital libraries forming the heart of their campus wide networks and information systems. The main tool of Information access by scientist, teachers and students is computer terminals providing access to campus wide information systems and networks as well as Internet. The Kerala University also has Information Systems and Networks, which includes Library LAN, Campus LAN etc, and the university in its libraries gives Internet facility. There is awebsite of the university providng some information and services. The students and teachers have access to Internet through universiy's Intranets as well as their home computers or Internet cafes available near their residence.

"Information in itself has no inherent value. It only has a value when it becomes accessible". The valuable information contained in the ancient manuscripts and records preserved in Oriental Manuscript Library, Kerala Collection of University Library, the PhD theses Collection of Kerala University etc are remaining underutilized due to their in accessibility caused by fear of destruction, undue importance to preservation of the physical form of the material, bureaucratic hindrances and lack of awareness about their existence; as well as misconceptions about networks and development of campus wide information systems.

The study is done with the belief that application of Digital Library Technology can improve the situation. It can provide a cost effective solution to conservation of indigenous documents and knowledge held by the university and organizations associtaing with it. It can make them accessible to teachers, students and researchers inside and outside the university, make them useful to the society and contribute for creation of new knowledge and development. More than that digitization of our documents and establishing a digital library as the central hub of university's network and information system can give meaning to the Information Infrastructure that the university has developed and is further developing; by bringing our own information into it.

1.2 Indigenous Content of Kerala University

A digital archive can be established under Kerala University with required digital storage capacity and network connectivity that can enable its accessibility throughout the campus as well as from the residence of teachers and students. Kerala University possesses very valuable content that is records of knowledge generated inside the university during more than a century as well as records of knowledge that originated in the region through many centuries. They are at present held in traditional media like palm leaf, paper, etc as well as microfilm, computer hard disk, etc at various institutions and they form part of existing library collections. From this the content of importance and relevance that requires digitisation and organization in a retrievable way is to be identified and selected according to their value and priority to be assigned in the context. The portions of the collections that are to be digitised and which should form the content of the Information System and network of the university are identified here as follows.

1.3 Holdings of Records Geneated in the Region

There are many institutions under the university, affiliated to the university as well as in the geographical regions covered by the university holding very valuable records of knowledge that originated in the region. University can take the initiative for establishing a digital library of their holdings. The following are the institutions that have been considered for this study.

1.3.1 Oriental Research Institute and Manuscript Library

The Collection contains about 60 000 manuscripts, which includes palm leaf manuscripts, paper manuscripts and other records. It is a very valuable collection on ancient science and technology in Kerala, and covers subjects like Ayur veda, Siddha, architecture, astronomy, tantra, astrology, Vedanta, Mimamsa, and Nyaya etc. Ninety percent of the documents in the collection are unpublished and of these most of them have no duplicate copies existing anywhere else.

1.3.2 Kerala Collection of University Central Library

The Kerala Collection contains books on various aspects of the region. There are many old and rare books and out of print books on various aspects related to Kerala. The collection comes to about 75000 books. Of these approximately 15000 books may require digitisation when their conservation, reference value, demand relevance etc are considered.

1.3.3 PhD Theses Collections

The Theses collection at the university comes to about 5000 dissertations approved by the university for awarding Doctoral Degree. Presently the complete collection is not available at a single place, the use of some titles submitted some forty years back are difficult due to their condition which needs urgent conservation work. As university should possess at least one copy of the theses accepted by the university for providing reference services; ensuring the safety of old theses has become very important which presently causes restrictions on their use.

1.3.4 Rare Items in other Institutions

Some of the institutions affiliated to the University also possess rare and valuable records in their collections the digitisation of which can enable the university to possess copies of such records and make them accessible in their information system

1.3.5. Affiliated Institutions

There are many colleges and other institutions affiliated to the University, which have very valuable, rare and ancient collections related to Kerala. Examples are Centre for Development Studies, University College, Government Ayurveda College, and Government Women's College etc.

1.3.6 Private Collections Around

There are many private collection in the areas covered by the university like Church Libraries, Temple Libraries, Publishers Collections, Collections in various families etc. One of the very important collections of old Malayalam publications that existed near the university has been lost recently. It was that of Kamalalya Press, which is one of the earliest publishers who have published the first editions of many famous, works in Malayalam. Thousands of rare titles in dozens of copies have been sold out from their go down recently as waste paper when the building of Kamalalya Publications was transferred and modified. A comparative review of the catalogue of kamalalya Publications and Kerala University Library can reveal that not even 50% of the books they have now weeded out are existing in university collections. As we were having no system for watching such incidents and collections this was not even understood by any. The owners of such collections would have been happy to transfer them to university free of cost or even for a higher price than waste paper if university would have contacted them in time. Many such collection owners may not agree to transfer; but may permit the university to copy or digitise on terms and conditions agreeable to them, which may enable them to conserve their records as well as enable the university to possess copies of such records and make them accessible in their information system. Such activities of the university require tough and competent professionals with a vision at the helm of university's library and information system. They should have required finacial and administrative powers to take action immediatley in situations in which such collections can be aquired.

But university is not giving that much important to its library and information system which has resulted in the keeping the managerial position of the library system vacant for about two decades. University would have saved a subsistent amount that would have gone as salary for a higher post like University Librarian for two decades. But the loss in quality of the information support and the loss of our recorded knowledge that would have lost due to the in efficiency of the system during the last 20 years may be a hundred times greater than the savings effected in terms of money.

1.3.7 Museums, Archives, Archaeology

State Archives, Sree Chitra Art Gallery, Napier Museum, State Central Library, public libraries like Avittam tirunal Smaraka Granthsala, Chittira Tirunal Smaraka Granthasala, Legislature Library and many other institutions possesses valuable ancient documents, which are highly relevant to research on Kerala. University can join them in some digital library development project, which will enable all these institutions also to conserve their records and make them accessible to the public thorough a common digital library project.

2. RECORDS DIGITIZATION

The documents contained in the collections of Kerala University and affiliated institutions mentioned above are of high relevance not only to the research conducted in the university but also all over India. But these are not accessible to academic and research community smoothly. But now Information Technology offers unlimited possibilities for increasing their utility to society.

The main purpose of this study is to focus attention on this aspect as well as suggest measures to ensure conservation of these valuable records as well as maximizing their utilization by applying digital technology by establishing necessary infrastructures for digitizing and networking of records and other materials held in the collections mentioned above under the Kerala University and other institutions.

2.1. Digital Technology

Digital Library Technology can ensure the accessibility as well as conservation of recorded knowledge for present and future generation. For developing digital information systems we have to bring together traditional scholars, language specialists, archivists, scientists, artists, etc on the one hand, and information systems people on the other.

There is a need for urgent utilization of high technology - including information technology and computer communication networks for conservation of our ancient records, art and cultural heritage. In much the same way as there is a movement for saving the endangered species of flora and fauna, so also there is a felt need for saving the endangered species of manuscripts, ancient books, art and culture. In the text sub-domain, a number of our books, manuscripts and other records stand the risk of environmental onslaught every day. Several thousands of these manuscripts become unusable or vanish without any trace. For very similar reasons, old paintings and sculptures are getting degraded and even lost. In the dynamic visual heritage sub-category, traditional folklore dances are vanishing every year through loss of continuity of new generation of artists. A very good example is Teyyam. Music is also meeting a similar fate. Even ancient systems of life styles are getting wiped out through imperatives of modernization. We also need to use digital library technology to maximize the utility of the results of current research in Science and Technology by organization and dissemination of the records reporting research and development through our information systems.

2.2 Forms of Records/Information to be digitized

Knowledge existing in the University of Kerala as well as the institutions and society, served by it and the expression of cultural and scientific heritage in general, looking from the informatics angle naturally falls into texts, images and sound categories. In Kerala University Collections as well as in institutions connected to it, recorded information of all these categories exist.

The text information may be palm leaf manuscripts, texts inscribed in carved stone tablets, handwritten paper manuscripts, old printed records and books, thesis and many others. Hundreds of thousands of such documents exist in South Kerala in regions covered by the Kerala University.

Image sub-domain may be paintings as 2-dimensional example, and sculptures/temples as 3-dimensional examples. It may also be dynamic like the various forms of dances like, Katha kali, Teyyam, Kudiyattam etc. The sound sub-domain encompasses vocal and instrumental music, historical speeches, to mention a few.

In the setting up of such a digital archives and information system, a standardized inventory across all the recorded information resources under Kerala University and other institutions, which have, numerous correlation, is most essential. Starting of a planned digital archiving programme is essential if any information system and network built up by the university is to become meaningful. There are inherent correlations among the three major sub-domains- texts, images and sound. There are situations where, the historical study would require all the three to be simultaneously presented, simultaneously analyzed and correlated. This can be made possible through the technology of multimedia systems. Digital Technology can combine graphics, animation, speech synthesis and video with multi media technology, which can support the archiving, and interchange of texts, images and sound based information, mainly heritage information.

3. INTERNATIONAL AND NATIONAL DIGITIZATION EFFORTS

There are many national and international examples of digital library development projects, which we should know about before starting such a programmes or selecting a solution for developing digital content for our information systems.

3.1 International Efforts

UNESCO Memory of the World Programme: This programme seeks to safeguard documentary heritage of the world. Naturally, it reflects the diversity of languages, peoples and cultures. 'It is the mirror of the world and its memory'

American Memory: American history in words, sounds and pictures and extensive online exhibitions of historic photographs and documents.

Digital Libraries Initiative (DLI): The National Science Foundation, Department of Defense Advanced Projects Agency and the National Aeronautics and Space Administration, USA funded six research projects in 1994 aiming at developing new techniques for creating digital libraries.

Ankorvat Heritage Conservation Project: It is part of World Heritage Inventory and Management project. It is meant for ancient site of Angkor, Kampuchea and specifically related to conservation a twelfth century temple complex in the ancient city of Angkor, Kampuchea.

3.2 National Efforts

In India, several institutions and national level

organizations have taken steps to develop digital libraries. Projects aimed at digitizing rare and out of print publications and manuscripts have been taken up in institutions like Indira Gandhi National Centre for Arts, Indian Institute of Science, National Library, Kerala Agricultural University, Centre for Informatics Research and Development, Centre for South Indian Studies etc.

Ragamela: It is a multimedia archiving project. With support from Unesco; Indira Gandhi Centre for Arts has developed a programme for archiving cultural and historical environment for enabling the future to experience the past using virtual technology. A digital archive on Indian culture has already been developed at IGNCA.

National Library: National Library at Calcutta has initiated programmes to digitize its rare collections. A number of utilities have been developed there to facilitate creation of digital libraries using solutions offered by various groups.

3.4 Regional Level Digitization Efforts

KAULIS: Kerala Agricultural University has developed a digital library. In it; the digitized collection of PhD these accepted by the University forms the indigenous content. Developed in 1998 it is the first functional Digital Library of PhD Thesis in India. KAULIS also has digitized content on world wide Agricultural Research from 1971 to present and course materials meant for various specialized Information Technology programmes.

Kerala History DL: It is a digital library of reference materials on Kerala History. It is a joint venture of Centre for South Indian Studies and CIRD. This library was first demonstrated during the South Indian History Congress held at Trivandrum in December 2001.

Kerala Forestry Documents: A proto type of archives of Working Plans exisitn in the Kerala Forest Department has been developed using Nitya Archives in 2002.

Mathrubhoomi Weekly: A digital Library of Mathrubhoomi Weekly for a few years has been developed using

Nitya Archives on experimental basis. This is a fine example of application of language technology for local scripts. This digital library has a search mechanism for original Malayalam script.

TPL Digital Library: A digital library of old Malayalam and English documents available in Trivandrum Public Library has been developed using Nitya Archives in 2005. It has the facility to search using Malayalam and English script. The library is functional now with a few selected documents from both languages. Approximately 5000 books are expected to be added to the digital library in first two years.

Biodiversity of Kerala -Flora, Herbarium: It is a proto type of digital library of Flora of Kerala. It has been developed under a joint programme of Forestry College, Thrissur and Centre for Agricultural Informatics using Nitya Archives.

KSDP Archives: A digital archives of Minutes of Board Meetings, Kerala State Drugs and Pharmaceuticals, Alappuzha has been developed using Nitya Archives.

KINFRA Archives: Minutes of Board Meetings, KNFRA, Thiruvanatnhapuram has been digitally archived using Nitya Archives.

Brennen College DL: Brennen College has prepared in 2004 a complete database of its Malayalam Books in Malayalam script based DBMS named M/ISIS. It has been released as an electronic Publication and available to other institutions on exchange basis. It has also developed a proto type of the digital library of Malayalam books of the college connected to this database using Nitya Archive.

Kerala Sahithya Akademi DL: Kerala Sahithya Akademi has started in 2004 a digital library project, which will include old and rare Malayalam and English books available at the Academy Central Library and Appan Tampuran Smarakam. The work has been allotted to CDIT. The solutions are under development.

4. SOLUTIONS FOR RECORDS DIGITIZATION

There are many national and international computer

programs and solutions for developing digital libraries, archiving of museums, monuments, text, and multimedia. The concept of library has gone far beyond digitization of text or library materials to incorporate other institutions and environment to the library like, art galleries, museums, and even cultural environments or incidents as they are. Digital technology enables the conservation of heritage by creating and preserving heritage items by copying the environment for preservation using virtual technology. Cultural heritage information management has become more sophisticated and efficient.

4.1 World Heritage Inventory Management Program

One important system is World Heritage Inventory and Management Program. The programme was tested at the ancient site of Angkor, Kampuchea. The conservation of built heritage requires the identification of items and the subsequent recording as an organized management tool for the care and conservation of items. The heritage records are a precise and reliable dossier of graphic and written documentation of an historic resource. This basic information should be used to guide conservation analysis, design and maintenance activities. The use of a computerized database is integral to the quantitative management of resources, and to the basic requirement of centralizing the wealth of information that the system is designed to accommodate. The prime objective of the programme was to function as a central inventory of buildings, relics and moveable objects and could be used as the basis for an accessible register and management tool for the conservation of the Monuments. The main components of the World Heritage Inventory And Management Program are as follows:

The linking of the graphics files to the databases information is facilitated. The program is primarily designed for tangible arte facts and buildings. Hence the programme is capable to retrieve a plan or a photograph easily, and from wherever one may be in the program. Establishing a consistent method of recording is a fundamental starting point of any computer system. Using this database, information can be organized into an appropriate hierarchy. The selected options become more sophisticated as site knowledge increases. With single keystrokes, words, paragraphs or graphics can be introduced or retrieved. The system is designed to be applicable to a variety of cultural heritage items or artifacts and to provide project management in addition to the inventory program. Archival documentation can be scanned into the system, there is a library of slides, drawings and photographs and these resources are linked to the inventory and can be found using keywords. They are planning to make this system accessible by network. Such a system can be used to conserve the records and knowledge on Padmanabha Swamy temple, and our ancient buildings and monuments.

4.2 Basis Plus/Techlib Plus Package

One of the powerful packages available in India and used worldwide is Basis Plus. It can be used for creating and maintaining digital libraries. Basis Plus is a Relational Database Management System (RDBMS) that combines many features normally not available together in any other similar packages. It combines the three key technologies; full text retrieval, relational database management system, and object management in a single platform. The Information Dimensions who has produced the package has also developed Basis Web server that can be overlaid in Basis Plus. Basis Plus' sophisticated search mechanism lets us get to the information we seek instantly, rather than being at the mercy of a haphazard hyperlink path. Its navigation features can enable us to move through a display or from document to document with a dexterity not found in most other Web server packages.

4.3 The Digital Library Toolkit

The Digital Library Toolkit developed by Sun Micro Systems is used in some digital Library projects. The systems and software are dependent on solutions offered by Sun Micro systems. In India University of Hyderabad had used this Tool kit.

4.4 Greenstone Digital Library Software

Green stone is a suit of software, which has the ability to build digital library collections. It provides a new way of organizing information and publishing it on the Web. The New Zealand Digital Library Project at the University of Waikato has produced Greenstone. It is now open source software supported by UNESCO.

4.5 University of Michigan Digital Library Extension Service (DLXS)

University of Michigan Digital Library extension Service provides foundation and the framework to develop digital library collections. It is an impressive and comprehensive suit of tools including a search engine and an array of middle ware some of which are free and some of which are priced.

4.6 Nitya: For Text and Images

Nitya Archives is a digital library package developed by Centre for Informatics Research and Development (CIRD). It can digitally record millions of records, books, different types of manuscripts like palm leaf, tablets, typescripts, metal or stone inscriptions, etc.; and manage them in an efficient way that enables full text retrieval within in seconds. Nitya has various programmes meant for text, manuscript, images, heritage etc.

5. RECOMMENDATIONS ON SELECTION OF SOFTWARE

The digitization of information is an efficient, effective and accessible means by which information can be compiled in a readily accessible manner. The information can be made available to many, and at minimal cost.

5.1. Evaluating Digital Archiving Systems

A Package selected for developing digital library in an organization should fulfill some basic functions. The requirements are that the solution must be:

* Adaptable: In scope and application
* Easy to use: In data input and retrieval
* Current: Using the best system available and standardizing input methods

* Low Cost: affordable to more people and therefore widely accessible
* Expandable: with options for enhancements and up gradation
* Compatible: with other programs enabling data transfer and networking
* Multi-media: ability to store text and graphics in one relational system
* Managerial: with capabilities to track time, budget and tasks
* Filing System: ability to maintain, modify, update and protect data
* Support: opportunity to obtain help or training
* Networking: communicate with others regardless of geographic Limitation
* Interdisciplinary: applicable to the various disciplines with minimum customization requirements.

We have to use these points as criteria for the selection of an appropriate system for the digitization of almost any record of any media or for digital library or museum projects.

5.2. The Problem with General Solutions

Although, several packages are in vogue for materializing digital archives, they lack efficient search mechanism. Devoid of a search mechanism, digitally stored information in hard disks and compact discs will remain as dump places of information, just the same way as documents converted into microform existing in our libraries. The full potential of digital archiving can be exploited only if selective access to content is made possible. Then only it can perform the traditional functions of a library.

Depending upon commercial agencies always for the creation of digital libraries is neither practicable nor cost effective. Therefore, it is necessary to make professional approaches towards the development of appropriate utilities and to train a new generation of library professionals to create and maintain digital archives.

5.3 Advantages of Nitya

When compared with the possibilities offered by the available packages for digital library development and electronic publishing Nitya fulfils most of the requirements mentioned above. In digitization projects of Kerala; our language and script is very important. Ninety percent of the manuscripts and records up to 1950, which any digital library project of Kerala has to deal with, are in original Malayalam Script. The only solution available for computerization of original Malayalam Script is Rachana. Nitya can incorporate this language technology and hence it makes Nitya a unique solution for digital library projects in Kerala. Also Kerala may require a solution that can process Tamil and Devanagari Script used for Sanskrit; as a considerable amount of documents in these languages are contained by most of the archives and library collections. As Nitya Archives is capable to scale up accepting more regional scripts of India it can be used for digitizing documents in other Indian languages also. So Nitya can succeed in achieving the goals of digital library package in any institution in Kerala as well as India.

5.4. Nitya for Digitization in University of Kerala

Centre for Informatics Research and Development (CIRD) has developed the NITYA the package meant for digital archiving. CIRD is a Research and Development organization functioning under the Act XXI of 1860 of Government of India. It consists of a group of professional librarians, lingusticians, historians and IT experts.

5.5. Contributions of Sri. K.H. Hussain

Nitya is the result of research by Sri. KH Hussain, an information scientist from Kerala, India. It is based on his research conducted at Amoudi Electronic Systems Jeddah, Saudi Arabia as well as for CIRD. He has structured more than 15 databases (majority of them Bibliographic) since 1985and is an expert in CDS\ISIS (Unesco package for documentation) and information system development. He has developed interface between Ventura and CDS\ISIS. He is also involved in developing Rachana software which recreated the original / full character set of Malayalam language in word processing and typesetting. He has coordinated linguistic and technical works involved (Digital typography, Designing keyboard layout and internal mapping, programming, etc). He has also developed a DBMS in Malayalam interfacing CDS/ISIS and Rachana, which will be instrumental in future bibliographic control of Malayalam literature and other information systems for Folklore, traditional medicine, agricultural systems, etc. Using this DBMS a Digital catalogue of 21000 Malayalam books available in Government Brennen College has been published in CDROM. This forms the first successful application of a search mechanism for Malayalam Language.

Nitya is programmed in Delphi as an interface between CDS/ISIS and Adobe Acrobat. Nitya combines high-level text compaction techniques and sophisticated free text search and retrieval procedure. The most outstanding aspect of Nitya is that any piece of information graphics, sound or video, contained in any page of the millions of documents stored in this archival system can be searched out within seconds. University should test such technology developed in the region as well as provide fcility for research and further development of such packages and products.

6. REASONS FOR CONSIDERATION OF NITYA ARCHIVES

6.1. Objectives of Nitya

Main objectives of Nitya as listed in its manual are :

* fast search and retrieval of documents from digital libraries.
* Can create stand alone Digital Archives.
* ideal for publishing digital collections in CDROM.
* elevates the status of CDS/ISIS by making it a powerful tool for digital libraries.

6.2. Physical Infrastructures and Front End

Kerala University should develop in the University Library minimum infrastructures required for developing and organizing digital content. Physical system of the digital library should have capacity to digitize, organize and manage content or information resources available at various centers of the university as well as permit access to it through Intranet and also from anywhere through Internet.

The infrastructure may consist of the Digital Library, connected to Building LAN of the University Library that will be linked to main campus network and through WAN to automated libraries in distant campuses of the university connected to concerned campus networks. The project should also consist of leased line connectivity or V-sat connectivity to the LAN consisting of the digital library. This will give to the campus networks strong communication capabilities to access information from their own Digital library and also from various outside sources.

6.3. Storage of Digitized Collections

The digital library storage systems that can manage storage in a cost effective way and disseminate information efficiently consist of three types of hard wares; meant for highly used information, middle level usage information and less or rarely used information. On best model for this that Kerala University can also adopt is the systems developed at Kerala Agricultural University. In KAU Electronic Library the storage systems with Alpha Server 1000A; under high security stores very costly specialized software and databases and agricultural research information received and downloaded under various MOUs and licenses. The PhD dissertations of KAU are available in this electronic library. The Electronic Library has a storage capacity of approximately 6.5 crore printed pages and it already has content copied under various MOUs and books and other documents acquired in electronic medium consisting of approximately 5.5 crore pages and about hundred and twenty hours video/ audio files in its storage systems. Course materials on agriculture and ICT related topics are also stored in the digital library, which was used by the university for conducting about 12 specialized courses on different aspects of IT.

6.4. User Interface in Digital Library

Paradigm used to develop Nitya Archives is adapted from the user approach to books in traditional libraries. When a user enters a library, he goes to the catalogue first and searches under appropriate access points such as author, title, subject, etc. This enables the user to get the documents he want. He locates relevant chapters/pages of the book with the help of table of contents and index. In the same way, when one opens Nitya, a dictionary of keywords similar to traditional catalogue appears. Terms in the dictionary are used to form queries. Search yields hit of relevant documents with bibliographic details. From them reqired full text is selected. Full text is then opened and the entire text can be navigated through bookmarks. Any Digital Library solution used should have a similar functionality.

6.7. Organization of Digitized Records for Use

Unlimited number of documents can be digitized, stored and managed using Nitya Archives. Older books, manuscripts in palm leaves, research reports, conference proceedings, parliament/legislative proceedings, hospital records, theses/ dissertations, government orders, journals, newspaper clippings, etc can be added to digital archives and stored either in hard disks or in compact discs. Retrieval of a document or a page using Nitya is accomplished in seconds. Any solution used should give this power.

6.8. Information Retrieval from Digital Library

Nitya Archives is so versatile that both Reference Retrieval System and Document Retrieval System are achieved in one step. As software tool that achieves these two high ends, Nitya but represents half the picture. Other half is application of documentation principles in archiving. Different kinds of materials demand different methods of indexing in order to achieve maximum benefits out of archiving. For example, documentation methods applied to archive and retrieve old printed books, PhD theses, technical reports etc should be different from that of archiving palm leaves of our Oriental Manuscript Library. It will be still different in archiving government orders. Digitizing the exhibits in our Sree Chitra Art Gallery, or the exhibits in the Archeological Museum requires different solutions. For bringing out the Kerala University Publications in CDROM we require another solution. So the package used by the Kerala University should have modules for all these, should be viable for customization of similar different requirements that may come up in the system, should be viable to the local scripts used by the manuscripts and books, and should enable pooling of all the digitized resources for use.

Unless proper documentation methods are applied, any archival system would be ineffective in retrieving relevant information. In this aspect the advantage of Nitya is that proven practices of traditional librarianship in organizing Universe of Knowledge has helped in designing Nitya. Since Nitya uses CDS/ISIS, defining databases and applying indexing methods are naturally adhered to cataloguing and documentation principles.

6.9. Incorporation of Traditional Library Practices

Nitya Archives; from the digital archives, databases and libraries developed is found to be committed to translate age old practices of traditional libraries archives and museums to modern IT practices in organizing knowledge. It is a flexible archival system. Documentation methods, dictionary building and query methods are to be changed depending upon the nature of materials and collection. As the archival and retrieval of Theses, Conference proceeding, Manuscripts in palm leaves, etc. are different from each other, Nitya is seen in the above libraries and prototypes developed using it; customized according to the need and vision of participating museums, libraries and archives. Nitya applications are getting developed in other Indian languages too. Already techniques have been developed to search in Malayalam especially in its original scripts in which most of our ancient documents and publications that arose before 1950 are available.

7. DIGITIZATION OF INTERNALLY GENERATED RECORDS

Kerala University has websites and Intranets. Ninety percent of the people from all over the world that access Kerala University web site check for university publications, its library and digitised content of knowledge generated by its academicians and researchers available in the web sites. But nothing of that sort is available in the site. Nothing of that sort is available in our Intranets. None of our own resources are available even in the Library LANs. This will be a disgrace to the university in this age of Cyberspace. The networks and automated information systems end as mere systems, cables and connectivity, which may enable access only to information other institutions, may permit us to access.

Hence in developing Information Infrastructures of the university, which includes, Campus Wide Information Systems, Building LANS, Campus Networks, Automated Libraries etc Kerala University should take development of a Digital Library of its own content as a priority item.

7.1. Digitisation of Indigenous Records at the University

University should undertake a digitisation project of its own content with specified time frame. In the first phase to be completed in three years university should digitise complete PhD dissertations accepted by the university and full text of selected rare manuscripts and books that originated up to 1925 available in all its collections. Of this priority is to be given to PhD dissertations of the University. The author has attempted a digitalisation of PhD thesis of a selected period of a university in 1999 when digital library packages where rare and Nitya was only in its development phase. A simple programme has been developed using MSAccess at front end and approximately fifty dissertations have been digitised all in four months. Later Nitya became available and the data has been transferred to Nitya with more facilities. By author's experience and by the trend in current technology it is calculated that if well planned Kerala University can digitise all its PhD dissertations in one year. That is if the university starts the work today by this date of next year any PhD dissertation accepted by the university will be available online for reference for our academic community.

Then the digitisation of remaining documents should be under taken and completed in a reasonable period so that every record generated in the university becomes accessible from anywhere at any time.

7.2. Use of Nitya Package for Digital Library in the University

For digitization' after a discussion on available packages and their use this study recommends Nitya solutions. Nitya represents a new generation of CDS\ISIS applications supported by UNESCO. It not only exploits the power of search and retrieval of CDS\ISIS, but also explores its potentialities in developing digital libraries. It simplifies the looks and functionalities of CDS/ISIS, there by making it user-friendly and more acceptable outside the realm of library professionals.

For different types of materials, concerned prototypes of 'Nitya archives' like those for Heritage Information Systems, Theses, Research Reports, Technical Reports, Conference Proceedings, Historical Documents, and Manuscripts in Palm Leaves, Journal Articles, Paper Clippings and Internet Downloads etc which already been developed by Nitya are recommended.

Use of Nitya for digitization in Kerala University can check the accumulation at Kerala University like in some others who have recently undertaken such digitization projects, the development of non-documented digital collections that only 'dumps' thousands of scanned pages in CD without proper retrieval mechanisms.

For bringing our e-versions of University Publications also Nitya is recommended. Digital collections developed using Nitya can be distributed to any number of users along with Electronic Document Reader. This will facilitate effectively organized and electronic publishing of University publications with information retrieval mechanism attached to each will become possible.

No digital Library solution except Nitya Archives has

presently the power to deal with Malayalam manuscripts and other publications especially those with scripts used prior to 1950. Nitya's customization for Original Malayalam script and other Indian languages will be a milestone in the history digital library movement and CDS\ISIS applications in India. As most of the research and development on Nitya occurred in Kerala; the university should make use of the technology.

8. INTERNATIONAL STANDARD AND LOCAL SUPPORT

Following of International standards as well as locally available support are two important aspects for selecting a digitization solution. Nitya has consultancy and training by CIRD available in Kerala. CIRD aims transfer of technology to professional librarians and archivists. The five types of institutions in need of digital archive creation identified by CIRD are the following.

* Archives and libraries, which plan to develop digital collections, but do not want to setup digitization unit.
* Institutions, particularly larger ones, which will outsource the work now, but have the potential to develop its own infrastructure later.
* Institutions having all the necessary equipment, software, etc., but do not have the digital archiving know-how.
* Institutions already started digitizing records using other packages, but decided to change to NITYA after seeing its capability.
* Institutions who want to publish ancient manuscripts, books, etc. in CD using Nitya software.

Kerala University can select one of the options from those given above that will be convenient to it. CIRD has also various schemes to support all these types of institutional requirements. CIRD consultancy for Nitya includes:

* Designing and customizing Nitya to meet special needs of the collection, users and librarians.
* General training in CDS\ISIS and Nitya.

* Specific training in digitization, adding documents to the archive, publishing in CD, etc.

The above schemes will be of high relevance to Kerala University and can be availed for its digitisation programmes.

9. NEED FOR ABSORBING NEW TECHNOLOGIES

Archives, libraries and museums as they exist now in Kerala University and other research institutions limit mainly to collection, preservation and services using original exhibits, printed documents, manuscripts and non-print materials like microforms. Services through these mediums are loosing their relevance and cost effectiveness. What we actually require is collection, preservation, organization and dissemination of the thought content of these records or a facility for viewing the exhibits online. Now electronic mediums are in a better position to fulfil all these functions. Any archive or museum or library providing support for research also should transform it by accepting new technology and should form the heart of any information system or network the organization develops. Availability of locally developed solutions using programmes like CDS/ISIS supported by Unesco and of International standard can give to University of Kerala and other institutions the power to enter the Information Superhighway in a deserving way. A competent professional as per UGC specified standards at the managerial position of the library and information system of the university and skill, imagination, motivation, sincere effort and devotion of a large number of people to be involved will be necessary to achieve this goal.

REFERENCES

1. Chen Li Liew and Gaunkun Sun. Electronic documents: What lies ahead. In the *Proceedings of the 4th International Conference of Asian Digital Libraries*. Bangalore, IIIT-B, 2001.

2. Brennen College. Malyala Granthasooji 2004: An Electronic Catalogue of Malaylam books in the College with a Search Engine for Malayalam Script. Tellycherry, the author, 2004.

3. Griffin, Stephen M. Digital Libraries and the NSF/DARPA/NASA Digital Libraries Initiative. In: Raitt, David. Ed. Libraries for the New Millennium. London, Library Association, pp 115-147.

4. Harris, C.D. Area studies and library sources. In *Proceedings of Conference on Area Studies*, London, 1965.

5. Hussain, K.H, *et al* Importance of search and retrieval CD-ROM full text publishing: Experiments using PDF documents and 'Nitya' archival system. (Co-Author) Information Studies 8(3) (July 2002): 173-180.

6. Lohuizen, Van C.W.W. Knowledge management and policymaking. *Knowledge.* V.8, No1. 1986.

7. Perry, J.W. Characteristics of recorded information. *In Documentation in Asia.* Ed. by J.H. Shera, New York, Reinhold, 1956.

8. Raitt, David. Ed. Libraries for the New Millennium: Implications for managers, London, Library Association, 1997, 288p.

9. Raman Nair, R. Developing Digital Libraries: Need for Proper Strategies. In Advances in Library and Information Science, V5: Digital Library. Jodhpur, Scientific Publishers, 2005.

10. Raman Nair. R. Establishment of an electronic library to support agricultural research education and extension in India. Proceedings of the FID Congress, Vignan Bhavan, New Delhi, 1998.

11. Ravindran Asari, K; *et al* Nitya Archives: Innovative Blending Techniques for Selective Access to Information fom digitally Organized Text. Proceedings of the National conference on Information management in e-Libraries, February 2002. IIT, Kharagpur.

12. Rawale, N.P. Technology information service, *University News.* V.33, No.19, 1995. 2. Rowley, Jennifer. The Electronic Library. 4th ed. London, Library Association, 1998.

13. Sasikala Subbarao, V. Electronic thesis and dissertations: digitising of the Phd dissertations by IIT_B. In the Proceedings of the 4th International Conference of Asian Digital Libraries. Bangalore, IIIT-B, 2001.

14. Sulochana Devi, L. Application of Digital Technology for Conservation and Utilization of Ancient Manuscripts and Archival Materials. In the Proceedings of the South Indian History Congress, Tvpm, December 2001.

15. Vijayan, K. Organizing Manuscript Collections for the People. In Public Library Development. New Delhi, Ess Ess, 1993.

16. Witten, Ian H. Visions of the digital library. International Conference on Asian Digital Libraries, 4th,Bangalore, 2001. Proceedings: Digital Libraries, ICDAL 2001, pp 3-15.

12

Sociology of Rural Information Services

Dr.G.Devarajan

0. INTRODUCTION

Information is an important resource and vital input for soci-economic and cultural development of a nation. The globalization of Information flows is in intensifying competition, raising the danger that poorest countries and communities will fall behind more rapidly than ever before. Today, even developing countries like India speak more and more about cyberspace and information superhighway. But, third world countries like India should not forget the real situation prevailing in our villages and slums. Many villages are still with out electricity, telephone, primary schools, and even with out primary facility like safe drinking water and sanitation. For the poor the promise of the Information age 'knowledge for all' can still is as remote as a distant star[1]. To bring the promise of Information age close to reality the implications of the Information revolution must be thought of in the proper perspective in the development programmes of developing countries like India.

1. INFORMATION AS A SOURCE OF SOCIETAL DEVELOPMENT

Information is an essential component of growth and improvement in living standard. In modern society, information is closely interrelated with growth and development which is reflected in the areas of economic, political, social, occupational and cultural spheres. A sea change is taking place in society due to the application of information and knowledge for development. Information technology with all its spectacular advances has been the chief instrument of these revolutionary changes leading societies to its third phase of development known as 'Information age'. Libraries and information centers should their activities in such a way as to meet the new challenges and fast and sweeping changes taking place in the society.[2]

A number of factors are attributed for the value of information in the present day society. They are mainly research and development, fusion of science and technology, societal, information, information technology and information demand. There are number of catalytic pressures such as growth of population, social differentiation and reorganization, technological innovation, growth in education, life expectancy increases, social welfare provision etc which have brought forth many demands for information. Today information has become a source of economic and political power and driving force for acquisition of wealth and political strength. In fact, information –rich countries of today are becoming more and more richer and powerful than before on account of expertise in creating new knowledge and information and its effective and efficient utilization. But the poor countries and poor people cannot compete with rich ones not only because they have less capital but because they have less knowledge. Knowledge is often costly to create, and that is why much of it is created in industrial countries.[3]

2. STRUCTURE OF INDIAN SOCIETY

India is a democratic and secular country with a population of more than 103 crores . Nearly three fourth of the people are living in villages and occupation of the majority is in the field of agriculture. About half of population is illiterate which constitute half of the total illiterate at the global level. The GNP is low (Us$.278.7bn).quite a good percentage of people are living below poverty line. Unemployment among the educated is high and superstitious belief, child labour and atrocity towards women and children are still prevalent especially in the weaker sections of the society. With all these adverse situations for prospective development India is moving towards the 21st century. Is it possible for such a nation to develop at the desired level it ought to be? In India, the majority are village populace.

The village is the basic unit of social, economic and cultural life of the Indian society. It is also a centre of political and administrative activity. Rural India has continued to remain neglected for centuries together has now come to be recognized for its immense economic potential. Economists, policy makers, planners and government have come to the conclusion that no socio-economic development can be achieved unless rural masses are fully involved in the programmes and process of economic development. This ultimately led to the ideas of people's participatory planning. Thus the village is now the unit for grassroot level planning as envisaged by Gandhiji as Panchayat Raj. People's participatory planning denotes the involvement of the people from the stage of initiation to the completion of the plan. It consists of people's participation in decision making, implementation of decisions, sharing of benefits are and evaluation and monitoring of plan. In such a society there would be genuine participation of people in the decision making process in all levels of government. In people-centered development, objectives like improvement of health, education, housing, safe drinking water and social welfare assume paramount significance. For the proper implementation of all these, information input is required by the community. The information requirement of people in one village is different from other village depending upon various social setups. Hence it is imperative to chanalize the need-based information for a multidimential social development of the country as a whole.

3. INFORMATION NEEDS OF THE SOCIETY

For an overall development of a society, information input becomes imperative especially in the present day information environment. Local libraries and Information centers under the local Government have a crucial role to play in this regard. As rightly observed by B.S.Kesavan the library is no longer a passive institution, but a dynamic institution and it has become an integral part of the society. This concept has changed the nature of the library architecture. Library is now a place where one is completely at home, where the entire family comes along with the *laughter* of children for the enjoyment of life. Unless the libraries are built in beautiful surroundings, they can't perform effective service in the matter attracting readers to activate their minds.[4]

A rural library is a rural information centre which should not respond to the need of the community it serves. It has been rightly observed by Bloss that "the conviction is that when people know the facts, they are more apt to make a better life for themselves and to easier to leave with what they don't. A skillfully selected and usefully organized collection of books is a source of ideas for rational action and for improved living. Such a collection can become an active force for good in the community when aggressively and imaginatively exploited"5

As a service centre a village library should ascertain the nature of information need-based, efficient and effective information service. Information need may be in the area of agriculture, industry, education, health, employment, developmental programmes of the Government for the uplift of the down trodden and weaker section of the society etc. the information needs should be ascertained through community survey by local libraries. Based on this baseline data information should be collected from various agencies and information sources and disseminated to the people in the society. Hence attempts should be made at the local level with the initiative of the local government for the establishment of rural information centers (RIC) as an extension of local libraries for the supply of information and for the development of rural community.

4. RURAL INFORMATION CENTRES IN KERALA

Attempts were made in Kerala for the establishment of

rural information centres viz "Sevana" by the Kerala State Library Council in fourteen districts in Kerala on an experimental basis. This is in addition to the district information centres established by the Government at the District head quarters. The services of these centres cannot always be utilized by the rural community due to the distance between the centres and the villages. Considering this aspect Kerala State Library Council launched the programmes of rural information centres. The structure, objectives and function of these centres are given below.

As part of the First phase of the programme 14 rural libraries were selected by the State Library Council to function as the rural information centres and as extension to these libraries. In the selection of these libraries preferences are given to libraries which are situated in places where the weaker section of the society live and that are functioning effectively in the region. For the functioning of each centre an annual grant of rs.5000/- is given by the council. The centre is controlled by an advisory body and services are rendered by the Librarian/ Information Assistant. The person who is in charge of the centre has been given necessary training in the collection, organization and dissemination of information. The Kerala State Library Council is the focal point in the collection of information generated at the State level in the field of agriculture, industry, education, health, employment and other developmental programmes for the weaker section of the society announced by the government from time to time etc. this information will be routed to the various local information centres in the State by the council.

The sphere of activities or services of the centres include the following:

I. To disseminate information that are useful to the rural community and which are generated by the various departments of the government.

II. To disseminate information pertaining to education and labour to the rural community.

III. To provide information pertaining to the welfare programmes intended for the weaker section of the society announced by the government from time to time.

IV. To conduct seminars, conferences and workshops on various subjects such as agriculture, animal husbandry, fishery, public health, industries etc.

V. To prepare students in the rural areas for attending competitive examinations conducted by the State Government and Central Government.

VI. To provide publicity among the rural community regarding the welfare programmes of the government.

VII. To ensure public participation in the developmental programmes at the village level etc. The establishment of rural information centers in Kerala is a pioneer attempt. The activities of these centres are so much linked with information support to people's participatory planning for grass root level development in Kerala which is recently launched and is a model to other states in Indian Union. According to Prof. Neelameghan there are three distinct but interrelated aspects to be taken note of in considering information support to grass root level development of rural communities. They are:

- * Provision for and communication of pertinent data and information to support rural people's efforts for their own development is in agriculture, literacy, health, housing, employment, natural resources conservation or environment matters.
- * Rural people possess a fund of valuable native knowledge –food, health and medicine related plants and animals, social and cultural value systems, ethnic, music and arts etc. which need to be recorded, processed, disseminated and utilized on a much wider scale. A good part of such information may not be in written or printed form but transmitted orally.

* Information required for preparing development plans at the national and sub national levels-data on demographic aspects, agriculture and other economic activities, human settlement, health and family welfare etc. to be provided to the planners, plan implementers and managers and supporting agencies.[6]

In order that the rural information center function as true instruments for planning at the local level the activities of the centers should strengthened. For this, each village should establish a rural information centre as the pivot of information generating centre and support the role of local development of state and thereby country as a whole. The Kerala State Library Council should take up a leading role in this regard and shows this as a model to other States in India

5. CONCLUSIONS

The significance for information for rural development need not be emphasized. Information condusive to local situation should be provided to the populace on important rural issues in the field of agriculture, industry, education, employment, health and sanitation etc. The local government should identify and establish the rural information centres as vital element in the promotion of socio-economic and cultural development of the society. In the present day information environment a network of rural information centres, with district and national information centres become necessary for overall development of the country. The future of 21st century will highly depend on information know-how and those countries which are able to collect organize and utilize the information effectively and efficiently is going to rule the world. Third world countries like India should concentrate more attention on rural development. For this, information access at the local level is imperative for grass root level planning and sustainable societal development.

REFERENCES

1. UNESCO: World Information Report. Paris, UNESCO,1998.
2. Sarada,K: Rural library services in India. New Delhi,ESS ESS, 1986.
3. Sharma,Pandey SK: Libraries and Society. New Delhi,ESS ESS, 1992.
4. Sathyanarayana,M: Public library and community analysis. New Delhi,Reliance Publishing House,1997.
5. Bloss, Meredith: Responding to manifest needs. Library Journal. 89(16),1964.
6. Neelameghan,A: Information Technology and Rural development. Information tudioes.4(1) 1998.pp.55-61.

13
Bridging the Digital Divide

Dr.G.Devarajan

0. INTRODUCTION

Information is a vital and regenerative resource. It is a basic component of societal development. The information and communication technology (ICT) is relied upon heavily by the information centres in order to satisfy the varied information needs of the user community. In all spheares of information activities of mankind there is a significant investment in the Internet as an enterprise and with wide utility to support teaching, scholarship and administrative matters. The application of new technology has accelerated and widened the existing information gap between the rich and poor is growing within a country or even region itself. This leads to "digital divide" between the information "haves" and "Have-nots".

1. BRIDGING THE DIGITAL DIVIDE"

The avenues of information and communication technology have helped in the democratization of information. But more than 80% of people in the world have never even heard a dial tone, let alone surfed the web. In fact the gap between information "haves" and "have-nots" is widening. As far as developing countries are concerned the stratification of information rich and information poor is going to be a big social problem. Various countries and organizations are making attempts to bridge the information gap.

2. BRIDGING THE DIGITAL DIVIDE-INDIA:

National and state-level agencies in India are making attempts to bridge the digital divide. In 2000, the Government of India in collaboration with an information technology started a project, known as the "Hole in the wall" experiment, to provide computer access to the city's street children. An outdoor five-station computer kiosk was set up in one of the poorest slums of New Delhi. Though the computers themselves were inside a booth, the monitors protruded through holes in the walls, as did specially designed joysticks and buttons that substituted for the computer mouse. Keyboards were not provided. The computers were connected to the Internet through dial-up access. A volunteer inside the booth helped to keep the computers and Internet connections running. No teachers or instructors were provided, in line with the concept called 'minimally invasive education'. The idea was to allow the children unfettered 24-hour access, and to learn at their own pace and speed. According to report, children who flocked to the site taught themselves basic computer operations. They worked out how to click and drag objects; select different menus; cut, copy, and paste; get on the Internet; and change the background "wallpaper". A number of projects are being undertaken in various states in India to bridge the Digital divide. The AKSHAYA is a project in Kerala inaugurated by the president of India, Dr.A.P.J.Abdul kalam on 18th November 2002. The project envisages the establishment of 9,000 community information centres across the State as part of a campaign to bridge the digital divide. These centres are to be established through private initiative, with the objective of having one centre within two km. of each household. The project would commence in Malappuram and Thiruvananthapuram in January 2003 and the entire state is proposed to be covered by May 2004. As part of the project, one person from each family will be trained to enable him to use the computer for day-to-day communication and information needs.

A shot in the arm for n-Logue is the mandate from the Tamilnadu government to network and put in place the infrastructure required in ten districts. Tamilnadu's Rural Access to services through Internet (RASI) project has already got 70 villages in each of the two districts-Madurai and Cuddalore –

networked and running. And nearly 5-10 villages are getting networked every month in these districts. RASI project seems to be different from other government projects that start with a bang and die even before inaugurations some to an end. It has attracted attention from corporate, educational institutions, hospitals and private telecom companies.

Akin to a PCO booth, the telephone cum Internet access point for a villager will be housed in a kiosk is equipped with a PC with CD-ROM and multimedia, web camera, printer, corDECT wall set, speaker microphone and power backup for four hours. The language barrier has been taken care by providing local language software. Networking rural India with telephone and the Internet is becoming a reality with "Chiraag".

3. IMPLICATIONS AND ISSUES"

Digital divide is marked not only by physical access to computers and connectivity, but also by access to the additional resources that allow people to use technology well in the real sense of the term "digital divide". It gives overriding importance to the physical availability of computers and connectivity, rather than to issues of content, language, education, literacy, or community and social resources. A problem with the digital divide concept is in its implication "haves" and "have-nots" but rather a gradation based on different degrees of access to information technology. As Henry Jenkins argues, "the rhetoric of the digital divide holds open this division between civilized tool users and uncivilized non users. As well meaning as it is as a policy initiative, it can be marginalizing and patronizing in its own terms". He also opined that the notion of a digital divide implies a chain of causality i.e. lack of access to computers and the Internet harm life chances. While this point is undoubtedly true, the reverse is equally true; those who have already marginalized will have fewer opportunities to access and use computers and the Internet. In fact, technology and society are intertwined and co-constitutive, and this complex in interrelationship makes any assumption of causality problematic. The digital divide framework provides a poor road map for using technology to promote social development since it overemphasizes the importance of the physical presence of computers and connectivity to the exclusion of other factors that allow people to use ICT for meaningful ends.

4. CONCLUSION

The division of information rich and the information poor is more serious and dangerous than economic stratification of rich and poor. A critique of the notion of a digital divide is necessary to fully inform and unleash efforts to use technology to promote social inclusion. A framework of technology for social inclusion allows reorienting the focus from that of gaps to be overcome by provision of equipment to that of social development to be enhanced through the effective integration of information and communication technology into communities and institutions. This kind of integration can only be achieved by attention to the wide range of physical digital, human, and social resources that meaningful access to information and communication technology entails. A society that is free from digital divide and societal divide would have ways for holistic development of a nation and global society.

REFERENCE

1. Deverajan, G. Information technology in libraries. New Delhi, Ess Ess Publications, 1999.
2. Vengan, R, *et al, Ed.* CALIBER-2000 : Information Services in a networked environment in India. Ahmedabad, INFLIBNET Centre, 2000.

14

Scientific Productivity of Agricultural Scientists : A Scientometric Study

Sarala. K. R.

0. INTRODUCTION

Agriculture is a subject of priority and concern to all the nations of the world especially developing countries. Among the developing countries, India occupies a place of pride in agricultural education and research. Various agencies in the country are responsible in carrying out teaching, research and extension activities in agriculture and allied fields. India has the largest number of scientific and technical manpower in the field of agriculture and our National Agricultural Education and Research system is one of the largest in the world, training more than 10,000 graduates and 5500 post graduate students annually in different disciplines of agriculture and animal husbandry.

An enormous quantity of agricultural information is being produced by various organizations concerned with agricultural production. Publications form the source of information. These publications come from all fields of agriculture, food, forestry and fisheries in many forms: article in journals, research reports, government documents, patents etc. in different languages. The immediate and tangible output of sciences & technology into public domain is literature. Scientific productivity in the form of intellectual contributions to the advancement of science, ultimately communicated in a written form is commonly considered to be important to the scientific community. It is interestingly being measured through publications and citation data. Publications to exchange the research findings is an important aspect of science and is a basis of methods to evaluate scientific productivity. Scientometrics involves quantitative studies of scientific activities, including among other publications and so overlap bibliometrics to some extent.[1] The essence of scientometrics is summarized by Price in the introduction to "Little Science Big Science" as follows "Science is a measurable substance, consequently the manpower engaged in science, the scientific literature, talent and expenses afforded to science can be measured by properly selected statistical methods"[2] Scientometrics includes all quantitative aspects of science of science, communication in science and science policy.

Many methods have been suggested to evaluate the scientific productivity of countries, universities, research institutions, research teams, research fields. In the recent years several formal analytical and predictive models have been developed for describing the phenomenon of scientific productivity. It is frequently measured in terms of published output, perhaps because the data on number of publications by the authors can easily be collected and also quite reliable. Therefore the number of publications by the authors can be taken as a measure of scientific productivity.[3] Quite a large number of studies have been carried out in the different parts of the world and literature on scientometric studies shows that the studies are conducted in varying subject fields. Scientific productivity studies in the field of agricultural science are few when compared to other sciences and technologies.

The various research activities of the College of Agriculture, Vellayani are carried out under the leadership of the faculty members. They engage in teaching, guide and supervise research, undertake projects, contribute to agricultural literature and participate in extension activities. They have a large number of publications to their credit. The faculty members of the College are regularly publishing their research findings in national and international journals. They are also participating in various national and international seminars, symposia etc. to present their findings. So far specific studies have not been conducted about the publishing features of these papers. It is at this situation, the present study is planned to be conducted taking the College of Agriculture as a representative institution contributing to agricultural literature.

The title of the present study is "Scientific Productivity of Agricultural Scientists in the College of Agriculture, Thiruvananthapuram". In the present study, the number of papers published by the agricultural scientists of College of Agriculture which appeared in the Annual Report of the Kerala Agricultural University has been chosen as the source data.

1. OBJECTIVES OF THE STUDY.

The following objectives were formulated for the study.

1. To examine the scientific productivity of agricultural scientists of College of Agriculture, Vellayani during 1977 to 2004, in terms of publications that they have produced.
2. To identify the year- wise distribution in the output of literature produced by the agricultural scientists.
3. To determine the authorship pattern and to identify the gender- wise distribution
4. To understand the most productive journal selected by the agricultural scientists to publish the articles and their country - wise distribution.
5. To ascertain the subject - wise distribution of publications in agricultural science.
6. To find out the extent of collaboration among the scientists.
7. To evaluate the factors influencing the publications of papers

2. DATA SOURCE AND METHODOLOGY

Since annual reports of academic as well as research organizations usually present a synoptic appraisal of research publications, the same have been used as the source data. The main source for evaluating the scientific productivity is thus the Annual Administration Report published by the Kerala Agricultural University.

A database was compiled by collecting data manually from each year's Annual Report. 27 years from 1977-2004 is taken into consideration. Normal count procedure was followed based on a common format: author (s), title of the sources item and title source under different heads. All the entries were written in separate 5"X3" index slips. All the forms of publications like journal articles, conference/ seminar presentations, science congress presentations, books, popular articles and participation in Radio / Doordarshan were considered for evaluation. The entries were arranged in chronological order under subject headings and then alphabetically author-wise and further title-wise. The data thus collected have been used for further analysis and interpretations. In the case of total data, giving full credit to every author of paper, a total of 3795 authors contributing 1548 papers including first authors and co- authors were considered. A questionnaire was also designed, distributed and collected data from the faculty members presently working in the College. 102 questionnaires were delivered personally and out of it 79 have responded, the percentage of response being 77.45.

3. HYPOTHESES

The study proceeded with the following hypotheses.

a) Solo research will be less in agricultural science

b) The output of female scientists will be quantitatively equal to that of their male counter parts in terms of publications.

c) There is significant association between scholarly productivity and gender.

4. LIMITATIONS

1. The study takes into consideration only the scientific output from a single representative institution under the

Faculty of Agriculture of Kerala Agricultural University (KAU).

2. The study is limited to the data available in the KAU's Annual report.

Therefore findings have to be viewed in this context and may not be generalizable.

5. FINDINGS

The major findings of the study evolved out of the analysis and interpretation of the data are summarised below.

5.1 Scientific productivity

All the faculty members have contributions in different media of publications. 3795 authors are responsible for contributing 1548 publications during 1977 to 2004. 41.92% authors have contributed. 596 articles in scientific periodicals, while 242 articles in popular magazines are contributed by only 9.14% of scientists. 34.2% authors presented 499 papers in conferences / seminars/ workshops etc. and 11.94% scientists are responsible for producing 165 papers in science congress. 2.8% authors are responsible for producing 46 books/ book lets and chapters in books. On an average 57.33 papers have been published every year since 1977. They have also contributed through audio visual media.

5.2 Year- wise distribution of publications

The year 1994-95 was found to be the most productive year, followed by 1979-80 and 1980-81 with equal number of publications. The year 1979 had the highest number of journal publications; conference papers are highest in number during 1982. 1991 and 1992 had the highest number of papers in science congress. Articles in popular magazines are found to be highest during 1980

5.3 Authorship pattern

Authorship pattern among agricultural scientists showed a general agreement with the world trend of decreasing number of contributions by single authors. Single authored contributions come only to 20.61%. Two authored papers

(38.31%) are higher than three authored papers (26.61%). Four and above authored papers constitute to 14.47%.

5.4 Subject –wise distribution

When number of papers in periodicals are considered, Agricultural Entomology has the highest number of publications (20.3%) followed by Plant Pathology (18.62%) and Plant Breeding (16.95%). Home science has the least number of publications. Analysis of papers in Malayalam language shows that the subject "fruit and vegetables" are well represented with 27 articles followed by coconut (27) and articles on plant protections. There are 12 articles dealing with sericulture and 11 on floricultural aspects.

5.5 Ranked list of periodicals.

596 articles are published in scientific periodicals by 1591 scientists, which accounted for 38.5% of contribution. 132 journals are preferred by the scientists to publish their articles. Only 24 journals are preferred to publish four articles or more. The ranked list of these 24 journals show that the first position is occupied by the inhouse journal of Kerala, Agricultural University, "Journal of Tropical Agriculture". Next three journals are also Indian journals. Among the ranked list, only two foreign journals are included: IRRI Newsletter and Pesticides.

5.6 Extent of collaboration

Sharing responsibility of a paper, as given in its author statement, can be considered as an indication of collaborative efforts behind the paper[4]. The extent of collaboration is measured with the help of multi authorship of papers. Collaboration coefficient is the ratio of the number of collaborative research papers to the total number of research papers in a discipline during a certain period of time. Degree of collaboration is calculated by the formula given by subramonyam[5] as $\frac{C = NM}{Nm + Ns}$.

Where,

C = degree of collaboration in a discipline

Nm = number of multi authored research paper in a discipline published during a year.

NS = number of single authored research papers in a discipline published during the same year.

As per the formula, the value of C will be between 0 and 1. Using the formula, the degree of collaboration in the field of agricultural science has increased from 0.93 during 1977 to even one in some years. But decreased in certain years, indicating no steady increase or decrease.

5.7 Factors affecting and influencing publication

Majority of the respondents are of opinion that there exist a conducive environment for publication in Kerala Agricultural University. But a minor portion experiences some factors which affect their publication such as service issues including administrative hurdles, delay in publication, lack of support from the institution, lack of time etc.

Providing weightage for promotions, monetary benefits, certificate of merit, medals, cash incentives, publicity are some factors which can influence productivity increase according to the scientists.

5.8 Gender and productivity.

Gender –wise distribution by questionnaire method shows that 49% of the respondents are females and there is only 37.97% males.

The study shows difference in scientific productivity between male and females. Males are more productive than females even though the percentage of female scientists are more. Out of the total 3795 authors responsible for the publication of 1548 contributions, 60.50% are male authors and 39.5% female authors. There are 2296 male contributors (60.50%) when compared to 1499 female contributors (39.5%). This difference in proportion is seen in different forms of publications also.

There is significant association between the gender of the respondents and productivity. It is studied by confidence level as computed by chi- square and found to be 2.76259×10^{-38}. The total number of female teachers is not reflected by the total contribution they made in academic publications.

5.9 Relative Growth Rate.

Relative growth rate, which is related to growth study, is applied in this study.

Relative growth rate is the increase in the number of publications / pages per unit of time. If the number of publications of subject doubles during a given period, then the difference between logarithms of the number of the beginning period and end of period must be logarithm of the number 2.

The average relative growth rates of articles decreased from 0.8 to 0.00448 from 1978 to 2003. The Mean Relative Growth rate for the beginning period shows a growth rate of 0.139567 but reduced to 0.05996 during 1999-2003.

These findings are fruitful in substantiating the objectives formulated for the study.

6. SUGGESTION

The teachers, the consumers of information are the generators of information also. Publication of articles is one form of information generation. Considerable measures should be initiated at the University level to motivate publication skills of the faculty especially the female members, as their participation shows a lesser contribution when compared to their total number.

7. CONCLUSION

It has been widely recognized that an analysis of the published output of scientists is a good indicator of their research activities, in terms of both volume and quality. The present study attempted to examine the scientific productivity of only one representative institution under the Kerala Agricultural University. It is recommended that similar studies if extended to other faculties of the university would yield fruitful answers related to productivity of scientists.

REFERENCES

1. Hood, William W and Wilson, Concepcion, S. (2001). The literature of bibliometrics, scientometrics and informetrics. Scientometrics 52(2) : 291-314
2. Price, De Solla, (1963). Little science, big science. New York, Columbia university press.
3. Ravichandra Rao, I.K. (1980). The distribution of scientific productivity and social change. Jl. Of the American Society for Information Science 31 (2) : 111-122
4. Suriya, M and Manimekalai, A. (1997). Research productivity of the academic community of the Marine Biological Centre, Annamalai University. Kelpro Bulletin 1 (1) : 20-26
5 Subramanyam, K. (1983). Bibliometric studies of research collaboration : a review. Jl. of Information Science 6(1) : 33-38.

15

Organisation and Utilisation of Media Libraries

Shibu M Das

0. INTRODUCTION

The term "media" is the means of mass communication regarded collectively [1]. The medium, which communicates to a mass, is considered as mass media. Mass media consists of both print and visual media. Visual media is new in or Mesopotamia, the country between the Tigris and Euphrates rivers, introduced writing to the world. The Sumarian people who inhabited Mesopotamia used the cylinder seal to mark and identify their property [2]. Other cultures developed early forms of writing, which were of two basic types: cuneiform and hieroglyphics. Cuneiform writing resembled wedge shaped characters and was used by the Sumerians, Akhadians, Babylonians, Assyrians and the Persians. Egyptian hieroglyphics used figures or objects to represent sounds or words [3] over a thousand years passed from the development of syllabic writing until alphabetic writing was developed. Although a contribution of the Near East alphabetic writing was adapted as an instrument of communication by the Greeks. The twenty six-character alphabet used today in western cultures was developed by the Romans [4].

Non-print media probably originated in the Orient, where shadow shows entertained the people for over two thousand years [5]. Reliance upon visuals has been demonstrated since early history through cave wall drawings, Egyptian pictographs, Babylonian maps, clay tablets, medieval art works, Renaissance woodcuts, and early illustrated books[6].

In a democracy, the print media as well as visual media plays a vital role in building public opinion by way of dissemination of information to the public. Compared with visual media, print media is less costly. Among print media, Newspapers are cheapest in cost. So it can go along with and make a great impact on public. Uncensored news, fearless editorial criticisms and other articles published in the newspapers and magazines influence the day-to-day governance of the country to a great extent. In India also, the significance of the "fourth estate" as the inevitable pillar of democracy and the freedom it enjoys, have contributed to the consistent growth of the print media. It is the print media, which is easily accessible and has an ever-lasting effect on the people than any momentary or of repeated events in the visual media. This media has now mounded itself to suit the requirements of the recent Internet revolution and is growing with its readership always on the raise.

1. RELEVANCE OF THE STUDY

The presentation of news and current affairs to the public at large can be seen as the most important informational activity in a democratic society. A great part of the ideas, reactions and emotions of our daily lives, the cultural air we breath, derive from last night's television, the morning newspaper or the car radio.

News does not just happen: it is made. The romantic concept of a reporter at the scene of great events is only the starting point of a highly complicated and vulnerable chain aided by electronics and sometimes by satellite, shaped and sharpened by sub-editors leading to the publication of news by adding some techniques which makes the public to accept. In these days of homely radio news it is many years since anyone cried 'hold the front page' if ever he did. What count in the competitive arena of the media is organization and editing, and the application of technology within a rigid time scale. Eyewitness accounts of war demonstration or sporting contests, a great source of news is not primary source material.

In spite of the significance and specialties, no systematic studies have been undertaken about the media libraries in Kerala. Hence it is felt appropriate to take up a study on the resources, organization, services, utilization and accuracy of news in media libraries in Kerala. The present study is conducted for evaluating the collection, facilities and information needs of the user groups, adequacy of the infrastructure, up-to-datedness of the information.

2. OBJECTIVES

The aim of the present study is to assess the information needs of the users of the media library and to assess the functioning of the media library. The leading newspapers, audio and visual media situated in Kerala are covered for the study. The study is based on the data collected through questionnaires from librarians and users of the media library. The analysis of questionnaire is done in order to attain the following objectives.

1. To identify the resources of the media libraries in Kerala.
2. To examine the organization of the media libraries.
3. To ascertain the services and utilization of the media library.
4. To examine the adequacy of the facilities available in the library to meet the requirements of the users.
5. To study, how fast the information retrieved from the media libraries.
6. To discover the role of media libraries for the professional development of its users.
7. To examine the up-to-datedness of the information received from the media library.

3. FINDINGS OF THE STUDY

The major findings derived from the analysis are categorized into the following heads.

Professional Qualification

Majority of the media librarians working in the media libraries possess B.LISc Degree [24 persons (36.92 %)]. Only one person has M.Phil Degree in Library Science.

Professional qualification of librarians in print media, 50 percentage of them possess other qualification, 34.38 percentage possess BLISc and only 3.13 percentage have MPhil Degree. In the case of audio media, all of them have professional qualification (BLISc / MLISc). In visual media libraries 40.74 percentage have BLISc Degree and 29.62 percentage possess MLISc Degree.

Library facility

100 percentage of the media have library facilities

Classification Schemes

Only 25 percentage of the media library uses the classification scheme for the systematic arrangement of information sources.

Media wise analysis reveals that most of the print media library (60 %) do not follow any classification scheme. In audio media, 100 percentage of the libraries are following classification schemes whereas in visual media, no one follows any classification scheme.

Type of Classification schemes

From among the libraries which are following classification schemes, 66.67 percentage are following their own system. Only 33.33 percentage of the media libraries is following colon classification.

Catalogue in media libraries

Only 33.33 percentage of the media libraries are using catalogues. Majority of the media libraries are not using catalogues. In the case of print media, 60 percentage of the libraries are not using catalogues. But 100 percentage audio media libraries have catalogues for the collection. In visual media, 83.33 % of the libraries are not using catalogues in their libraries.

Category of users

Major users of the media libraries are news producers /

Programme producers (43.51 %). Advertisement staff are the least user group from among the users (1.56 %).

Media wise analysis reveals that in print media, editorial staff are the major users (50.2 %) whereas in audio media, most of the users are news producers / programme producers (54.55 %). In the case of visual media, major users are news producers / programme producers (66.13 %).

Access method

Only 25 percentage of the media library follows open access method. Media wise analysis reveals that 60 percentage of the print media library following closed access system. In the case of audio media, 100 percentage follows open access system whereas in the case of visual media, all of them following closed access system (100 %).

3. NATURE OF COLLECTION

Book Collection

Most of the media libraries have book collection (58.33 %). Media wise / collection wise analysis reveals that 33.33 % have below 5000 collection. Only 8.33 % have book collection above 10,000. in print media, 80 percentage of them have book collection. Audio media possess the high place in book collection. In the case of visual media, 66.67 % have no book collection.

Back volumes of newspaper collection

Only print media library has back volumes of newspaper collection. Among them, 60 percentage has back volumes of newspaper collection. Among print media libraries, only one (20 %) of libraries have above 2000 back volumes of newspaper collection.

Newspaper clippings collection

Out of 12, 41.67 percentage have newspaper clipping collection. Media wise analysis reveals that most of the print media library (60 %) have newspaper clipping collection whereas in visual media, 66.67 percentage have no newspaper clipping collection.

Collection wise analysis shows that only 16.67 percentage have above 10,000 newspaper clippings.

Photograph collection

Here 15 percentage of the media libraries have photograph collection. Collection wise / media wise analysis reveals that only two media libraries have above 10,000 photograph collection (16.67 %). They are belonging to print media.

Audio cassette collection

In media library, 41.67 percentage of them have audio cassette collection. In print media, 20 percentage of them have less than 1000 cassettes in their collection. 80 percentage of them have no collection at all. Audio media have above 1000 number of cassette collection. In visual media libraries, 50 percentage of them have cassette collection.

Video cassette collection

Among the media libraries, only audio visual media contains video cassettes.

Magazine subscription

Most of the media libraries (66.67 %) subscribes magazines for their libraries. 80 percentage of the print media libraries are subscribing magazines / journals. Whereas audio media library do not subscribe magazines. In visual media library, 66.67 percentage are subscribing magazines. Only 8.33 percentage of the media libraries are subscribing journals / magazines upto 40 no.s. Most of the libraries (33.33 %) are subscribing upto 20 no.s of journals / magazines.

Report collection

Only 25 percentage of the media library have report collection in their library. Media wise analysis shows that audio media have no report collection and 40 percentage of the print media and 16.67 percentage of visual media have report collection in their libraries.

Collection of press cuttings on cassette

Only 8.33 percentage of the media libraries have

collection of press cuttings on cassette in their library. Only one of the visual media (16.67 %) among six from the three kinds of media possess the collection of press cuttings on cassettes.

CD Rom collection

About 8.33 percentage of the media libraries have CD Rom collection in their libraries. Media wise analysis shows that 80 percentage of the print media, 100 percentage of the audio media and 83.33 percentage of the visual media have the collection of CD Rom.

DVD collection

Only visual media library have DVD collection (8.33 %).

Adequacy of furniture

About 83.33 percentage of the media library have adequate furniture.

Computerization

About 91.66 percentage of the libraries are computerized.

Internet access facility

Majority of the media library provides Internet access facility (58.33 %). All print media libraries provide internet access facility for users, even though there is internet connection in front of the desk.

Website

It is found that all of the media libraries have their website except audio media (Akasavani).

Computer training for librarians

About 75 percentage of the media libraries provide computer training to their librarians.

Online version

Only 41.67 percentage of the media have online version. They belongs to print media.

Networking of libraries

The study reveals that most of the media libraries are not undertaken networking.

Special methods of preservation

It is found that only one media library had special preservation method for their library materials.

Job satisfaction

Most of the media librarians (83.33 %) are satisfied with the present job. But (16.67 %0 of the librarians in Jeevan TV and Doordarsan have reported that they are not satisfied with the job.

4. QUESTIONNAIRE FOR USERS

Library collection

Most of the users responded that their library collection was partially adequate to meet their information requirements. Only 2.29 percentage of the users responded that the collection is inadequate.

Information sources

In print media libraries 60 percentage of the users preferred periodicals for their use. Whereas, in audio media only 40 percentage of the users preferred periodicals. In the case of visual media, most of the users preferred video tapes (51.02 %).

Designation wise analysis reveals that 58.3 percentage of reporting staff use periodicals. Whereas in the case of editorial staff, 42.86 percentage uses periodicals. In the case of news producers and programme producers, most of them use video tapes (68.96 % and 58.62 % respectively).

Technical organization of resources

It is found that out of 218 responses, 54.13 percentage were unsatisfied with the present system of technical organization. Media wise analysis shows that 55 percentage of the print media staff and 64.28 percentage of the visual media staff are unsatisfied with the technical organization of resources. Whereas in the case of audio media, all are satisfied.

Classification system

Most of the users (64.22 %) in media libraries are

unsatisfied with the present library classification system. Media wise analysis shows that 72 percentage of the print media staff were unsatisfied with the present system of classification. In visual media, 69.39 percentage were unsatisfied with the system of classification. Only in audio media, 100 percentage of the staff were satisfied with the present classification system

Catalogues

It is found that 59.63 percentage of the media libraries possess catalogues for their library holdings, whereas 40.37 percentage do not use any catalogue

Locating books

Among the respondents, 67.89 percentage have difficulty in locating books from the library.

Frequency of library visit

It is found from the study that, most of the users (77.98 %) visit the library daily. Among them, all news producers (100 %) visit the library daily whereas majority of the daily users are from editorial staff (85 no.s).

Purpose of visit

From the analysis, it is found that most of the users gave first preference to news production (58.26 %). Second preference goes to programme production and third preference to research purpose.

Use of other libraries

From the analysis it is clear that majority of the users (68.81 %) are using other libraries and information centers for their information requirement.

Up-to-dateness of the information

It is found that majority of the media library users (68.81 %) mentioned that they need up-to-date information.

Professional improvement

Eventhough the functioning of the media library is unsatisfactory, most of the users (86.24 %) got professional improvement.

5. DISCUSSION

It was found from this study that only the news producers are the frequent visitors of the library. The news-producing category is coming under the audio-visual media. In print media, the news producers are the editorial staff. Reporting staff of the media are the least visitors of the library.

It was revealed that majority of the users suggested that the collection of media library is partially adequate for their use.

It was clear from the analysis that no particular classification system was followed in the media libraries and hence the users find difficulty in locating the materials.

Majority of the users reported that the purpose of library visit is for news production and even some of the users use the media libraries for leisure time spending.

Information is the vital force behind a news producer or programmer. For that a challenged news maker or program producer rush into wherever he get the information. But the users of media libraries are not fully satisfied with the collection and also the media libraries fail to give current up-to-date information to the users. Hence the users and librarians have to depend on other library and information sources other than their media libraries and majority have membership in other libraries.

Most of the media libraries are computerized with Internet facility and opened their own website.

Another difficulty is that when a user approaches the library to get a particular visual, the librarian is supposed to provide the item without any failure. But lack of a proper system, it is very difficult to locate an information like this. Majority of the users and librarians are not satisfied with the present system in media libraries and overall changes in the organization are needed.

Another thing concerned with the news library is the timing of the retrieval or dissemination of information to the users. If the user/news producer asks the librarian to give him a back file, the librarian must give the information at once. This is only happening in the visual media library.

The analysis based on the data collected proved that the hypothesis and objectives are substantiated.

6. RECOMMENDATIONS

On the basis of the survey made through the questionnaires and personal interviews with the librarians and users of the media library, the following recommendations are made, in order to improve the services and functioning of the media library.

1. Sufficient number of professionally qualified librarians should be appointed
2. An efficient indexing system inorder to get visuals with speech must be created for the media libraries.
3. There should be a standard software system to be followed by the media librarians.
4. Collection should be enhanced inorder to meet the information requirements of the media library users.
5. The librarian must have to keep a directory of different websites for the frequent and easy usage for the users.
6. Installation of a hard disk of more capacity is needed for locating more information.
7. The librarian must find some techniques to keep the magnetic cassettes for longer use.
8. Proper training in software use in media library to be assured.
9. There must conduct evaluation studies by the officials.
10. A media library network is essential to utilize maximum resources to the users.

7. CONCLUSION

The study was started with the hypothesis "media libraries are not technically organized and resources are not adequate to satisfy the requirements of the media library users"

In the case of services, majority of the users opined that they are satisfied with the present services. But while examining the details it is clear that most of the users are not satisfied with the present system. Most of them reported that there is no adequate resources to satisfy their requirements. These observations indicate that the hypothesis formulated by the investigator is valid.

REFERENCES

1. **Readers Digest Oxford: Complete Word finder,** New York: Clarenden press, 1990.
2. **Hostrop, Richard W.** Education Inside the Library Media Center, Hamden: Shoe String Press, 1973.
3. Ibid. p. 2-4.
4. **Grove, Pearce S.** Nonprint Media in Academic Libraries, Chicago: American Library Association, 1975. p. x.
5. **Hostrop, Richard W.** Education Inside the Library Media Center, Hamden: Shoe String Press, 1973, p. 4-5.
6. **Nolan, John L.** Audio-Visual Materials, ***Library Trends*** 10, (October 1961). p. 262.
7. **Readers Digest Oxford: Complete Wordfinder**, New York:Clarenden Press, 1990.
8. **Rogers, Rutherford and Weber, David** University Library Administration, New York: H.W. Wilson Co., 1971.